A233 Telling stories: the novel and beyond

Book 1

Realism

Edited by Jonathan Gibson

This publication forms part of the Open University module A233 *Telling stories; the novel and beyond.* Details of this and other Open University modules can be obtained from Student Recruitment, The Open University, PO Box 197, Milton Keynes MK7 6BJ, United Kingdom (tel. +44 (0)300 303 5303; email general-enquiries@open.ac.uk).

Alternatively, you may visit the Open University website at www.open.ac.uk where you can learn more about the wide range of modules and packs offered at all levels by The Open University.

The Open University, Walton Hall, Milton Keynes MK7 6AA

First published 2019.

Edited and designed by The Open University.

Typeset by The Open University.

Printed and bound in the UK by Page Bros Group Ltd.

ISBN 978 1 4730 2493 9

1.1

Contents

Introduction to Book 1: Telling realist stories

Jonathan Gibson

Figure 1 Lovis Corinth, *Woman Reading*, 1888, oil on canvas, 67 × 55 cm. Private collection. Photo: © Christie's Images/Bridgeman Images.

Stories

Stories, or **narratives**, are everywhere around us – in our conversations with friends, in the news, in advertising, in the way we think about other people and ourselves. They are, as the critic Peter Brooks says, one of the fundamental ways in which every one of us makes sense of the world:

> Our lives are ceaselessly intertwined with narrative, with the stories that we tell and hear told, those we dream or imagine or would like to tell, all of which are reworked in that story of our own lives that we narrate to ourselves in an episodic, sometimes semi-conscious, but virtually uninterrupted monologue. We live immersed in narrative, recounting and reassessing the meaning of our past actions, anticipating the outcome of our future projects, situating ourselves at the intersection of several stories not yet completed.
>
> (Brooks, 1984, p. 3)

It's no surprise, then, that stories in literature – in novels, poems, plays and short stories – can have such a strong effect on us, meshing in complicated ways with the stories we tell ourselves about our lives, our attitudes, our emotions, the world and other people. It is the power of literary storytelling – something that can seem simultaneously an intimate part of ourselves and something at one remove from reality – that is the starting point for this module. The overall aim of this module is twofold: to introduce you to a range of stimulating stories, written in a variety of different periods and contexts; and to help you become a more thoughtful, self-aware reader, sensitive both to the ways in which you respond to stories and to the multitude of different ways in which writers *tell* their stories.

Realism

In this first part of the module, you will read books that depict the actual world lived in by their authors. These **texts** are examples of a type of writing often referred to as **realism**. Although realist novels are by definition works of fiction – and therefore, put crudely, untrue –

their key characteristic is their authors' ability to make us believe otherwise, to relate to a novel's characters, events, places and things as if they genuinely exist.

The basic idea behind realism is easy to understand, and of course we're used to talking about a book (or another fictional narrative, on film or TV, for example) as being more 'realistic', more like the life we know, than another one. But further examination shows that realism is not as simple or straightforward a concept as it might first appear.

What exactly does realism involve? What are the key 'realistic' features of a realist novel? If you were to make a list, you would probably come up with characteristics belonging to the following two categories:

- The events and characters that are depicted in a novel. A story about two people meeting in a café in Cardiff and falling in love is likely to seem more realistic than a story about a knight using a magic sword to kill a dragon.
- How these events and characters are presented to the reader – the techniques used by the writer to convince the reader about the reality of the story. Some methods, you might have felt, are better at conveying a sense of reality than others.

Both of these ways of thinking about realism have changed over the years. Ideas about what aspects of the real world can or should be depicted in literature have developed, along with ideas about what exactly 'reality' is. The precise techniques and devices used by realist writers have altered over time, too. Society's view of acceptable subject matter for fiction has also changed, and literary techniques that once seemed fresh and innovative have come to seem obvious and stale, and been superseded by new ways of writing. This process of change highlights one obvious fact, which is all too easy to forget while immersed in the world of a gripping realist novel: that there is a distinction between a novel and actual life. As Pam Morris says in her book, *Realism*, 'realist novels *never* give us life or a slice of life' (Morris, 2003, p. 4). Instead, these novels present us with an *illusion* of life, creating in the reader's mind the sense of things actually happening, which is done by using a large number of agreed ways of doing things, or **conventions**. The fundamental point is made very clearly by the Victorian philosopher and critic (and partner of the novelist George Eliot), G. H. Lewes (1817–1878):

> Art is a Representation of Reality – a Representation which, inasmuch as it is not the thing itself, but only represents it, must necessarily be limited by the nature of its medium; the canvas of the painter, the marble of the sculptor, the chords of the musician, and the language of the writer, each bring with them peculiar [i.e. unique] laws.
>
> (Lewes, 2001, p. 37)

A realist writer, then, must *choose*: they must decide both which aspects of life to write about, and which literary conventions to use.

Realism is usually linked with the downbeat, the middling – with 'everyday life'. A realist plot is generally felt to be a sequence of events that would be likely to happen, and realist characters to be like people we can imagine coming across in real life. The reader will often also get from a realist novel some sense of the interior life of its characters – their feelings, motivations and ideas.

Narrators

One of the best-established realist conventions is the use of a particular kind of **narrator** to tell the story. Many realist novels use either a **third-person omniscient narrator** or a **first-person narrator**. A third-person omniscient narrator has the following characteristics:

- They seem to know everything about the characters, events, places and things in the novel (which is why they are referred to as 'omniscient' or 'all-knowing').
- They refer to the characters of the story as 'he', 'she' or 'they' (they use, that is, the grammatical 'third person').

Here is an example of omniscient third-person narration by Thomas Hardy (1840–1928), the author of the first book you will read on the module. The extract has been taken at random from Hardy's short story 'The Distracted Preacher':

> Stockdale was so excited by the events of the evening, and the dilemma that he was placed in between conscience and love, that he did not sleep, or even doze, but remained as broadly awake as at noonday. As soon as the grey light began to touch ever so faintly the whiter objects in his bedroom he arose, dressed himself, and went downstairs into the road.
>
> (Hardy, 1995, p. 174)

Referring to Stockdale as 'he', Hardy's narrator knows about the precise state of Stockdale's restless mind (the tension in it between 'conscience' and 'love'), about his physical movements (failing to sleep and then getting up and going out at a particular moment) and about the behaviour of light in Stockdale's bedroom.

As a contrast, here is a passage written in the voice of a first-person narrator: this is a narrator who is also a character in the story and refers to themselves as 'I'. The extract is taken from *Villette* (1853) by Charlotte Brontë (1816–1855), and the narrator is the main character in the novel, Lucy Snowe, who has just boarded a ship called the Vivid:

> I took off my bonnet, arranged my things, and lay down. Some difficulties had been passed through; a sort of victory was won: my homeless, anchorless, unsupported mind had again leisure for a brief repose: till the "Vivid" arrived in harbour, no further action would be required of me, but then … Oh! I could not look forward. Harassed, exhausted, I lay in a half-trance.
>
> (Brontë, 2000, p. 51)

The situations described in the two extracts are broadly similar: their minds full of the worries of the day, both of the main characters are unable to sleep. But the contrast in narrative point of view distinguishes the two passages from each other and, as a result, we experience Stockdale's wakefulness very differently from Lucy Snowe's. Both extracts convey a strong sense of things genuinely happening, but they do this in quite different ways. Throughout the history of the novel, both first-person and third-person narratives have been used, one or the other being preferred by different writers at different times.

A short history of the novel

We are so used to reading this sort of narrative, whether in the first or the third person, that we tend not to register its reliance on set literary conventions, or to notice how different reading a realist narrative is from the way in which we experience 'real life'. The twentieth-century novelist E. M. Forster (1901–1970) points out just one of these ways:

> In daily life we never understand each other ... We know each other approximately, by external signs, and these serve well enough as a basis for society and even for intimacy. But people in a novel can be understood completely by the reader, if the novelist wishes; their inner as well as their outer life can be exposed. And this is why they often seem more definite than characters in history, or even our own friends; we have been told all about them that can be told; even if they are imperfect or unreal they do not contain any secrets, whereas our friends do and must, mutual secrecy being one of the conditions of life upon this globe.
>
> (Forster, 1976, pp. 56–7)

The novel is a genre that has always been extremely fluid, always taking on new techniques, new characteristics and new subject matter. (It is surely no accident that word 'novel' means 'new'.) The basic requirements of the genre allow for a vast number of variations – in order to be a novel, a text really only needs to be relatively long, in prose, and fictional or made-up. The critic James Wood compares the novel's ability to evade critical ideas about what it should be to the skills of an escapologist, a 'great virtuoso' who 'always wriggles out of the rules thrown around it' (Wood, 2009, p. 83).

The development of the genre of the novel took place in eighteenth-century England. This period saw the writing of many novels with settings in ordinary life, with a large number being written using a first-person narrator, like Daniel Defoe's *Robinson Crusoe* (1719). Literary realism's high point, however – what we could call 'classic realism' – is usually taken to come with the **canonical** fiction of the nineteenth century, especially in the writings of the period from about 1840 to 1870 and the novels of Charles Dickens (1812–1870), Elizabeth Gaskell (1810–1865) and George Eliot, the pen-name of Mary Anne Evans (1819–1880). These books explored ordinary lives, favoured the use of omniscient third-person narrators, and described places and things in vivid terms, highlighting particular 'telling' details. They were also highly critical of problematic social institutions and practices, from the moribund legal system to conditions in factories. Meanwhile, in continental Europe, particularly in France, sophisticated forms of literary realism were being pioneered by novelists such as Gustave Flaubert (1821–1880) and Honoré de Balzac (1799–1850). This led, in turn, to the development of a rigorous documentary realist style called **naturalism**: this dwelt on some of the bleakest facts of life, and sought to show, using a supposedly scientific method, how forces in wider society shaped individual lives. It is broadly within these nineteenth-century contexts that the first two books you will read on this module, Hardy's *Far from the Madding Crowd* (1874) and Edith Wharton's *The Custom of the Country* (1913), were written.

From the end of the nineteenth century, and increasingly around the time of the First World War (1914–1918), new kinds of writing began to challenge well-established realist norms. Reality was increasingly felt by many writers and readers to be fractured and uncertain, and more dependent on the different perceptions of different individuals than nineteenth-century realists had allowed. Reflecting this view, new impressionistic and **subjective** literary forms emerged, a development which has become known as **modernism**. A key feature of many modernist novels is **stream of consciousness** – a technique developed particularly by Virginia Woolf (1882–1941) and James Joyce (also coincidentally 1882–1941) – in which the thoughts and feelings of a character, their interior life, seem to have been written on to the page in a fluid, often hardly coherent, continuous flow. Modernist narratives are often fractured and complex, told from multiple points of view. Here is an example of modernist writing, from *As I Lay Dying* (1930) by the American novelist William Faulkner (1897–1962): 'In a strange room you must empty yourself for sleep. And before you are emptied for sleep, what are you. And when you are emptied for sleep, you are not. And when you are filled with sleep, you never were. I don't know if I am or not' (Faulkner, 1996, p. 73).

Modernist concerns and devices influence two of the books on the module, Ali Smith's *Hotel World* (2001) and Edmund Blunden's First World War **memoir** *Undertones of War* (1928), in different ways. *Hotel World* is also influenced by a late twentieth-century movement known as **post-modernism**, which took a very sceptical view of our ability to understand and describe reality adequately. This movement also distrusted sweeping generalisations about the world. Post-modernist writers often mix up genres, media and literary conventions – both old and new – in a stimulating way. In *Hotel World* you will find snippets from newspapers, pop songs, a hotel review and extracts from a training manual, as well as first-person, third-person and stream of consciousness narrative.

Modernist and post-modernist techniques can be interpreted as attempts to make fiction seem more real than realism – in other words, truer to how we experience life than the **objective** representational methods of realism. From this point of view, some critics have attacked what I have referred to as 'classic realism' as having an over-simplistic view of the world, and a complacent confidence in the ability of realist conventions to depict it accurately. The oldest realist novels you will read on this module, *Far from the Madding Crowd* and *The Custom of the Country*, however, seem to me to be far more subtle, interesting and complex than this caricature would suggest. The critic George Levine argues that nineteenth-century realism 'was not a solidly self-satisfied vision based in a misguided objectivity and faith in representation, but a highly self-conscious attempt to explore or create a new reality' (Levine, 1981, pp. 19–20). It is, meanwhile, easy to read modernist novels as simply employing new forms of realism, rather than throwing realism out of the window.

Summing up

Today, in the twenty-first century, it is clear that literary realism – whether 'classic realism' in a narrow sense or realism in a broader sense that includes the aspirations of modernism – is still very much with us. Most fiction is still written using recognisably 'classic realist' conventions and techniques that would be recognisable to Hardy and Wharton. The final text in this first module book, Arundhati Roy's *The God of Small Things* (1996), like much of the most interesting contemporary fiction, combines modernist, post-modernist and classic realist methods in a heady and richly enjoyable brew designed – quite as much as the novels of Dickens, Gaskell, Eliot, Flaubert, Balzac, Hardy and Wharton – to make us believe in a specific fictional world comparable to our own.

References

Baldick, C. (2015) *Oxford dictionary of literary terms*. 4th edn. Oxford: Oxford University Press. Available online via the OU Library.

Brontë, C. (2000) *Villette*. Edited by Margaret Smith and Herbert Rosengarten, introduction and notes by Tim Dolin. Oxford: Oxford University Press.

Brooks, P. (1984) *Reading for the plot: design and intention in narrative*. Oxford: Oxford University Press.

Faulkner, W. (1996) *As I lay dying*. London: Vintage Classics.

Forster, E.M. (1976) *Aspects of the novel*. Edited by Oliver Stallybrass. Harmondsworth: Penguin.

Hardy, T. (1995) *Wessex tales*. Edited by Michael Irwin. Ware: Wordsworth.

Levine, G. (1981) *The realistic imagination: English fiction from Frankenstein to Lady Chatterley*. Chicago: University of Chicago Press.

Lewes, G.H. (2001) 'Realism in art: recent German fiction', in Regan, S. (ed.) *The nineteenth-century novel: a critical reader*. London: Routledge, pp. 36–8.

Morris, P. (2003) *Realism*. London: Routledge.

Wood, J. (2009) *How fiction works*. London: Vintage.

How to use this book

The chapters that follow, both in this book and in Book 2, have been designed to help you build on your initial responses to the set texts and develop your awareness of such techniques and devices as characterisation, plot, imagery, symbolism, theme and style, introducing you to a variety of different critical approaches.

In this first book, you will study four novels: *Far from the Madding Crowd* by Thomas Hardy, *The Custom of the Country* by Edith Wharton, *Hotel World* by Ali Smith and *The God of Small Things* by Arundhati Roy. You will also study *Undertones of War*, a non-fiction, autobiographical book by Edmund Blunden.

Each chapter in this book is an invitation to join a conversation about the set text for the week, rather than an infallible summary of everything you need to know about it. As you read this book, you will encounter a variety of different views about the set texts: not just the views of the authors of each chapter, but also the views of a range of other critics and writers. Try to remember that the chapters have been designed to start you thinking about the set texts – and about your responses to and ideas about them – rather than to provide the 'last word' on the subject. At key points in each chapter, the author will invite you to join the debate by completing a short activity. These activities are important opportunities for you to get to grips with your thoughts about the texts, so you should avoid the temptation to skip them. Many of the activities are designed to help you improve your skills of textual analysis, by looking in detail at particular passages, so don't worry if you disagree with what the author of the chapter says from time to time!

You will find a glossary at the end of this book that explains some of the specialised words and phrases used in the chapters. You will see that each term explained in the glossary is shown **in bold** when it first appears in the text. You can find mentions of glossary items in the chapters by looking them up in the index. You may find that there are other specialised terms used in this book that you don't understand. If that's the case, you will find Chris Baldick's *Oxford Dictionary of Literary Terms* (available online via the OU Library website) a good place to look them up. Additionally, *The Oxford Dictionary of English* (also available online via the OU Library website) is a good basic dictionary and an excellent first stop to find out the meanings of any words you're puzzled by.

Chapter 1 Thomas Hardy, *Far from the Madding Crowd*: Reading the novel

Sue Asbee

Contents

Introduction

Realist novels tell us stories which invite us to believe that the fictional characters we are reading about – their relationships, their actions and their emotions – are real. Paradoxically, even though novels are by definition fictional, we tend to become most involved in reading when we care about characters and their fates, as if they were 'real'. Often we are so familiar with the way stories are told that, unless we are studying rather than simply reading for entertainment, we rarely stop to question how or why we become so involved with a novel. We may read to 'lose ourselves' in a book, or we may find ourselves unwilling to put it down, so intent are we on finding out what happens next. We may sympathise and identify with particular characters and dislike or despise others. Events in a realist novel take place during convincing timescales, to characters that are believable, in locations and situations we recognise and may even imagine and visualise as we read. But there is nothing 'real' about realist novels: they are, unquestionably, fictional.

Figure 1.1 Early photograph of Thomas Hardy, aged 32, close to the time he wrote *Far from the Madding Crowd*. Photo: Courtesy of Dorset County Museum.

In the chapters that follow this one, you will learn more about the author Thomas Hardy (1840–1928), and the settings used in his fiction. You will also discover different approaches to interpreting and analysing his novel *Far from the Madding Crowd* (1874) and the circumstances in which the novel was written. But in this chapter, the focus is on the organisation and mechanics of the text, which will provide you with ways of approaching other prose fiction texts you will read on this module, and indeed elsewhere. The use of narrative techniques – such as **characterisation**, **dialogue**, **imagery** and time – are fundamental ways in which the complex, detailed illusion of the real world is constructed. This chapter aims to consider each of those elements separately, even though it will rapidly become apparent that in one way or another they are all interdependent.

Figure 1.2 Mary Hardy, 'Thomas Hardy's Birthplace at Bockhampton, Dorset, Showing his Mother and Sister', oil on canvas, 47 × 64 cm. Dorset County Museum, gift from Messrs Lock and Mann as part of the Kate Hardy Collection, 1941, acc. no. 1941.7.67. Photo: Courtesy of Dorset County Museum. The cottage, painted by Mary Hardy (1841–1915), the elder of Hardy's two sisters, was where he wrote *Far from the Madding Crowd.*

The discussion which follows in the next four sections assumes that you have read the first four chapters of *Far from the Madding Crowd*. If you haven't, then you should read them now. Novels are by definition long prose works, and nineteenth-century novels conventionally have complex plots that cover a lengthy time span. Novels demand an investment of time from readers too, and different approaches to reading them. As you read the following sections, you will discover that besides having an overall grasp of the story, you will also need to develop your close reading skills. This means looking closely at specific passages in the text, particularly at its use of language, considering the word choice and the style of writing: looking for sentences that are especially long or short, and asking whether the length and rhythm of a sentence affects the meaning; considering if particular images are striking when they recur; looking at whether the narrative point of view changes. Close analytical reading like this will help you to develop your critical awareness – something that is invaluable no matter what you are reading.

Narrative and narrators: introducing Gabriel Oak

Every story needs a storyteller: a narrator who shapes, orders, organises and presents the events and characters whose story they are telling. Thomas Hardy's *Far from the Madding Crowd* has a third-person, or 'omniscient', narrator; in other words, god-like, knowing everything, able to enter any character's mind and tell us what they think, while also reporting what they say and explaining what happens. A third-person narrator is not a character present in the story but a voice that stands apart, uninvolved in the action. In *Far from the Madding Crowd*, the narrator may share some characteristics or opinions with Hardy himself, but in the same way as when we read a poem, we should not automatically assume that it is written in the poet's own voice, neither should we assume that author and narrator are one and the same when it comes to storytelling.

How does the narrator tell this story? Each character is introduced in turn until a whole population of both major and minor, but nevertheless important, background characters are assembled. These characters' lives, relationships and actions intertwine and become more complex as the drama of the novel unfolds, but it begins as the title of Chapter I 'Description of Farmer Oak: An Incident' suggests: with Gabriel Oak and the first indication that something will happen to set the story in motion. In the short opening paragraph, the narrator describes Gabriel's face when he smiles. His mouth appears almost to reach his ears (a wide smile), while his eyes become 'chinks' and the resulting wrinkles look like 'the rays in a rudimentary sketch of the rising sun' (p. 9). Gabriel is a farmer, so comparing his smiling wrinkled face to the sun may also suggest an outdoor complexion; certainly it conveys a genial, pleasant disposition. He will be a major character in this story, so the details and the images the narrator employs work to convey Gabriel's importance. It is also clear that the narrator is taking a leisurely approach to this story, taking time to establish the way readers envisage and begin to understand what kind of character Gabriel is. The treatment of the passage of time is always significant in any novel, and that will be considered later. But for now it is worth noticing the amount of time and words the narrator is prepared to expend in telling this story; the other side of that unspoken contract is the time that readers will invest in reading it.

On working days, Gabriel is, we are told, 'a young man of sound judgment, easy motions, proper dress and general good character' (Hardy, 2002, p. 9). That description coincidentally also tells us that the narrator is someone who understands and values moral qualities. There is also an unspoken suggestion that readers will understand and share those same values. Of course, there may well be places where you find that you simply do not, which introduces the idea that texts produce a kind of 'ideal' reader, while each individual reader (you and me) in reality is different.

A long, complicated sentence with a number of **subordinate clauses** describes Gabriel on Sundays in a mildly comical way: he is a man 'of misty views' who is 'hampered' by his Sunday-best clothes; he attends church but his attention wanders to 'what there would be for dinner' when he should be listening to the sermon (p. 9). In other words, his character is being constructed as a man who conforms to expectations of respectability – he will dress appropriately and attend church – but he is human, practical and far from pious. That long and winding sentence is interesting too because of the asterisks in the set text edition which indicate no less than three places where explanatory footnotes have been provided: for 'Laodicean neutrality', 'the Communion people' and the 'Nicene creed' (p. 9). All of these relate to the Christian religion, appropriate since the subject is church on Sunday, but they also provide readers with context and background to the fiction – this is a novel set in a rural, Christian community. The narrator knows their Bible and Book of Common Prayer and expects their readers to share that familiarity – whether we do or not. The fact that many footnotes appear in this 2002 edition suggests that, over a hundred years after the novel was first published, this familiarity for the readers is no longer necessarily the case. Nevertheless the text imagines – or constructs – a reader who understands everything, even though you and I may have to rely on explanatory notes.

So leisurely and whimsical is the narrative that time is spent not only on describing Gabriel's waterproof boots, but also on the 'conscientious' bootmaker who made them. Even more time is invested in the history and inadequacies of Gabriel's fob watch and the comedy of his expression as he draws it with difficulty, incongruously, by its chain from his pocket 'like a bucket from a well' (p. 10). Readers may remember this later when discovering how adept Gabriel is at telling the time by the movement of the sun and the stars. The silver watch therefore has no practical application, but it provides telling detail of possession, status and family history; Gabriel's own comical lack of skill with it and its inaccuracy all contribute to establishing our sense of his place in society. More extended lengthy description of Gabriel is then summed up with surprising speed, economy and precision: 'In short he was twenty-eight and a bachelor' (p. 11).

That short sentence signals the beginning of the 'Incident' of the chapter title: the arrival of a young, very attractive woman, who is another major character in the novel – Bathsheba. The third-person narrative point of view moves almost imperceptibly away from describing Gabriel to observing him – a young unmarried farmer – observing her, something he does on more than one occasion. Throughout the novel, whether we are aware of it or not, the narrator shapes the way readers respond to events. We will look further at how character is established by considering how Bathsheba is introduced and depicted in the next section.

Characterisation: Bathsheba and the looking glass

How is Bathsheba characterised and what exactly does that word mean? During your literary studies there will be times when you are asked to stop and think about ways in which a character is presented, or 'characterised'. That means looking at how they are described, their appearance and character, as well as what the narrator tells us about them, including what and how they think. Once we begin to consider their actions within the story and what they say when they speak for themselves, we build up a sense of a recognisable character. It can be helpful to think of the narrator's descriptions as direct, and of our observations of the character's dialogue and interactions with others as more dramatic or indirect.

We learn about Bathsheba Everdene in the same way that Gabriel does and initially, though not entirely, through his point of view. The third-person narrative shifts perspective slightly and focuses on Gabriel's interest, as he watches the young woman arrive in a horse-drawn waggon, in which she is surrounded by household items and articles of furniture. Many novels begin in this way, with the arrival of a stranger and the subsequent disruptive effect they then have on the community. Like Gabriel, we don't discover her name until the beginning of Chapter IV; the narrator withholds it for much the same reason as Bathsheba later teasingly refuses to tell it to Gabriel: it is a way of making her even more interesting and intriguing, and like Gabriel, we want to know more about her. It adds a small element of **suspense** to the story – who is this woman? Apart from the waggoner's remark that they have stopped because the tailboard of the waggon has dropped off, hers is the first voice we hear in *Far from the Madding Crowd* – she addresses the waggoner, and like Gabriel we 'overhear' her. Left alone and unaware that she is being watched, she cannot resist investigating 'an oblong package tied in paper' (p. 11) which lies between a caged bird and a cat in a basket. The package contains a looking glass 'in which she proceeded to survey herself attentively. She parted her lips, and smiled' (p. 12). 'What possessed her to indulge in such a performance ... nobody knows' (p. 12), the all-seeing, all-knowing narrator remarks, pretending ignorance.

Figure 1.3 A more conventional place for contemporaries of Bathsheba to use a mirror: an engraving from the French fashion magazine *La Mode Illustrée*, 1885. Photo: Liliana Fichter/Alamy.

Activity 1.1

Allow around 20 minutes to complete this activity

Read and make notes on the following short passage, and try to identify the narrator's attitude to Bathsheba and her actions. There is a great deal to notice, and you may well find a dictionary useful for some of the vocabulary – *The Oxford Dictionary of English* is recommended.

> What possessed her to indulge in such a performance in the sight of the sparrows, blackbirds and unperceived farmer, who were alone its spectators – whether the smile began as a factitious one to test her capacity in that art – nobody knows: it ended certainly in a real smile; she blushed at herself, and seeing her reflection blush, blushed the more.

> The change from the customary spot and necessary occasion of such an act – from the dressing hour in a bedroom to a time of travelling out of doors – lent to the idle deed a novelty it did not intrinsically possess. The picture was a delicate one. Women's prescriptive infirmity had stalked into the sunlight, which had clothed it in the freshness of an originality. A cynical inference was irresistible by Gabriel Oak as he regarded the scene, generous though he fain would have been. There was no necessity whatever for her looking in the glass.
>
> (p. 12)

Discussion

The scene being described is visually simple and quite charming, if unusual: a young woman sitting in a cart, alongside her belongings, smiles at herself in a looking glass. But the language is not simple or straightforward: 'fain', for example, is an old-fashioned **adverb** meaning 'gladly', which is being used here in a mildly amusing way. Another difficult word is 'factitious', meaning something that is created artificially and is only pretending to be natural. So Bathsheba is only practising to smile; her expression is not genuine. The all-seeing, all-knowing narrator pretends ignorance when they remark that 'nobody knows' what possessed her to admire herself, smiling and blushing with only 'sparrows and blackbirds' (and the hidden Gabriel) as an audience. Bathsheba blushes because she is so delighted with the image the mirror presents – fully aware of the attractive face she will present to the world – and her blush intensifies at her own awareness of her beauty.

Later again the narrator claims that they can only 'conjecture' (or guess) Bathsheba's reasons. This assumed ignorance is a strategy, like withholding her name, designed to tease and increase our desire to know more about her. For the moment readers only see her from the outside and the narrator pretends that they, like Gabriel, only have a limited point of view. But the narrator also expresses the opinion that women in general are preoccupied with their appearance, using the difficult phrase 'prescriptive infirmity'. The second definition of 'prescriptive' in *The Oxford Dictionary of English* is the relevant one here: 'having become legally established or accepted by long usage or the passage of time' (Stevenson, 2015). 'Infirmity', meanwhile, means 'weakness'. So 'women's prescriptive infirmity' is a weakness that has become conventionally associated with women. It is clear from the context that the weakness in question is 'vanity', or excessive pride in

Figure 1.4 Jean Louis Forain, *At the Milliner*, *c.*1885, pastel on paper laid down on board, 55 × 46 cm. Private collection. Photo: © Lefevre Fine Art Ltd, London/Bridgeman Images.

one's own appearance. The formal, awkward language the narrator uses here lends a kind of scholarly authority to their opinion that attention to appearance is a weakness (an opinion with which I for one don't agree – this is one place where my values and the narrator's part company).

Personification is the technical term for suggesting that something inanimate has human characteristics, and that is what happens next in this passage: for, as if 'prescriptive infirmity' were an entity in its own right instead of being an idea, it 'stalked' into the sunlight as if it had two legs. There is then a gap between the simple scene the narrator describes and the language they choose to express it. The effect is to insist that even though the narrator is someone of education and learning, they cannot fathom Bathsheba's actions. At the same time that they disapprove of what seems to be a display of self-love, they are also attracted by the sight of her smiling and blushing in her mirror. The fact that she does this out of doors, rather than in her bedroom where (it is suggested) women would normally preen themselves in private, 'clothed' her act 'in the freshness of an originality' – it makes what Bathsheba is doing seem fresh and original. The narrator ascribes a 'cynical inference' to Gabriel as he watches the same scene, against his instinct to be 'generous'. The narrator and Gabriel are both captivated by her appearance, but both have reservations which, as we shall see, Gabriel articulates very soon.

In spite of Gabriel's cynicism, when he moves from his 'point of espial' and realises there is a dispute going on between Bathsheba's waggoner and a turnpike keeper, he is interested enough in her to resolve it and pays tuppence to allow her waggon to pass through. This is their first encounter. She does not deign to thank him, though 'she might have looked her thanks … on a minute scale' – again, the **omniscient narrator** pretends to be unsure. Gabriel's and Bathsheba's relative heights in this exchange, 'He looked up at her then; she heard his words, and looked down' (p. 13), prefigures ways in which their relationship will develop and the changes in their relative social positions that occur later in the novel. They also prefigure Gabriel's words the first time he proposes to her: 'whenever you look up there I shall be—and whenever I look up there will be you' (p. 34).

In the same way as the narrator summed up a lengthy and discursive description of Gabriel with a short and pithy sentence, the dialogue here achieves a similar effect at the end of this first 'incident': as the waggon moves off, the turnpike keeper remarks that the young woman is 'handsome' and queries Gabriel's comment that she has her faults. Gabriel replies crisply with one word: 'Vanity' (p. 13). We learn something about her then, from simply watching her when she is unaware that she is observed, and from Gabriel's reaction to the looking glass incident.

Gabriel sees, or rather spies on, Bathsheba twice more before he talks to her. At night, through a crevice in a shed wall, he watches two women ministering to a sick cow and its calf. His curiosity and interest in the young one increases when he overhears her say that she can ride without a side-saddle. The next morning, he is astonished to see her drop backwards on her pony's back to avoid overhanging branches: her movement is as swift as a 'kingfisher' and '– its noiselessness that of a hawk: Gabriel's eyes had scarcely been able to follow her' (p. 21). Once past the obstacle of trees, she springs upright 'like a bowed sapling' and significantly 'satisfying herself that nobody was in sight, she seated herself in the manner demanded by the saddle, though hardly expected of the woman' (p. 22). Gabriel is amused, 'astonished' and intrigued at this performance, as well he might be. The images the narrator uses to describe her are taken from nature – the kingfisher, hawk and 'bowed sapling' attest to beauty, strength and youthful suppleness – while her disregard for a conventional side-saddle and the fact that she seemed 'quite at home anywhere between a horse's head and its tail' (p. 21) testify not only to her independence, but also her scant respect for convention.

Much later in the novel, when Bathsheba takes charge of her own farm and takes her place in the market, the narrator tells us unequivocally that she is a 'woman with some good sense in reasoning on subjects wherein her heart was not involved' (p. 119). We also learn about her from different characters who hold different opinions. On the night of Boldwood's Christmas Eve party, she is several years older, much wiser, and believes herself to be a widow. One man says what a fool she was to have gotten married, commenting on her being 'so self-willed and independent too'. His friend does not agree: 'She was no otherwise than a girl' when she married, and he asks reasonably enough 'how could she tell what the man was made of' (p. 358). Laban Tall, one of her agricultural workers, says 'she's never been anything but fair to me. She's hot and hasty, but she's a brave girl who'll never tell a lie however much the truth may harm her' (p. 359).

Therefore, we learn about the main characters in different ways, all of which work to build up complex portraits of motivation and psychology. Characterisation is developed by what the narrator tells us the characters are doing and thinking, and what they themselves say, as well as what others say about them.

Figure 1.5 Still from *Far from the Madding Crowd*, Julie Christie as Bathsheba riding side-saddle, not astride her horse, dir. John Schlesinger (Metro-Goldwyn-Mayer, 1967). Photo: Vic/Appia/Kobal/Shutterstock.

Dialogue: Gabriel and Bathsheba in conversation

Gabriel and Bathsheba's dialogue when he proposes to her reveals a great deal about both characters at that particular stage in their lives.

Activity 1.2

Allow around 20 minutes to complete this activity

Reread Chapter IV, starting from 'When Gabriel had gone about two hundred yards …' (as Bathsheba runs after Gabriel to tell him her aunt was wrong about her having a dozen young men after her), to the end of the chapter (pp. 32–7). Pay close attention to the dialogue between the characters and see what you notice.

Discussion

Bathsheba's first words are breathless and ambiguous enough for Gabriel to mistake her meaning:

> I didn't know you had come to ask to have me, or I should have come in from the garden instantly. I ran after you to say —that my aunt made a mistake in sending you away from courting me … It was quite a mistake—aunt's telling you I had a young man already … I haven't a sweetheart at all—and I never had one, and I thought that, as times go with women, it was *such* a pity to send you away thinking that I had several.
>
> (pp. 32–3)

She puts her hand on her bosom 'to still her loud-beating heart' (p. 33), but as Gabriel tries to hold her hand, she slips it away. Her actions mimic her speech: the dashes indicate words tumbling out without a great deal of thought; Bathsheba is excited at the idea of being desired and of a proposal; she is also keen to dispel her aunt's misinformation. She is not, however, quite as excited at the prospect of Gabriel as a husband, and it is her action of removing her hand, rather than what she says, which makes him less confident of her meaning.

Figure 1.6 Still from *Far from the Madding Crowd*, Alan Bates as Gabriel and Julie Christie as Bathsheba, dir. John Schlesinger (Metro-Goldwyn-Mayer, 1967). Photo: Vic/Appia/Kobal/Shutterstock.

Nevertheless, as he explains his prospects, 'a nice snug little farm' and his financial situation with regard to it, his confidence builds once more: 'When we be married, I am quite sure I can work twice as hard as I do now' (p. 33). At this point the narrator intervenes: this is the moment that Bathsheba edges behind the holly bush 'seeing his advance take the form of an attitude threatening a possible enclosure'. Her clear statement

'I never said I was going to marry you' dismays Gabriel, and prompts her really interesting explanation:

> 'What I meant to tell you was only this,' she said eagerly, and yet half-conscious of the absurdity of the position she had made for herself: 'that nobody has got me yet as a sweetheart, instead of my having a dozen as my aunt said; I *hate* to be thought men's property in that way – though possibly I shall be had some day. Why, if I'd wanted you I shouldn't have run after you like this; 'twould have been the *forwardest* thing! But there was no harm in hurrying to correct a piece of false news that had been told you.'
>
> (p. 33)

A narrative comment breaks up her speech at the beginning of that extract, because it would be difficult for her to convey quite so clearly her own sense of the 'absurdity' of her position. But what she goes on to say is more dramatic in her own words, especially in this situation, than had it been conveyed by narrative. Her speech demonstrates her independence of mind: how much she would hate (and the word is italicised in the novel for emphasis) to be a man's property. It shows the extent to which she is aware of modesty and convention and contrariness: had she actually wanted Gabriel, she would not have chased after him. She also foresees fate eventually taking a hand – 'possibly I shall be had some day' – marriage is almost inevitable but thinking of it in terms of being 'had' shows that her ideas about marriage are not necessarily romantic.

Gabriel's ideas of love and marriage are comically sadly limited. As inducements he offers a piano, a gig for market, flowers, birds, a cucumber frame and an announcement of the marriage in the newspaper. Carried away with his own eloquence and enthusiasm, he plans to publish 'the babies in the Births – every man-jack of 'em!' (p. 34). This is too much for Bathsheba, whose answers to each of his increasingly elaborate suggestions have been brief, 'Yes: I should like that', 'I should like it very much', and 'Yes'. But the idea of babies is a step too far: 'Wait, wait, and don't be improper!' (p. 34). Her self-awareness is clearly apparent when she says that marriage would be 'very nice in one sense' (p. 34). She would enjoy being talked about, people would think she had won her 'battle', and she would feel 'triumphant'. But she baulks at the notion of having a husband: 'Well, what I mean is that I shouldn't mind being a bride at a wedding if I could be one without having a husband. But since a woman can't show off in that way by herself I shan't marry – at least yet' (p. 35).

When Gabriel counters Bathsheba's statement 'I don't love you' with the unrealistic 'But I love you – and as for myself, I am content to be liked' (p. 35), she has the wisdom to tell him that he would grow to despise her. This uncomfortable comic scene draws to a close after she has pointed out their inequalities: she is better educated than he, but has barely a penny to her name; he would be prudent to marry a woman with money who could help him enlarge his farm. Her speech is thoughtful and she demonstrates practical insights – as well as emotional ones – to explain why their marriage would not work. Their dialogue has dramatised their unsuitability, their different views, and Gabriel's curiously romantic yet hopelessly impractical attitude to what his love for her might achieve. What narrative description could have told us about these two characters has been brought to life by their conversation.

Imagery, repetition and patterning

Imagery is a rather general term that covers figurative or decorative language in poetry and prose writing. It includes **metaphors** and **similes** which in one way or another appeal to the senses. The example we will consider in this section focuses on colour, but imagery is not exclusively concerned with the visual. One important aspect of close reading and analysis of language involves recognising ways in which images enrich the narrative and how, through repetition, they can work as a patterning device.

We have already noticed how Hardy used nature imagery to construct the idea of Bathsheba's supple grace of movement on horseback; the use of colour is equally important in conveying her attractive appearance. She wears a crimson jacket when she is first seen, which the sun illuminates, casting a 'soft lustre upon her bright face and dark hair' (p. 12); later, in the cow shed, Gabriel identifies her by her 'tumbled ropes of black hair over a red jacket' (p. 20). She blushes when she smiles at her reflection in the looking glass, but it is Gabriel who blushes when they actually first meet (p. 23). The red of repeated blushes indicates different degrees of awkwardness, embarrassment, passion, or sometimes just consciousness of having revealed feelings. It all depends on who is doing the blushing. Red and black are arresting colours: they demand attention, but do not always have the same resonance. When we meet Sergeant Troy in Chapter XXIV, his uniform is scarlet (p. 162) – this is an accurate detail for a cavalryman of his rank at the time – but the colour of Troy's uniform accrues different associations from Bathsheba's red jacket. In this way, the colour red acquires metaphorical meanings from repetitions within the text. Troy is devious, he is 'moderately truthful towards men, but to women lied like a Cretan' (p. 166). So, in his case, red signifies danger – as well as realism.

Activity 1.3

Allow around 20 minutes to complete this activity

Thinking about the points that have just been made, reread the passage from Chapter IV, from the paragraph beginning 'When Gabriel had gone about two hundred yards along the down …' to the end of the chapter (pp. 32–7). This time, focus on the description of the scene rather than the dialogue, and think about the use of colour and the movements of Gabriel and Bathsheba as they talk.

Discussion

Bathsheba waves her white handkerchief as she catches up with Gabriel; his colour deepens, while hers is 'deep' already but from running, not from emotion. The narrator's subsequent description of her as 'panting like a robin' with a face 'red and moist from her exertions, like a peony petal before the sun dries off the dew' (p. 32) must be the most poetic and appealing way of describing sweat ever devised. It is one of many ways in which narrative reminds us of how astonishingly attractive she is. Gabriel blushes 'with gladness' (p. 33) to hear that she does not have countless suitors and assumes her hasty arrival means that she will marry him, but Bathsheba puts a 'low, stunted holly bush, now laden with red berries' (p. 33) between them. This splash of bright colour on the prickly leaves is so potent that Gabriel 'regarded the red berries between them over and over again to such an extent that holly seemed in his after life to be a cypher signifying a proposal of marriage' (p. 34). This is exactly what the narrative is doing with images: they come to stand for more than just themselves, and often they evoke quite complicated emotions. As Gabriel moves round the holly to reach Bathsheba, she looks hopelessly around for escape from her moral dilemma: he seemed to be coming 'by the force of his words straight through the bush and into her arms' (p. 35). Ploughing straight through a holly bush would be an uncomfortable if not painful experience – this encounter is equally painful for him. The courtship country dance round the holly bush is over. Red spots appear in Bathsheba's cheeks, and Gabriel challenges her with making her colours 'come up' in her face and of getting 'crabbed' with him (p. 36). Her laughter eventually convinces him that his proposal is a lost cause, and on that note the chapter ends.

The outdoor setting among farmland is appropriate and convincing for this episode: Bathsheba's aunt lives in a rural cottage, Gabriel's proposal takes place outdoors as he leaves and Bathsheba runs after him. The description, however, owes everything to technical artistry. The use of the colour red in the shared blushes of the couple and the bright red berries of the holly bush punctuates, structures and gives shape to the episode, enriching it in a way that might better be described as poetic rather than realism. The choice of a red-berried but prickly 'stunted' holly bush only adds to the difficulties and awkwardness of Gabriel's proposal.

Conscious that I was going to write a chapter on *Far from the Madding Crowd*, I made notes as I read about anything that I found particularly striking. Before I got very far I noticed the number of times the colour red was mentioned, so skimmed back over the first chapters again, adding to my list wherever I came across 'scarlet', 'red', 'blushing' and other related words. My notes only consisted of a page number and (usually) the word 'red', but when I reviewed them I was able to return to particular passages to think about, analyse and choose the example I thought could be most useful – hence the section above. Together with one or two wider examples taken from my notes, I could support an argument about the way in which the repetition of this colour imagery worked in the novel. Note-taking like this means that you are much better equipped to produce your own independent work. Hardy's novel is rich with strands of repeated imagery, so your own notes are likely to provide many different examples demonstrating your own close analytical reading. As you continue your reading, you might notice (for example) how often the weather, time of day or night, clothes, or even dogs are repeated. You will have to decide whether all your examples are equally significant and choose the ones most convincing for your argument.

The discussion in the rest of this chapter assumes that you have finished reading the novel.

Time

Time is always important in any realist novel, in various different ways. We have already noticed the amount of time the narrator can expend on pages of detail, and how this dictates the amount of time we spend reading the text: the approach to the way this tale is told is a leisurely one. Some incidents which happen over a short space of time are described in depth and detail, yet in other places periods of time are passed over. These instances are fundamental to the time span of the novel, which is in turn fundamental to its structure. *Far from the Madding Crowd* begins in winter, and the movement of time is governed appropriately enough by the rhythm of the agricultural year: lambing, calving, sheep washing, shearing and harvest. The action takes place just over a three-year span, beginning on 20 December, the eve of St Thomas's Day. Bathsheba inherits the lease of a farm; meets, marries, and believes she is widowed during the first year; Boldwood shoots her husband, Sergeant Troy, the following Christmas; and not long after the third Christmas, Bathsheba and Gabriel are married. So whereas many nineteenth-century novels follow a character from childhood to adulthood (a **genre** that has become known as ***Bildungsroman***), Hardy's characters are already adults: Gabriel is 28 and Bathsheba is 20 when the story begins; and Bathsheba is 24 when it ends. Boldwood is at a different time of life, about ten years older than Gabriel, while Sergeant Troy is a young man. This represents time in a different guise, the maturity (or not) of the characters, and the extent to which their response to events changes them. For example, Bathsheba's apparent wisdom about marriage goes to the four winds when she meets Sergeant Troy in his dangerous scarlet uniform. But for the moment we will focus on a different aspect of time: time of day, or indeed night. Day, night, time of year and seasons can all also be considered as 'setting', as important as 'time' and slightly different from 'location'.

Glancing down the chapter titles on the contents page confirms this: 'Night: the flock', 'A morning meeting', 'Eventide: a second declaration' and 'Particulars of a twilight walk'. The chapter 'Night: horses tramping' begins with the first paragraph establishing the silence of the village of Weatherbury, as the church clock strikes 11: 'quiet as the graveyard in its midst, and the living were lying well-nigh as still as the dead' (p. 206). But Bathsheba's servant Maryann's sleep is disturbed and as a result she sees a 'gray moving figure' apparently stealing a horse. As Gabriel and Jan Coggan, riding bareback, gallop off in pursuit, the episode takes on the character of adventure. In the dark, tracks are only visible by dismounting and examining the ground by the light of matches. As this is too 'difficult to describe in words' (p. 208), the narrator resorts to a series of diagrams representing hoof marks, which the pursuers interpret as a gallop, a canter, a trot, a walk, and finally indications that the horse has become lame. The 'thief' is unmasked as Bathsheba herself, who responds to their astonishment with 'the trick she could do so well in crises not of love, namely, mask a surprise by coolness of manner' (p. 211). Secretly, she is on her way to Bath to warn Sergeant Troy not to return to Weatherbury in order to protect him from Boldwood, an escapade she could not undertake under watchful eyes in daylight. As Coggan says, 'ladies don't drive at these hours, miss, as a jineral rule of society' (p. 211). Bathsheba drives on without any more explanation, while Coggan and Gabriel, 'fanned by the velvety air of this July night', retrace their steps. Coggan is understandably curious, but Gabriel suspects the truth behind Bathsheba's secret journey and suggests they 'keep this night's work as quiet as we can'. For their part they can be home before 3 a.m., 'and can creep into the parish like lambs' (p. 212). Under cover of the night, society can be protected from the knowledge of Bathsheba's reckless actions.

Putting things together: the characterisation of Farmer Boldwood

In this section we are going to put together the ideas we have looked at so far – about narrative, dialogue, imagery and time – to see how Farmer Boldwood is characterised in the novel. The **plot** depends on his reaction to Bathsheba's frivolous valentine, sealed with the fateful words 'Marry me'. His is the second marriage proposal she refuses, choosing instead to marry faithless Sergeant Troy. Boldwood's jealousy eventually leads him to imprisonment for killing Troy, thus relieving Bathsheba of two troublesome men in her life and leaving her free to marry Gabriel. How then is Boldwood's character constructed, and how does the story convince us of his transformation from a dependable, respectable member of the community to a murderer? Careful examination of the text reveals that the potential for his deranged state of mind is present from the start, but it is latent, only triggered by Bathsheba's meddling.

As we first observed Bathsheba through Gabriel's eyes, so we are introduced to Boldwood through hers. He arrives on horseback at Bathsheba's new home to enquire if anything has been heard of Fanny Robin, who is missing. Bathsheba only overhears his conversation with Liddy; Bathsheba questions Liddy closely about him after he has left. She learns that Boldwood is single, about 40 years old and handsome. As Fanny's protector, he took responsibility for her schooling and he found her work with Bathsheba's uncle. Liddy confirms that he's 'a very kind man' (p. 76). She also gives a lively account of Boldwood's romantic history: 'Never was such a hopeless man for a woman! He's been courted by sixes and sevens – all the girls gentle and simple for miles round have tried him' (p. 76), but he remains impervious to their attractions. Neither narrative nor dialogue hint that this might be significant, but Boldwood's lack of a romantic past, together with Bathsheba's vanity and sense of her own attraction, provide toxic potential.

While Bathsheba is conscious that every farmer at Casterbridge market views her with interest, there is one who fails to notice her at all. Only when Boldwood's carriage overtakes hers at the end of the day does Liddy confirm his identity. Even then he 'never turned his head once, but with eyes fixed on the most advanced point along the road, passed as unconsciously and abstractedly as if Bathsheba and her charms were

Figure 1.7 Still from *Far from the Madding Crowd*, Peter Finch as Boldwood, dir. John Schlesinger (Metro-Goldwyn-Mayer, 1967). Photo: MGM/Kobal/Shutterstock.

thin air' (p. 93). Though Boldwood is oblivious, he might as well have thrown a challenge at Bathsheba's feet: it is left to readers to discern the extent of her pique, for just like all the young women 'for miles round' (p. 76) who tried to attract his attention, she is invisible to him.

'He wouldn't see any humour in it', Bathsheba says, debating whether to send the valentine to Boldwood. 'He wouldn't. He'd worry to death' (p. 97), Liddy replies – a throwaway remark which may pass unnoticed as we read, but which actually prefigures what happens. The valentine starts the sorry chain of events; it works away at Boldwood's psyche until Bathsheba becomes his obsession. That it 'was of the smallest magnitude compatible with its existence at all Boldwood of course did not know … The vast difference between starting a train of events and directing into a particular groove a series already started, is rarely apparent to the person confounded by the issue' (p. 99). Dwelling on the valentine, Boldwood, the 'solemn and reserved yeoman' (p. 100), reaches a state of 'nervous excitability' (p. 101). Even before he proposes to Bathsheba, his mind has already become 'a hotbed of tropic intensity' (p. 122), which only becomes angrier and more intense when she refuses him. His fury is ultimately redirected to Troy, once he learns of Bathsheba's preference for the younger man.

Boldwood degenerates from this point. When Bathsheba sees him, 'the very man she sought so anxiously to elude' (p. 198) walking over Yalbury Hill, his state of mind is evident in his physical appearance: he was 'stepping on, not with that quiet tread of reserved strength which was his customary gait …. His manner was stunned and sluggish now' (p. 198). His life becomes 'secluded and inactive' (p. 322), and even his crops fail to flourish:

> The strange neglect which had produced this ruin and waste became the whispered talk among all the people round, and it was elicited from one of Boldwood's men that forgetfulness had nothing to do with it, for he had been reminded of the danger to his corn as many times and as persistently as inferiors had dared to do.
>
> (p. 322)

While even the pigs refuse the rotten results of his failed harvest, this image of failed fertility is extended as hope having nevertheless 'germinated' in Boldwood (p. 323). In a perverse inversion of the biblical metaphor (note 324, p. 428), it flourishes 'like a grain of mustard-seed' after Troy is presumed drowned, and Bathsheba thought to be a widow.

Boldwood's conversation with Liddy leaves her 'thinking how very stupid Mr Boldwood was getting' (p. 325), as with his own self-interest at heart, he mishears or misinterprets her every answer to his questions about 'Mrs Troy', her general demeanour, and the possibility of her marrying again in the future. While the dialogue suggests his obsession, the narrative comment which follows *seems* to concur that Boldwood's thoughts are sensible. If Bathsheba is legally able to marry six years after her husband's disappearance and supposed drowning, then:

> This pleasant notion was now continually in his mind. Six years were a long time, but how much shorter than never ... He tried to like the notion of waiting for her better than that of winning her at once. Boldwood felt his love to be so deep and strong, and eternal, that it was possible she had never yet known its full volume, and this patience in delay would afford him an opportunity of giving sweet proof on the point. He would annihilate the six years of his life as if they were minutes – so little did he value his time on earth beside her love.
>
> (p. 326)

In this passage, the omniscient third-person narrator shifts to Boldwood's point of view and presents the deranged character's thought processes without comment, without intrusion, and without approval or disapproval.

If Boldwood has changed from being a sensible man to an obsessive, Bathsheba has also changed. Her conscience never allows her to forget that she once 'seriously injured him in sheer idleness', realising that if she had 'never played a trick upon him' (p. 345), he would never have wanted to marry her in the first place. Subsequently, feeling 'coerced by a force stronger than her own' (p. 344), she promises to marry Boldwood in six years if Troy fails to return. When the scene is set at Boldwood's Christmas Eve party, melodramatically Troy stage-manages his own reappearance. An 'unearthly silence' (p. 366) falls as he enters, while Bathsheba sinks to the floor – and Boldwood shoots.

In the months before Boldwood's trial, it becomes evident that although the community in general was aware of his 'excited and unusual moods', no one had imagined the 'unequivocal symptoms of the mental derangement' (p. 373) which Bathsheba and Gabriel at times suspected. Clothes of rich fabrics and expensive jewellery – packed and labelled 'Bathsheba Boldwood' – which were discovered among his possessions, contribute to the suggestion of 'a mind crazed with care and love' (p. 373), and to the general feeling that, in spite of his 'guilty' plea, he had 'not been morally responsible' for his actions. 'Mental disease' (p. 373) and sheer 'madness' (p. 374) transmute Boldwood's death sentence to 'confinement during her Majesty's pleasure' (p. 375).

Conclusion

We have considered the third-person narrator and some of the narrative strategies used in Hardy's novel, and looked at ways in which the narrative shapes, develops and changes our sense of its characters. An omniscient narrator can tell us what individual characters think, so when they speak for themselves, we may notice a gap between what is said and what is thought. Boldwood's dialogue with Liddy, followed by the narrative point of view from his thought processes, are good examples of this. Dialogue between characters dramatises and brings them to life. We have also seen that *Far from the Madding Crowd's* time span conforms to ideas about realism, in that the **duration** of the novel is paced by recognisable annual events. But we have also noticed that the setting of an episode at a particular time of day or night has been chosen to generate atmosphere, and that the use of imagery – often rooted in the setting – nevertheless takes on a resonance of its own, adding poetic layers to the text beyond realism. Fiction, then, is an art and creating the illusion of realism is complex.

References

Set text

Hardy, T. (2002) *Far from the madding crowd.* Edited by Suzanne B. Falck-Yi, introduction by Linda M. Shires. Oxford: Oxford University Press. Oxford World's Classics.

Other references

Stevenson, A. (ed.) (2015) 'Prescriptive', in *Oxford dictionary of English* (2010). Available at http://www.oxfordreference.com.libezproxy.open.ac.uk/view/10.1093/acref/9780199571123.001.0001/acref-9780199571123 (Accessed: 11 April 2019).

Chapter 2 Thomas Hardy, *Far from the Madding Crowd*: ‘A pastoral tale’?

Jonathan Gibson

Contents

Introduction

The life of the countryside, both human and non-human, is a constant thread in *Far from the Madding Crowd*. Early reviewers praised its descriptions of landscape and rural activities in particular. The American novelist Henry James (1843–1916), for example, found little to interest him in either the story or the central characters of Hardy's novel. On the other hand, James felt that '[t]he most genuine thing in the book' was 'a certain aroma of the meadows and lanes—a natural relish for harvesting and sheep-washings' (Cox, 1979, p. 39). When Hardy was first asked to write *Far from the Madding Crowd* as a serialised story for *The Cornhill Magazine*, it was because the magazine's editor, Leslie Stephen, had read an earlier novel by Hardy, *Under the Greenwood Tree*, which was full of evocative descriptions of rural scenes and activities (Millgate, 2004, p. 135).

Many other readers over the years have particularly valued Hardy's depictions of country life, and many visit or long to visit Dorset to see for themselves the original of Hardy's 'Wessex' – the 'partly real, partly dream country' (Hardy, 2002, p. 3) – in which *Far from the Madding Crowd* and most of Hardy's other novels are set. Nostalgia for a lost rural past has often been seen as a defining feature of his works – frequently by critics themselves nostalgic for such a world. This is the view that sees Hardy as 'a traditionalist writer whose deepest affiliations are with the farmlands, animals, rocks, hills and simple people who live among them' (Howe, 1966, p. 17).

Pastoral literature and *Far from the Madding Crowd*

The depiction of the countryside as a harmonious, peaceful, idyllic place is often associated with a particular genre of writing: the **pastoral**. The word comes from 'pastor' – the Latin word for 'shepherd' – and the type of literature the word describes involves an idealised version of country life, focused particularly on the love affairs of shepherds and shepherdesses. Originating in ancient Greece, the pastoral genre has continued to be adapted in a variety of ways by more recent writers. The earliest pastoral work, the *Idylls* by the Greek poet Theocritus (*fl. c.*270 BCE), is the origin of the word 'idyllic' and set many of the genre's defining characteristics in place. The countryside in pastoral poetry becomes a place to seek refuge in and escape the corruption and complexities of urban life (Gifford, 1999, pp. 15–20), and often a strong contrast is made between the country life of the innocent shepherds and the corrupt life of cities. In Chapter 11 of this module book, you will find out about how the genre was adapted by Edmund Blunden for his First World War memoir, *Undertones of War*.

The main form pastoral writing originally took was a sequence of 'eclogues', poems in which two or more shepherds talked and sang: they might mourn the death of a friend; talk to one another about successes or failures in love; present a lamb to a beloved shepherdess; sing songs competitively; debate topics such as the difference between youth and old age; or simply play the flute. The world of these shepherds was felt to be close to that of the mythical **Golden Age** – a far-distant historical period in which humanity had lived in peace, prosperity, innocence and harmony with nature. The Greek region of Arcadia became particularly associated with this idealised pastoral way of life.

To a large extent, pastoral writing relies on images of the natural world. Pastoral poets and novelists draw on a storehouse of visual memories and emotions in their readers' minds that are associated with nature and often have strong cultural associations (Foley, 2012). In the western European literary tradition, for instance, rivers and streams are associated with the passage of time and 'greenness' with the self-renewing potential of nature itself (Siddall, 2009, pp. 24–5). Farm

Figure 2.1 Samuel Palmer, *The Magic Apple Tree*, *c.*1830, watercolour, 35 × 27 cm. Fitzwilliam Museum, University of Cambridge. Photo: Fitzwilliam Museum, University of Cambridge/Bridgeman Images. Palmer painted intensely romanticised pastoral scenes, inspired by the pastoral eclogues of the Roman writer Virgil (70–19 BCE), which he translated into English, and the pictures of the visionary artist and illustrator William Blake (1757–1827).

animals have also long had literary associations – for example, working horses are often associated with strength and hard work, and farm dogs with fidelity.

Pastoral writing has had a strong influence on British writers. In Shakespeare's *As You Like It* (*c.*1599), a banished duke escapes to the pastoral world of the Forest of Arden. Two centuries later, **Romantic** poets drew upon the pastoral's sense of country and city values being opposed to each other, in order to evoke the sense of 'loss and alienation' associated with the agricultural and industrial revolutions (Garrard, 2012, p. 44). This Romantic poetry expresses an anxiety that rural landscapes and traditions were under threat from an encroaching modernity. As the critic Raymond Williams points out, pastoral frequently takes the child's point of view (Williams, 2016, p. 16): descriptive passages of rural idyll in literature are often associated with childhood memories. They represent a nostalgic longing to return to a state of youth and innocence located in the writer's own life, to preserve in writing what otherwise would be irrevocably lost.

Activity 2.1

Allow around 20 minutes to complete this activity

This activity is in two parts.

When he first told Leslie Stephen about his plans for *Far from the Madding Crowd*, Hardy described the novel as 'a pastoral tale' (Millgate, 2004, p. 135). But exactly how 'pastoral' is *Far from the Madding Crowd*?

Part A

Look again at the description of pastoral literature just provided, and then look back over the notes you took while reading *Far from the Madding Crowd*. You may also want to reread any particularly relevant passages you can remember in the novel. Make a list of 'pastoral' elements in the book. Don't worry if the list isn't very long.

Discussion

The most obvious link between *Far from the Madding Crowd* and the pastoral is its focus on sheep and shepherds. (As we have seen in Chapter 1, the book follows the sequence of the sheep-farming year.) Gabriel Oak is a shepherd in love who plays the flute – and it's hard to think of a more 'pastoral' figure than that. When going to propose

SHE STOOD UP IN THE WINDOW-OPENING, FACING THE MEN.

Figure 2.2 Helen Allingham, 'She Stood Up in the Window-Opening, Facing the Men' from *The Cornhill Magazine*, 1874. British Library, London, Shelfmark no. RB.23.a.15320. Photo: © British Library Board. All Rights Reserved/Bridgeman Images. A pastoral idyll: Helen Allingham's illustration shows the occasion of the sheep-shearing supper in *Far from the Madding Crowd.*

marriage to Bathsheba, Gabriel takes a lamb along with him as a present (p. 31). Additionally, there are descriptions of landscapes and buildings that seem to present an idealised, pastoral view of the countryside, in contrast to cramped city life:

> It was the first day of June, and the sheep-shearing season culminated, the landscape, even to the leanest pasture, being all health and colour. Every green was young, every pore was open, and every stalk was swollen with racing currents of juice. God was palpably present in the country, and he had gone with the world to town.
>
> (p. 142)

There are other contrasts between country and city in the novel: for example, in Cainy Ball's wide-eyed account of Bath (pp. 216–19), and in the narrator's observation that time is different in the two places ('The citizens' *Then* is the rustics' *Now*' (p. 144)). At the sheep-shearing supper, there is something approaching a singing competition, between Jan Coggan, Joseph Poorgrass and (the clear winner) Bathsheba, accompanied by Gabriel's flute (pp. 154–7); Hardy makes a direct reference to a pastoral eclogue by the Roman poet Virgil (70–19 BCE) at this point (p. 156; note on p. 415). There are also episodes where a lover talks companionably, if sadly, about his lack of success with a woman (examples include Boldwood's conversation with Gabriel, on pp. 251–3, and Gabriel's with Coggan, on p. 221).

Part B

Now look back over your list. Are any of the pastoral elements you have listed also 'anti-pastoral'? In other words, do they undermine or clash with any of the attitudes or ideas characteristic of pastoral literature? According to the critic Stephen Regan, Hardy's 'version of pastoral' in *Far from the Madding Crowd* is 'one that functions in dark and unsettling ways' (Regan, 2009, p. 246). Do you agree with him?

Discussion

When Hardy writes about animals in *Far from the Madding Crowd*, things are often grim, and certainly not conventionally 'pastoral'. The reader is, as the critic Ivan Kreilkamp says, constantly made aware of the 'indecorous bodily life of the sheep in Gabriel's care': they 'are not fluffy baa-lambs but start out as membranous, slightly disgusting beings who [in Chapter II] must be coaxed to recognize and take hold of their own lives and bodily forms' (Kreilkamp, 2009, p. 475). Gabriel's flock is effectively killed by one of his own sheepdogs (Chapter V), and later on, Bathsheba's sheep break into the clover field and become bloated – 'Many of them foamed at the mouth, their breathing being quick and short, whilst the bodies of all were fearfully distended' (p. 137). As Bathsheba says, 'Sheep are such unfortunate animals!' (p. 137). The dog that befriends Fanny is equally unfortunate, 'stoned away' by the workhouse attendant (p. 263).

On my own list, I found that some of the 'pastoral' items I identified were 'darkened' by worry about money. Gabriel's flute-playing is an example of this. When he plays his flute at the hiring fair, we are told, in a direct reference to pastoral, that he could 'pipe with Arcadian sweetness' (p. 45). The context for this comment is dismal, however: Gabriel is only playing his flute to earn a few pennies, because he has failed to get a job as a shepherd; he is, in other words, a shepherd playing his flute because he can't be a shepherd. Money and the lack of it plays a crucial role in *Far from the Madding Crowd*: Gabriel's calculations about the amount Bathsheba stands to lose if her ricks are destroyed in the storm (p. 240) is only the most noticeable of such moments.

Despite all this, I felt that many of the other 'pastoral' moments remained resolutely undarkened, continuing to cast something of a golden glow on the surrounding narrative. Gabriel does after all end up playing his flute in happier surroundings than the hiring fair: at the malthouse (p. 67) and at the sheep-shearing supper (p. 157). Sometimes these golden moments connect up poignantly with terrible events in the story: Bathsheba's song at the sheep-shearing supper, for example, about a faithless soldier with 'a winning tongue' (p. 157, and note on p. 415) is followed in the next chapter by her first meeting with the eloquent but unreliable Troy (p. 161).

The country and the city: Wessex and London

Though the pastoral contrast between the country and the city appears only occasionally in *Far from the Madding Crowd*, it is extremely important in the circumstances *behind* the composition of the book itself – in Hardy's own anomalous, displaced position at the time of writing.

Hardy wrote *Far from the Madding Crowd* in the countryside, in the cottage in Higher Bockhampton in Dorset in which he'd grown up. At times the part played by the natural world in the composition of the novel was very direct: Hardy remembered later that he had written 'sometimes indoors, sometimes out – when he would occasionally find himself without a scrap of paper at the very moment that he felt volumes. In such circumstances he would use large leaves, white chips left by the wood-cutters, or pieces of stone or slate that came to hand' (Hardy, 1984, pp. 98–9).

Higher Bockhampton was a place with idyllic pastoral associations for Hardy. When later in life he reread the pastoral *Idylls* of Theocritus, they reawakened in him memories of his boyhood life:

> Cf Theocritus & the life at Bock$^{\underline{n}}$ – when I was a boy – in the wheatfield, at the well, cidermaking, wheat weeding, &c.
>
> (Hardy, 2009, p. 62)

While writing *Far from the Madding Crowd* in the autumn of 1873, Hardy had helped his father with the cider-making. It was

> a proceeding he had always enjoyed from childhood—the apples being from huge old trees that have now long perished, as well as the old outbuildings. It was the last time he ever took part in a work whose sweet smells and oozings in the crisp autumn air can never be forgotten by those who have had a hand in it.
>
> (Hardy, 1984, p. 99)

This was a life very different from the other one Hardy was simultaneously living in London. In 1874, London was the largest city

Figure 2.3 (Left) Gustave Doré, 'Ludgate Hill – A Block in the Street', 1872, wood engraving. Photo: Granger/Bridgeman Images. (Right) Gustave Doré, 'A Ball at the Mansion House', 1873, wood engraving. Photo: Granger/Bridgeman Images. Two faces of London shown in pictures by Gustave Doré (1832–1883) for *London, A Pilgrimage* (London, 1872). In *The Hand of Ethelberta* (1876), the book he wrote immediately after *Far from the Madding Crowd*, Hardy transports a Wessex family to London: while the sons work as jobbing labourers, the daughter, Ethelberta, flourishes in high society.

in the world, at the centre of an empire covering more than a quarter of the earth's land surface. The city was a vast and disorientating metropolis: in the words of the author and political theorist Walter Bagehot, London was 'like a newspaper. Everything is there and everything is disconnected' (quoted in Frawley, 2017, p. 387).

Hardy had arrived in the capital in 1862, aged 21, working at first as an assistant in an architect's office, but driven by the ambition to become a poet. His move from Dorset to London was not just a geographical one: it also entailed the crossing of class boundaries. The son of a jobbing builder, Hardy had moved across from the social world of the Dorset 'labouring classes' into polite, middle-class cultured London, a painful transition that inevitably left him, in the critic Roger Ebbatson's words, 'self-divided in respect of social class' (Ebbatson, 2009, p. 170).

Context in focus: Beginning as a novelist

Hardy had initially wanted to be a poet, but he found that prose fiction was more appealing to publishers. The first novel he wrote, *The Poor Man and the Lady*, seems to have explored class tensions more trenchantly than any of his later works. It was praised by a publisher's reader, the famous novelist George Meredith (1828–1909), but Hardy was nevertheless advised that it was 'too socialistic, not to say revolutionary' (Hardy, 1984, p. 63) to risk printing. *The Poor Man and the Lady* was not published and no text of it survives. Drastically changing tack, Hardy next wrote a plot-heavy, sensationalist novel – a thriller, in effect – called *Desperate Remedies* (1871), which *was* published. Hardy then focused in detail on a rural setting in *Under the Greenwood Tree* (1872), a distinctly pastoral story which Hardy himself referred to as an 'idyll' (Hardy, 1984, p. 88). His third published novel, *A Pair of Blue Eyes* (1873), was written while Hardy was negotiating with Leslie Stephen about the plans for *Far from the Madding Crowd*. It was based on Hardy's courtship of his first wife, Emma. *Far from the Madding Crowd* (1874) was Hardy's fourth published novel. You can find out more about Hardy's life and literary career by reading the entry on him in the *Oxford Dictionary of National Biography* (Millgate, 2006).

When Hardy told the *Cornhill*'s editor that the new novel he was planning would be 'a pastoral tale', he was effectively telling him what he wanted to hear, as Stephen had only become interested in Hardy because of *Under the Greenwood Tree* – perhaps the most purely 'pastoral' of all Hardy's works. Hardy was at an early stage in his career, and urgently needed to make money with his writing: *The Cornhill Magazine* was more prestigious than the publisher, Tinsley's, which Hardy had been writing for before. The founder of the *Cornhill* had envisaged it as a sort of print version of a middle-class London dinner party, full of brilliant and entertaining guests (Schmidt, 1999, p. 205).

In this context, the pastoral feeling of *Far from the Madding Crowd* looks then, in part, like an attempt by Hardy to play it safe and fit in with the preferences of his middle-class London readership. While there is much misery in the novel, meanwhile, Hardy airbrushed out a slew of social problems in Dorset – a county found by an 1867 report to be 'one of the areas where wages were lowest, cottages the least sanitary, landlords the most unenlightened, and the plight of the labouring class nearest to desperation' (Millgate, 1971, p. 98). Just before Stephen got in touch with Hardy about the possibility of writing for the *Cornhill*, Hardy attended a meeting in support of the activist Joseph Arch's attempt to get Dorset agricultural workers to found a trade union (Millgate, 1971, p. 98). Hardy's choice of Puddletown ('Weatherbury') as his main location may, his biographer Michael Millgate suggests, have been due to its reputation as a place where labourers were, like those on Bathsheba's farm, particularly well treated (Millgate, 1971, p. 101). The organisation of labour in Weatherbury, meanwhile, differs from actual practice: where most agricultural labour on farms depended on precarious short-term contracts, the labourers on Bathsheba's farm seem to be in permanent, stable employment (Plietzsch, 2004, p. 101).

Hardy's title for his novel comes from what was then perhaps the most famous poem in English, the 'Elegy Written in a Country Churchyard' by Thomas Gray (1716–1771). In the poem, the line 'Far from the madding crowd's ignoble strife' evokes the lives of country villagers now dead, lived far away from the great public world:

> Along the cool sequester'd vale of life
> They kept the noiseless tenor [i.e. course] of their way
>
> (Gray, 1966, p. 40)

As Linda M. Shires says in the Introduction to your edition of the set text, however, the events in the novel do not bear out this description of country life, instead involving 'murder, illegitimate children, crop and livestock loss due to carelessness, missing persons, emotional cruelty, the poignant obsessive hope of a man who collects dresses for a woman who will not marry him, and poverty and suffering leading to death in a workhouse' (Shires, 2002, p. xx). Another part of Gray's poem, however, gives a better idea of what Hardy might have been trying to do. Gray points out that obscure people buried in humble

Figure 2.4 'Mob Burns Hay Rick in Swing Riots', 1830. Photo: Chronicle/Alamy. In Chapter VI, one of Bathsheba's ricks catches fire by accident. Here, ricks are burnt as part of the 'Swing riots' of 1830, an example of the sort of agricultural protest studiously not mentioned by Hardy in *Far from the Madding Crowd.*

village churchyards may, for good or ill, have had qualities similar to prominent public figures, but have not – unlike the people he mentions in the poem (all vehement opponents of King Charles I) – had the opportunity to show them in the public world:

> Some village-Hampden, that with dauntless breast
> The little Tyrant of his fields withstood;
> Some mute inglorious Milton here may rest,
> Some Cromwell guiltless of his country's blood.
>
> (Gray, 1966, p. 39)

One way, then, of thinking of Hardy's novel as a whole might be to imagine it as bringing exotic, far-off Dorset to London: showing Hardy's middle-class London audience Bathsheba, Boldwood, Gabriel, Fanny, Liddy and the rest in all their complexity.

This geographical disjunction between Hardy's London and the Dorset of the novel's narrative, therefore, seems to be the major way in which pastoral works in *Far from the Madding Crowd*. Time and change (and therefore nostalgia) are less significant than they later become for pastoral writers like Edmund Blunden, and indeed for Hardy himself in other works. This is a little surprising, as *Far from the Madding Crowd* seems to have been set close to Hardy's birth date in 1840: two things familiar in 1874, when Hardy was writing – the railway and a female monarch (Queen Victoria (1819–1901), who began her reign in 1837) – are described as novelties. Throughout, Hardy's narrator stresses the contrast between the country and city more than the effect of change on the country. (On the other hand, the preface to the novel (pp. 3–4) that Hardy wrote twenty years later is shot through with nostalgia.)

Reading landscape in *Far from the Madding Crowd*

Gabriel on the hill

Hardy does not describe landscape in *Far from the Madding Crowd* in a straightforwardly 'pastoral' way. His descriptions are often extremely detailed and link in different ways to events and characters in the book. In the next activity, you will look at descriptions of two natural settings from the novel: the first one is quite lengthy, and the second is very short. In the second passage, the psychological situation of the human character seems to map very closely on to their natural setting. In this first passage, however, the relationship between person and nature seems less straightforward, and it is that relationship which you will now analyse.

Figure 2.5 Fields of sheep, Dorset. Photo: Joe Dunckley/Alamy. A hill like Gabriel's.

When reading Hardy's extraordinary descriptions, it's easy to let them wash over you and to have their effect without looking at them more closely. The following activity has been designed to slow you down a bit, to get you to separate out and think about the key things that are going on in a passage, so that you can get to grips with the ways in which Hardy's writing describes the world. The passage you will be looking at is the description of Norcombe Hill from the beginning of Chapter II (pp. 14–15). I've divided the passage up into two sections. Make sure that you reread each section before answering the questions on it. You will find it helpful to jot down short answers to each of the questions.

Activity 2.2

Allow around 30 minutes to complete this activity

This activity has two parts.

Part A

First, reread the first three paragraphs of Chapter II (from 'It was nearly midnight ...' to '... smart taps' (p. 14)). When you have finished, answer the following questions:

1 What are the three main natural features here? What is the relationship between them?
2 What signs of human activity are there in these paragraphs? Are people doing anything in it? Are any of the natural features described as if they are people?

Discussion

1 The three main natural features are the wind, the hill itself and the beech trees on it. It isn't a very harmonious rural scene – wind and trees appear to be in conflict: the 'desolating wind' comes from north and strikes the trees.
2 Below is my answer. You may or may not agree with my conclusion; you may, for example, feel that I am over-simplifying and finding things in these extremely rich paragraphs that point in a different direction.

   In the first paragraph, there is reference to something man-made and driven by humans: Bathsheba's yellow carriage. The only human presence in the second paragraph, apart from the mention of a human settlement ('the little town of Emminster'), is an imagined 'passer-by' who the narrator says would feel that the hill is indestructible, even in the face of some future day of natural disaster. Whether Hardy is thinking here of the Christian 'Day of Judgement' (when all humanity will be judged), or whether he is thinking in more scientific and geophysical terms, is left uncertain. Either way, the effect is to highlight the contrast between the temporarily present human passer-by and the immensity and apparent timelessness of the natural world. In the third paragraph, some of the words describing the actions of the wind can also be used to describe human activity and therefore appear to be metaphors: 'smote' (i.e. hit), 'floundered', 'grumbling', 'moan', 'tongue' and 'ferreting out'. The trees and the leaves, on the other hand (the poor victims of the wind), seem less human: the line of beeches looks like the 'mane' of an animal, while the leaves 'simmered' and 'boiled' like a liquid. This is perhaps a bit odd, as, unlike the wind, the beech trees are only there because they have been planted by people (they are a 'plantation'). Something with human origins (the plantation), described as if it's non-human, is being attacked by something non-human (the wind) that Hardy is describing as if it's human. (A quick note: the name for writing in the way Hardy does in the third paragraph, as if nature is capable of expressing human emotions, is **pathetic fallacy**.)

Part B

Now reread the next three paragraphs (from 'Between this half-wooded ...' to '... tiny human frame' (p. 14–15)). What relationship can you find between humanity and nature here?

Discussion

In the first paragraph, the human presence is there at first implicitly, in the act of classifying the different types of wind, 'one rubbing the blades heavily, another raking them piercingly, another brushing them like a soft broom', and then openly, 'The instinctive act of human-kind was to stand, and listen' (p. 14). The human observer grows quiet and lets nature take the place of humanity in singing like a cathedral choir. The imagined speaker is less obvious in the second paragraph, though their perceptions are present in the word 'perceptible'. In the third paragraph, nature – 'the panoramic glide of the stars' (p. 15) – vividly isolates the human observer from the rest of humanity, riding along in an imaginary 'progress through the stars' (p. 15).

If you reread the text following the passage you just looked at, you will find that the reader comes down to earth with a bump. In the narrator's description of Gabriel's slow and steady movements, there are a number of interesting contrasts that you can make with what has gone before in the description of the hill.

Bathsheba among the ferns

The quotation you are going to look at next comes from a manuscript of a chapter about sheep rot, which never made it into Hardy's finished text. (You will find the whole chapter, in which Troy and Gabriel briefly fight, as an appendix in the set text (pp. 390–8).) Though most of the chapter is complete, at one point what look like very rough notes for a description of fungi appear:

> Desc. these fungi thus. Then there was the—with its bloody skin &—spots. which .... There was also
>
> (p. 394)

Presumably Hardy intended to come back to this later and fill in the details. As it turned out, however, although the sheep rot chapter was dropped, a completed version of the fungi description did appear in the published version – but at a completely different point in the story. In this new location, rounded out and amplified, the fungi description makes perfect sense and eloquently develops the situation; it is as if it had always been intended to go where it ended up.

The full version of the description appears as part of the passage in Chapter XLIV that you will read in the following activity. Having confronted Troy over Fanny's coffin and been spurned by him, Bathsheba has just spent the night outside. She looks around and notices a 'hollow' which she has narrowly missed falling into.

Activity 2.3

Allow around 40 minutes to complete this activity

This activity has two parts.

Part A

Reread the passage in Chapter XLIV from 'There was an opening towards the east ...' to '... brink of so dismal a place' (p. 296), and then answer the following question:

How do you think the use of imagery in the passage might be related to Bathsheba's recent experience?

Discussion

The appearance of the fungi at this point doesn't look accidental: the disgust Bathsheba feels for the fungi seems very much like an echo of her wish to escape Troy, who has just told Bathsheba that she is 'nothing' to him (p. 293). The splotches of red echo the redness of Troy's coat, in the days before their marriage, and there is an air of fetid, fleshy, repellent ('moist', 'clammy', 'oozing', 'rotting', 'leathery') sexuality about the whole passage.

There are striking reminders in the passage you have just read of a very different evocation of Bathsheba's sexual relationship with her first husband: the description much earlier in the book of Troy's sword exercise (Chapter XXVIII). Both passages seem to take place in the same location, a 'hollow amid the ferns' (p. 181), although in different seasons: the sword exercise takes place on a midsummer evening, and Bathsheba's encounter with the fungi on an autumn morning.

Part B

Reread the sword exercise chapter, Chapter XXVIII (pp. 181–5), and answer the following questions:

1 What are the main differences between the plants of the hollow in midsummer (in the sword exercise chapter) and in the autumn (in the passage discussed in Part A of this activity)?

2 Do any features of the sword exercise chapter (the imagery it uses, for example) remind you of the description of the swamp?

Discussion

1 In the midsummer evening of the sword exercise, the ferns are freshly grown and therefore a bright, 'untainted' green colour (p. 181); in autumn, as seen by the recently-awakened Bathsheba, they are 'yellowing' (p. 296). In summer, the hollow is 'floored with a thick flossy carpet of moss and grass intermingled, so yielding that the foot was half buried within it' (p. 181). In autumn, the same place is less pleasant underfoot: it has become a 'species of swamp, dotted with fungi' (p. 296).

2 Here are the similarities that I noticed.

   In both passages, the ferns are attractive ('beautiful' in the autumn (p. 296), 'radiant' in the summer (p. 181)). At the start of both passages, Bathsheba is welcomed to the hollow by their 'feathery arms' (p. 296). Early on in the swamp passage, the 'species of flag' (or wild iris) that glistens in the sun 'like scythes' (p. 296) is reminiscent of Troy's flashing blade in the sword exercise. (There is a particularly strong link to Troy's fourth 'cut', made, he says, 'as if you were reaping' (p. 182): reaping was often done in Hardy's day with a scythe). Both scenes are lit by a low sun, but whereas in autumn there is a mist, in summer everything is bright and gleaming.

In both passages, Bathsheba avoids damaging contact with something: a fatal sword-point in summer, 'clammy' fungi in autumn (p. 296). Her responses to the two kinds of alien object are very different, however. During the sword exercise, she feels excited and physically overwhelmed by Troy ('He was altogether too much for her' (p. 185)); in the fungi passage, she is simply repulsed. There is also a strong contrast between the different kinds of liquid that appear in the two passages: a poisonous swamp in one passage, the 'liquid stream' of tears (p. 185) brought on by Troy's first kiss in the other. Intriguingly, however, the emotion of that kiss is said in the sword exercise chapter to have 'swamped' Bathsheba's thought (p. 185).

Vivid descriptions, like the accounts of Norcombe Hill and the hollow in the ferns, occur throughout *Far from the Madding Crowd*. Rereading and working through these passages, as in the previous two activities, is an enjoyable way of extending your work on Hardy.

Conclusion

In this chapter, we have explored some of the ways in which the popular caricature of Hardy as a nostalgic 'pastoral' writer can be challenged and complicated. Our approach has involved both the close reading of key descriptive passages and a broader consideration of the relationship between *Far from the Madding Crowd* and the genre of pastoral literature. You will find that your work on this module will continue to involve both of these elements – close textual analysis and more general ideas – and that literary analysis is at its most exciting when both work together, with broad conclusions grounded in evidence gained from close reading.

References

Set text

Hardy, T. (2002) *Far from the madding crowd*. Edited by Suzanne B. Falck-Yi, introduction by Linda M. Shires. Oxford: Oxford University Press. Oxford World's Classics.

Other references

Cox, R.G. (ed.) (1979) *Thomas Hardy: the critical heritage*. London: Routledge.

Ebbatson, R. (2009) '"A thickness of wall": Hardy and class', in Wilson, K. (ed.) *A companion to Thomas Hardy*. Oxford: Wiley-Blackwell, pp. 162–77. Available online via the OU Library.

Foley, S. (2012) 'Imagery', in Green, R., Cushman, S. and Cavanagh, C. (eds) *The Princeton encyclopedia of poetry and poetics*. 4th edn. Princeton: Princeton University Press. Available online via the OU Library.

Frawley, M. (2017) 'The Victorian age', in Poplawski, P. (ed.) *English literature in context*. Cambridge: Cambridge University Press, pp. 364–469.

Garrard, G. (2012) *Ecocriticism*. 2nd edn. Abingdon: Routledge.

Gifford, T. (1999) *Pastoral*. Abingdon: Routledge.

Gray, T. (1966) *The complete poems of Thomas Gray: English, Latin and Greek*. Edited by H.W. Starr and J.R. Hendrickson. Oxford: Oxford University Press.

Hardy, T. (1984) *The life and works of Thomas Hardy*. Edited by Michael Millgate. Basingstoke: Palgrave Macmillan.

Hardy, T. (2009) *Thomas Hardy's 'poetical matter' notebook*. Edited by Pamela Dalziell and Michael Millgate. Oxford: Oxford University Press. Available online via the OU Library.

Howe, I. (1966) *Thomas Hardy*. London: Weidenfeld and Nicholson.

Kreilkamp, I. (2009) 'Pitying the sheep in *Far from the madding crowd*', *Novel: A Forum on Fiction*, 42(3), pp. 474–81. Available online via the OU Library.

Millgate, M. (1971) *Thomas Hardy: his career as a novelist*. London: Bodley Head.

Millgate, M. (2004) *Thomas Hardy: a biography revisited*. Oxford: Oxford University Press.

Millgate, M. (2006) ‘Thomas Hardy (1840–1928)’, in *Oxford dictionary of national biography* (2004). Available at: https://www-oxforddnb-com.libezproxy.open.ac.uk/view/10.1093/ref:odnb/9780198614128.001.0001/odnb-9780198614128-e-33708 (Accessed: 5 June 2019).

Plietzsch, B. (2004) *The novels of Thomas Hardy as a product of nineteenth-century social, economic and cultural change*. Berlin: Tenea.

Regan, S. (2009) ‘The darkening pastoral: *Under the greenwood tree* and *Far from the madding crowd*’, in Wilson, K. (ed.) *A companion to Thomas Hardy*. Oxford: Wiley-Blackwell, pp. 239–53. Available online via the OU Library.

Schmidt, B.Q. (1999) ‘Introduction. *The Cornhill Magazine*: celebrating success’, *Victorian Periodicals Review*, 32(2), pp. 202–8. Available online via the OU Library.

Shires, L.M. (2002) ‘Introduction’ in Hardy, T., *Far from the madding crowd*. Edited by Suzanne B. Falck-Yi, introduction by Linda M. Shires. Oxford: Oxford University Press. Oxford World’s Classics, pp. xi–xxx.

Siddall, S. (2009) *Landscape and literature*. Cambridge: Cambridge University Press.

Williams, R. (2016) *The country and the city*. Introduction by Tristram Hunt. London: Vintage Classics.

Chapter 3 Thomas Hardy, *Far from the Madding Crowd*: Realism, serialisation and criticism

Jonathan Gibson

Contents

Introduction

This chapter looks at *Far from the Madding Crowd* from three different points of view. It begins by taking a step back from the previous two chapters' detailed textual analysis, to instead consider the relationship between Hardy's novel and the idea of realism. The second section of this chapter looks at the original publication of *Far from the Madding Crowd* as a serial in a magazine and the effects that serialisation had on the structure of the book. Finally, the third section of this chapter provides you with a framework for engaging with critical approaches to Hardy's work.

Hardy and realism

How realist a novel is *Far from the Madding Crowd*? How well does it fit the definitions of realism discussed in the Introduction to this book? Many people would classify Hardy's work as a 'classic realist novel', and would say that it conformed to the definition from Chris Baldick's *Oxford Dictionary of Literary Terms* for 'the 19th century novel of middle- or lower- class life': a novel 'in which the problems of ordinary people in unremarkable circumstances are rendered with close attention to the details of physical setting and to the complexities of social life' (Baldick, 2015a).

It's true that Bathsheba, Gabriel and the other characters are 'ordinary people' – they aren't royalty or great military heroes – and, as Chapter 2 of this book has shown, Hardy certainly pays close attention to 'the details of physical setting'. But are the events depicted equally ordinary? Bizarre (if, admittedly, not supernatural) things happen in the novel and these could be thought to be more **melodramatic**, **Gothic** or sensationalist than realist: the episode of the 'gurgoyle' (pp. 306–12); Troy's disappearance and transmogrification into Dick Turpin (pp. 330–5); his apparent return from the dead at Boldwood's party (pp. 366–7); and the gruesome scene at the coffin (pp. 288–94). Suffering, when it comes, is extreme: Gabriel's entire flock falls to its death (pp. 39–41); Boldwood goes mad and murders Troy (p. 367); and the pregnant Fanny dies after a horrifying last walk (pp. 258–63). As many critics have pointed out, meanwhile, chance and coincidence play what looks like a disproportionately large part in Hardy's stories. In *Far from the Madding Crowd*, examples include the lucky chance that Gabriel comes across Bathsheba's flaming rick (pp. 47–55), the accidental meeting of Bathsheba and Troy in the middle of the night (pp. 161–5), the mix-up over All Saints' and All Souls' (pp. 115–17), and the failure of Joseph Poorgrass to deliver the coffin (pp. 274–82). These do not seem like 'unremarkable circumstances'.

Hardy himself was aware of the contrast in his stories between his 'ordinary people' and the remarkable events he made them live through. A note on fiction written by him in 1881 includes this suggestion:

> The writer's problem is, how to strike the balance between the uncommon and the ordinary so as on the one hand to give interest, on the other to give reality.
>
> In working out this problem, human nature must never be made abnormal, which is introducing incredibility. The uncommonness must be in the events, not in the characters; and the writer's art lies in shaping that uncommonness while disguising its unlikelihood, if it be unlikely.
>
> (Hardy, 1984, p. 154)

Many readers of Hardy have felt that he was not very good at 'disguising' the 'unlikelihood' of his events!

The sense the reader gets in *Far from the Madding Crowd* that the progress of the novel is being driven by unusual chance events – more, perhaps, than the characters' willed decisions – is highlighted by the often rather oblique way in which the narrator talks about what is going on inside characters' heads. As Chapter 1's analysis of the opening chapters of the novel has shown, Hardy's narrator does not always tell us everything about a character's thoughts, feelings and motivations; some information is held back. This gap in information seems particularly striking, I think, as the novel draws to its close, in the narrator's unwillingness to go into any detail about Bathsheba's and Gabriel's feelings for each other; we also, for example, learn less than we might about the nature of Gabriel's reluctance to tell Bathsheba about Fanny's relationship with Troy, something he is clearly brooding on for much of the novel.

One element in the book, however, seems more 'realist' to a modern-day reader than it did to Hardy's earliest readers: the depiction of women, and, in particular, of female sexuality. Hardy was writing *Far from the Madding Crowd* in the middle of Queen Victoria's reign; while there were many women who led important and influential professional lives, their situation was 'hampered by prevailing medical myths that perpetuated the belief that women were "by nature" weaker, more prone to disease and debility, and suited to quiet lives [in the home]' (Frawley, 2017, p. 375). Any form of female sexual activity outside marriage was strongly condemned. 'Fallen women' who behaved in this way, like Fanny, were demonised. Tragically, among women who, like Fanny, had given birth to an 'illegitimate' baby, infanticide – the murder of the child – was an all too common response

(Higginbotham, 1989). In *Far from the Madding Crowd*, Hardy's narrator can sometimes seem misogynistic when making generalisations about women (as, for example, in the early part of the novel analysed in Chapter 1), and Gabriel's constant spying on Bathsheba can be seen as unpleasantly voyeuristic by modern-day readers. But there is a degree of sympathy for Fanny – a failure to condemn extra-marital sex – that would have struck many Victorian readers as incomprehensible. Many of these same readers would also have been puzzled by the book's apparent tolerance of Bathsheba's independent-mindedness and her continuing sexual desire for an unworthy partner.

Serialisation

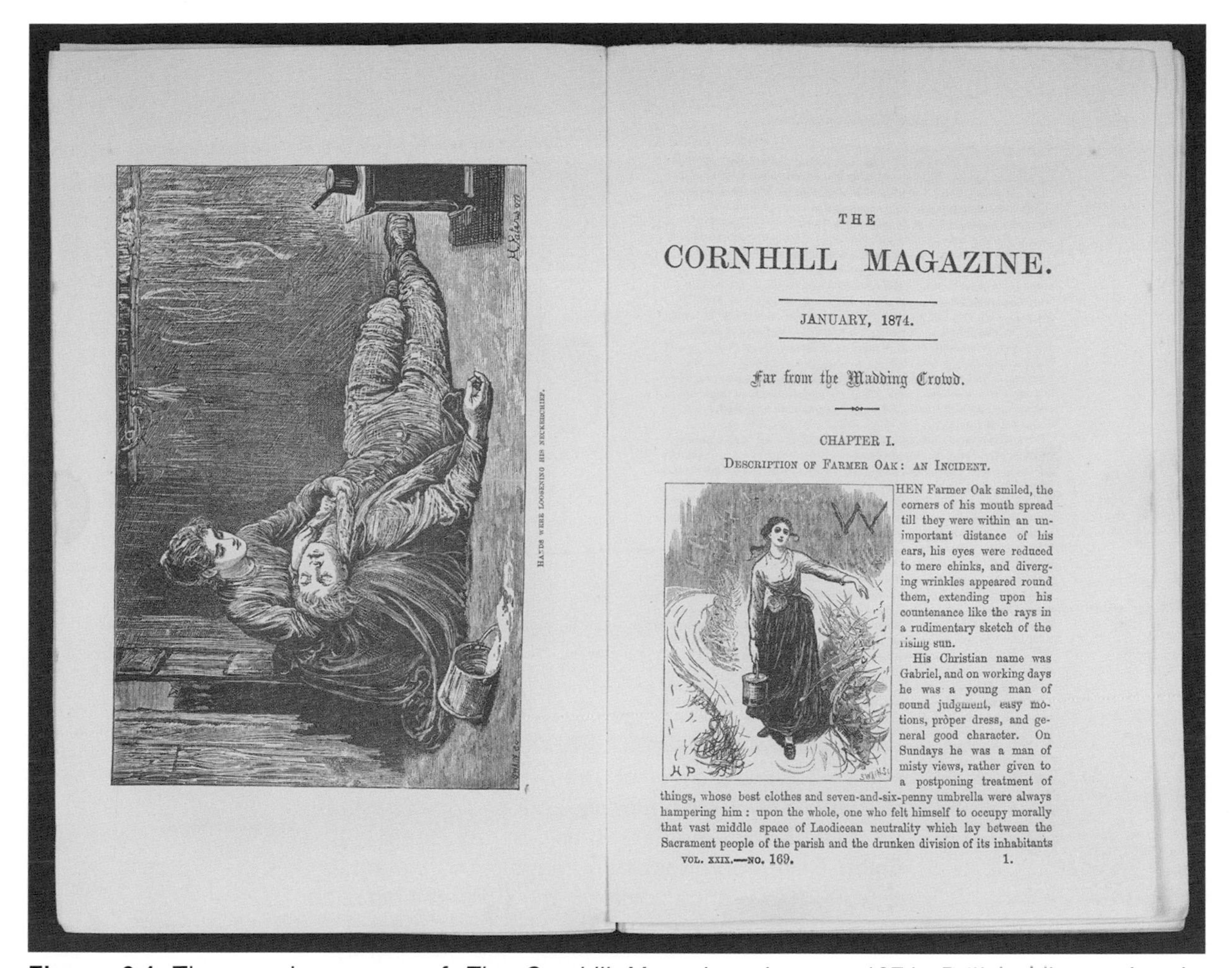

HANDS WERE LOOSENING HIS NECKERCHIEF.

THE

CORNHILL MAGAZINE.

JANUARY, 1874.

Far from the Madding Crowd.

CHAPTER I.

DESCRIPTION OF FARMER OAK: AN INCIDENT.

WHEN Farmer Oak smiled, the corners of his mouth spread till they were within an unimportant distance of his ears, his eyes were reduced to mere chinks, and diverging wrinkles appeared round them, extending upon his countenance like the rays in a rudimentary sketch of the rising sun.

His Christian name was Gabriel, and on working days he was a young man of sound judgment, easy motions, pròper dress, and general good character. On Sundays he was a man of misty views, rather given to a postponing treatment of things, whose best clothes and seven-and-six-penny umbrella were always hampering him: upon the whole, one who felt himself to occupy morally that vast middle space of Laodicean neutrality which lay between the Sacrament people of the parish and the drunken division of its inhabitants

VOL. XXIX.—NO. 169. 1.

Figure 3.1 The opening pages of *The Cornhill Magazine*, January 1874. British Library, London, Shelfmark no. RB.23.a.15320. Photo: © British Library Board. All Rights Reserved/Bridgeman Images. These pages begin the serialisation of *Far from the Madding Crowd*. The frontispiece depicts Bathsheba rescuing Gabriel from suffocation in his shepherd's hut (Chapter III).

Your set text edition of *Far from the Madding Crowd* includes all of Hardy's text along with an introduction, notes and two maps (Hardy, 2002). It has no illustrations, and the name of the author is prominent on the cover. When *Far from the Madding Crowd* was first published, however, it did not take this form. As mentioned in Chapter 2, it was serialised – that is, printed in sections of a few chapters at a time. Each section, or 'part', appeared in one of twelve successive monthly issues of *The Cornhill Magazine*, from January to

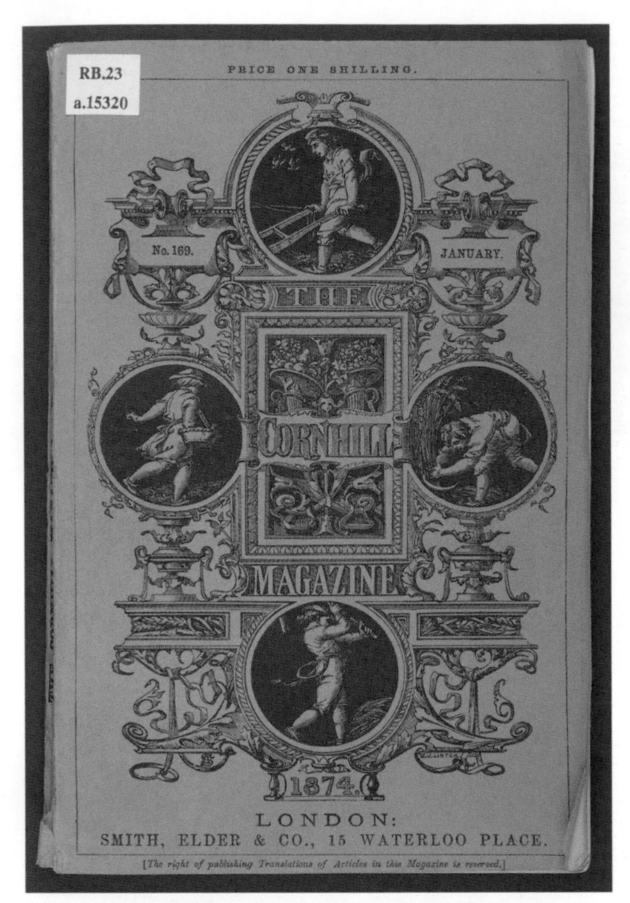

Figure 3.2 Front cover of *The Cornhill Magazine*, January 1874. British Library, London, Shelfmark no. RB.23.a.15320. Photo: © British Library Board. All Rights Reserved/Bridgeman Images. The instantly recognisable orange cover of *The Cornhill Magazine* is, like the plot of *Far from the Madding Crowd*, structured around the agricultural year: each of the four roundels depicts a different stage in the production of corn, in a pun on the magazine's title. The implication is that the magazine's articles will provide the reader with food for the mind (Cooke, 2016).

December 1874, each accompanied by two illustrations (see Figures 3.1 to 3.3 for images of the magazine and one of its readers). Table 3.1 shows how the chapters were grouped into parts. The story appeared anonymously: Hardy's name appeared neither next to the serial itself nor in the advertising for the issue. As the parts were published, reviews appeared in other newspapers (much as reviews of TV serials

Figure 3.3 John Everett Millais, *Effie Millais née Gray*, 1873, oil on canvas, 100 × 84 cm. Perth & Kinross Council, acc no. 3/149. Photo: The Picture Art Collection/Alamy. This image shows one of *The Cornhill Magazine*'s readers, in a portrait by her second husband. Her first, unconsummated, marriage had been to the art critic John Ruskin. Ruskin wrote for the *Cornhill*, but the magazine stopped publishing him because of the radical political arguments in his articles.

appear now). *The Illustrated London News*, for example, thought that the novel was slow to get under way, responding with impatience to the descriptions of Gabriel and Bathsheba in the early chapters: '[t]he most prominent characteristic of this story is, so far, its extreme minuteness of detail, evincing carefulness of composition rather than the glow of inspiration' (*The Illustrated London News*, 1874a, p. 10). By

July, the reviewer had decided that *Far from the Madding Crowd* was certainly 'not to be reckoned among the most successful novels of the *Cornhill*' (*The Illustrated London News*, 1874b). As the novel sped towards its **dénouement**, however, the reviewer cheered up: '*Far from the Madding Crowd* certainly improves in interest as it approaches its conclusion. There is more action, and less tediously minute elaboration of character' (*The Illustrated London News*, 1874c, p. 474).

Table 3.1 The parts of *Far from the Madding Crowd*, as printed in *The Cornhill Magazine*. The story was spread across Volumes 29 (January–June 1874) and 30 (July–December 1874). Page numbers refer to the equivalent text in the Oxford World's Classics edition (Hardy, 2002).

Date	Chapters	Page nos (set text)	Events
January 1874	I–V	pp. 9–42	Gabriel's failed wooing; loss of his sheep and Bathsheba's move away.
February 1874	VI–VIII	pp. 43–72	Gabriel saves Bathsheba's rick and is employed by her; Fanny; the malthouse.
March 1874	IX–XIV	pp. 73–102	Bathsheba, her labourers, and Boldwood; Fanny at the barracks; the valentine.
April 1874	XV–XX	pp. 103–135	Boldwood identifies valentine sender; rejected by Bathsheba; Gabriel fired.
May 1874	XXI–XXIV	pp. 136–165	Gabriel rehired; sheep-shearing and supper; Troy meets Bathsheba.
June 1874	XXV–XXIX	pp. 166–192	Troy and Bathsheba at harvest, bee hiving, sword exercise; Gabriel's advice.
July 1874	XXX–XXXIII	pp. 193–221	Bathsheba rejects Boldwood and he threatens to attack Troy; her night ride.
August 1874	XXXIV–XXXVIII	pp. 222–253	News from Bath; Troy tricks Boldwood; marriage revealed; the storm.
September 1874	XXXIX–XLII	pp. 254–283	Meeting Fanny on the road; her death; her corpse brought to Bathsheba's house.

Date	Chapters	Page nos (set text)	Events
October 1874	XLIII–XLVII	pp. 284–316	Troy finds Fanny, rejects Bathsheba; Troy and the gurgoyle; Troy swims off.
November 1874	XLVIII–LI	pp. 317–347	Boldwood hopeful; Greenhill fair, Troy and Pennyways; Gabriel and Bathsheba.
December 1874	LII–LVII	pp. 348–389	Christmas party and Troy's death; marriage of Bathsheba and Gabriel.

The experience of *Far from the Madding Crowd*'s first readers, then, would have been very different from ours. It's likely that you have been reading the book over a short, intensive period. There was nothing stopping you from flicking ahead at any point to see how the story ended. By contrast, what the reader of *The Cornhill Magazine* would have encountered was 'a continuing story over an extended time with enforced interruptions' (Hughes and Lund, 1991, p. 1). Their immersion in the world of Weatherby and the affairs of Bathsheba, Boldwood, Troy and Gabriel would have been a gradual, piecemeal one and they would have lived with the characters over many weeks. The purchaser of the first issue, in January 1874, would have only been able to read up to the end of Chapter V. After finding out about the loss of Gabriel's sheep, they would have had to wait for a month before discovering what happened next. They would have had to wait until the spring to find out about Boldwood's response to Bathsheba's valentine, and they would have been living in the world of the novel for four months before, in May, they could read about Troy's first meeting with Bathsheba. It would be winter again by the time they found out about the grim fates of Troy and Boldwood. As Hughes and Lund argue, 'Serialization … fostered an approach to narrative as a gradually developing story and pattern of significance, with pauses between parts for additional reflection and speculation, rather than as a finished aesthetic product to be read and considered as a whole all at once' (Hughes and Lund, 1991, p. 7). For much of the serial, the time of year described in the novel matched the time of year in the reader's real life. The two descriptions of the hollow in the ferns that you analysed in Chapter 2, for example, each appeared in the appropriate month: the midsummer episode (the sword exercise) in June, and the autumn one (Bathsheba and the swamp) in October. Additionally, some articles in the *Cornhill* strikingly echoed the concerns of the novel, and look as if they might have been deliberately chosen with that month's part of *Far from the Madding Crowd* in mind as a prompt for discussions around the dinner table. Examples include an article about workhouse schools and London maids-of-all-work in the September issue in which Fanny Robin dies at Casterbridge workhouse (or 'Union house'), and an article on 'Agricultural labourers' that appeared in July, the month of the corn harvest.

Stephen, Hardy and the challenges of serialisation

Records survive of some of the correspondence between Hardy and the *Cornhill*'s editor, Leslie Stephen (Figure 3.4), about the serialisation of *Far from the Madding Crowd*. From these, it is possible to trace some of the alterations made to the text, in the period between Hardy's initial writing of the manuscript (now in the Beinecke Library in America) and the publication of the text in the magazine. The available evidence is patchy – by no means have all the relevant letters survived – but there is enough to show clearly that the form *Far from the Madding Crowd* takes in *The Cornhill Magazine* was crucially influenced not only by the demands of writing for serialisation, but also by particular decisions made by Stephen.

When Stephen first commissioned the story, he explained to Hardy that the new serial would have to be different from *Under the Greenwood Tree* – the only previous novel of Hardy's that Stephen knew – a gentle pastoral romance full of amusing and picturesque scenes of country life: '"Under the Greenwood Tree" is of course not a magazine story. There is too little incident for such purposes; for, though I do not want a murder in every number, it is necessary to catch the attitude of readers by some distinct and well arranged plot' (Letter to Hardy, 30 November 1872, in Hardy, 1986, p. 340).

Hardy said that he was ready to take instruction from Stephen and to prioritise the needs of serialisation when writing his story:

> I am willing, and indeed anxious, to give up any points which may be desirable in a story when read as a whole, for the sake of others which shall please those who read it in numbers

> [i.e. monthly parts]. Perhaps I may have higher aims some day, and be a great stickler for the proper artistic balance of the completed work, but for the present circumstances lead me to wish merely to be considered a good hand at a serial.
>
> (Hardy, 1986, pp. 342–3)

Stephen's suggestions to Hardy took two main forms. First, he felt that some of the scenes involving Bathsheba's rustic labourers were too long, delaying the progress of the story. Accordingly, he persuaded Hardy to trim the following passages:

- the scene in the malthouse in Chapter XV (removing, Rosemarie Morgan shows, numerous references to rural hardship (Morgan, 1992, pp. 89–96))
- the scene in which Bathsheba pays her workers (Hardy, 1986, p. 341)
- the description of the sheep-shearing supper ('I think it rather delays the action unnecessarily' (Letter to Hardy, 17 February 1874, in Hardy, 1986, p. 342)).

Second, Stephen worried about how sexually explicit some of Hardy's text was, feeling it would offend the more genteel readers of the *Cornhill*. On one occasion, Stephen told Hardy that 'Three respectable ladies and subscribers' had objected to a particular passage early in the serialisation (Hardy, 1984, p. 101); this was probably the section about Bathsheba's father (p. 64). Stephen was also anxious about the episodes involving Fanny Robin:

> May I suggest that Troy's seduction of the young woman will require to be treated in a gingerly fashion, when, as I suppose must be the case, he comes to be exposed to his wife? I mean that the thing must be stated but that the words be careful—excuse the wretched shred of concession to popular stupidity; but I am a slave.
>
> (Letter to Hardy, 12 March 1874, in Hardy, 1986, p. 343)

Figure 3.4 George Frederick Watts, *Sir Leslie Stephen*, 1878, oil on canvas, 66 × 53 cm. National Portrait Gallery, London. Photo: © Stefano Baldini/ Bridgeman Images. Stephen (1832–1904) was one of the most prominent intellectuals of the period, writing prolifically on literary, historical, political and philosophical topics. He was also a keen mountaineer. After his term as editor of *The Cornhill Magazine*, he became founder editor of the *Oxford Dictionary of National Biography*, a key reference work that continues to be updated today (Bell, 2012). To take up a post at Cambridge University early in his career, Stephen had been required to become an Anglican priest. Like Hardy, however, he lost his faith. In 1875, when he formally renounced his clerical qualifications, he asked Hardy to be his witness. Stephen was the father of the famous modernist novelist Virginia Woolf.

Fanny's baby, when it appeared, was a particular worry for Stephen: 'I have some doubts whether the baby is necessary at all … I am necessarily anxious to be on the safe side; and I should somehow be glad to omit the baby' (Letter to Hardy, 13 April 1874, in Hardy, 1986, p. 344). Hardy kept the baby in the *Cornhill* text, but he did remove a long, lyrical description of the beauty and freshness of the dead baby and its mother in the coffin (the 'plump balls' of the baby's fists reminding Bathsheba 'of the soft convexity of mushrooms on a dewy morning' (p. 289)). (You will read the *Cornhill* version of this part of the book in Activity 3.3 later in this chapter.) Meanwhile, the episode in which Fanny and Troy fail, by accident, to get married (Chapter XVI, pp. 115–17) was only added to the serialised text at the very last minute, presumably to render the relationship between the lovers more respectable.

Context in focus: First, second and third thoughts

Some of the excised manuscript passages have been printed in your set text edition of *Far from the Madding Crowd*: the long passage cut from the sheep-shearing supper for *The Cornhill Magazine*, for example, runs from 'Boldwood being at the remote end …' (p. 152) to '… down a conjuror's throat' (p. 154), and the cut description of Fanny's baby appears from 'eager eyes …' to '… returned upon her mind' (pp. 289–90). You will read the *Cornhill's* original text of this episode in Activity 3.3.

Some of Stephen's adjustments were undone when *Far from the Madding Crowd* was published as a novel, taking a physical form much closer to that of your edition of the set text. Novels cost more than magazines and it was felt that their readers would be less easily offended.

Over the years, Hardy made many revisions to the texts of his novels, as they were published and republished. For a concise (but very complicated!) survey of the revisions to *Far from the Madding Crowd*, see the 'Note on the Text' in your set text (pp. xxxi–xxxvii).

Plotting *Far from the Madding Crowd*

When looking at the plot structure of *Far from the Madding Crowd* – the sort of action focused on within particular chapters, and how different events in the story were combined into a sequence – it is useful to bear in mind the requirements of serialisation within which Hardy was working. Serialisation encouraged the construction of 'multiplot' or 'multiple plot' texts, 'fictions with several plot lines among which the serial author could switch from part to part until all converged at the end' (Hughes and Lund, 2010, p. 149). Many novels and other types of narrative, not only serialised ones, tell more than one story at the same time and thus have multiple plots – they can have a number of different plots of equal significance, or perhaps just one 'main plot' and one **'subplot'** (a secondary plot usually involving some different characters). In Shakespeare's play *The Tempest*, for example, which you will read at the end of this module, the main plot involves nobly born characters from the ducal court of Milan. Meanwhile, the subplot revolves around three rebellious servants and their attempt to rebel against the ruler of the island, Prospero.

Activity 3.1

Allow around 25 minutes to complete this activity

Look again at your notes on *Far from the Madding Crowd*, and at Table 3.1 to remind yourself of the sequence of events in the book. Then answer the following questions:

1 Do you think *Far from the Madding Crowd* has a subplot (or subplots) as well as a main plot? If it does, what connection(s) are there between the subplot(s) and the main plot?

2 How does the arrangement of the plot(s) relate to the arrangement of the serialisation into parts, as shown in Table 3.1?

Discussion

1 The plot involving Bathsheba and the three men in love with her is the main plot. This plot has three strands, although I wouldn't classify these as subplots. These strands frequently overlap, when, for example, the action of one man leads to another man having to do something (such as when Gabriel rescues the ricks because of Troy's drunkenness (pp. 236–49)). What happens in Bathsheba's relationship with each man, meanwhile, depends in part on what happens in her relationships with the others (for example, she

ignores her promise to Boldwood because of meeting Troy).

I wouldn't classify the scenes involving Bathsheba's labourers as a subplot either. Sometimes one of these characters does something that has a significant effect on the main plot (for example, Joseph Poorgrass's fateful stop at the Buck's Head with Fanny's coffin (pp. 276–81), an event which leads ultimately to Bathsheba's confrontation with Troy (pp. 282–94)). Mostly, however, the scenes featuring these characters act more like a commentary on the main plot, providing little bits of information about such things as: Bathsheba's reputation and parentage (pp. 47, 63–5); the verdict on Boldwood (p. 375); and troubling changes in rural life ('Tompkins's old apple tree is rooted ... Ah, stirring times we live in' (p. 108)). (An early reviewer compared the role of this group of characters to the function of the 'Chorus' in an ancient Greek play – a character or characters who comment on the play's action from outside (Cox, 1979, p. 43).)

The events involving Fanny Robin and Sergeant Troy, however, do look like a subplot, at least in the first part of the book, where they seem separate from the events in the main plot involving Bathsheba and the three men. Later, this subplot links up with and begins to take over the main plot.

2 Here are a couple of things I noticed. Other things may have caught your attention.

First, I noticed the way in which the three strands of the main plot make their initial appearances. Gabriel is the only one of the three men to appear in the first two parts (January and February), while Boldwood enters the narrative in March and begins to dominate the story. Boldwood and Gabriel are now both 'on stage', as it were, both potential husbands for Bathsheba. At the end of April, however, Bathsheba gets rid of both of them, rejecting Boldwood and sacking Gabriel. Both men return the following month, but are temporarily bumped out of the narrative by Troy, who meets Bathsheba for the first time in May; this new volatile relationship occupies nearly all of June. The end of June marks the six-month midpoint of the serial. Bathsheba's three suitors and the nature of their interrelationship have now been comprehensively introduced.

The second thing I noticed was that the interleaving of the Fanny and Troy subplot into the middle of 'main plot' chapters occurs in three successive parts: February (the meeting with Gabriel (pp. 53–5)); March (the visit to Troy's barracks (pp. 85–9)); and April (the terrible mix-up over All Saints' and All Souls' (pp. 115–17)). In the next part, May, as we have seen, Bathsheba takes Fanny's place with Troy (pp. 160–5). There is one more chapter devoted entirely to this subplot – in September, Chapter XL (pp. 258–63) – in which Fanny walks to the workhouse. From then on, the Fanny–Troy subplot overwhelms the main plot.

Whose story?

It's worth further considering Hardy's arrangement of the different sections of the story, and in particular the choices he makes about what his novel should concentrate on most. Although I have described the Fanny–Troy episodes as having been identified as a separate subplot, they end up being crucial to the main plot – though the reader does not at first, of course, know that this will happen. Moreover, one key character, Sergeant Troy, hops over from the subplot into the main plot. Until Chapter XXIV, when Bathsheba bumps into him after the shearing supper, Troy has only appeared in the two chapters so far with Fanny. The rest of the narrative has been entirely taken up – apart from the odd glancing reference to the Fanny–Troy plot (e.g. p. 152) – with the manoeuvrings of Bathsheba, Boldwood and Gabriel (and Bathsheba and Gabriel only in the first eight chapters).

This way of arranging the material vividly reveals a secret, incriminating past for Troy (known about by Boldwood and Gabriel, but not by Bathsheba), something there is no hint of for Gabriel. (Interestingly, one of the early reviewers of the book complained that 'there is always a sense on the reader's part of not really knowing the background of [Gabriel's] character' (Cox, 1979, p. 35).) By being kept to very few chapters, however, Fanny Robin – arguably the only character in the book to be harmed directly, in a tragic way, by their low social status (and whose time with Troy could easily have taken up a large part of the novel) – is marginalised. The effect of this marginalisation of Fanny is highlighted by the book's repeated failure to name her. She first appears as 'a slim girl, rather thinly clad' (Hardy, 2002, p. 53), encountered by Gabriel on his way to the malthouse and keen for him not to tell anyone about her whereabouts. She is unnamed again throughout the chapter describing the failed attempt to get married (pp. 115–20). When Troy and Bathsheba, out driving in their gig, come across Fanny, Troy is naturally anxious to ensure Fanny's identity is hidden from Bathsheba. Strikingly, the narrator too fails to name her, referring to her only as 'A woman' (p. 255). The same is true in the description which follows of Fanny's gruelling walk to Casterbridge: rather than 'Fanny', she is simply: 'the woman'; 'the pedestrian' (p. 258); 'the wayfarer'; 'a shapeless heap' (p. 259); and finally 'the prostrate figure' (p. 263). Fanny's name appears in two chapter titles (Chapters XLI and XLIII), as she takes her 'revenge', and she has a splendid memorial in the churchyard; but by that point in the narrative, of course, she is dead. We, the readers, never enter Fanny's mind: in the chapter dedicated to her last journey, for example, in order to know how she is feeling, we can rely only on the moments in which she talks to herself ('I'll believe that the end lies five posts forward, and no further, and so get strength to pass them' (p. 260)), and on the narrator's description of her physical progress.

It could be said that Fanny is in a similar position in the story to the jovial drinkers at the malthouse: the lives and voices of these 'lower-class' characters are not explored in as much detail as those of the 'higher-class' characters of Gabriel (rich before the loss of his sheep), Boldwood, Bathsheba and Troy. None of the labourers' or servants' love lives are opened out into anything approaching a plot, whether tragic or comic: such things as Joseph Poorgrass's sexual timidity (pp. 60, 155), Maryann's desire for a lover (p. 150), the state of the Talls' marriage (p. 67) or the maltster's vigorous past (p. 149) function simply as gently comic topics for conversation.

In a later novel, *Tess of the D'Urbervilles* (1892), Hardy is perhaps making up for Fanny's marginalisation in *Far from the Madding Crowd*, providing, in the central figure of Tess herself, a more detailed version of Fanny and her problems (Shires, 2009, p. xxix).

The depiction of the labourers may seem patronising to modern-day readers, but it seems to have struck Hardy's Victorian reviewers in a completely different way: many were astonished to see such 'illiterate clods' (Cox, 1979, p. 30) allowed to display any individuality, wit or intelligence. As Ralph Pite says, though these characters were designed to make the reader laugh at them, they nevertheless 'reveal preferences, character, awareness, limitation, and personal taste' (Pite, 2009, p. 141).

Suspense and surprise: learning about the marriage

We will now look in detail at how Hardy took *Far from the Madding Crowd*'s first readers across the boundary between one month's part and the next. It is important here to bear in mind the difference between two key features in any serial narrative: suspense and **surprise**. These two elements work in quite distinct ways from each other. As Heta Pyrhönen describes, surprise occurs in a narrative when the reader has strong expectations about what will happen, only to find that they 'are violated by what in fact does happen' (2005, p. 578). Suspense, on the other hand, works differently. Suspense occurs when the reader is aware of a number of different possible outcomes and is anxious to see which will actually occur. As Pyrhönen says, '[t]he intensity of suspense is inversely proportional to the range of possibilities' (2005, p. 578). There is therefore most intensity of suspense when there are obviously and compellingly only two possible outcomes, one very desirable, the other not: for example, if, in a thriller there are only two wires to cut, and cutting one of them will set off a bomb.

In the following activity, you will be investigating the serialisation's transition from the July part (Chapters XXX–XXXIII) to the August part (Chapters XXXIV–XXXVIII), leading up to the revelation of Bathsheba's marriage to Troy. The July part begins with Bathsheba arriving home after saying goodbye to Troy, who has gone to Bath for two days. She writes a letter to Boldwood saying she cannot marry him, and then quarrels with Liddy and her other servants about Troy, the nature of her feelings for him, and his bad reputation (Chapter XXX). Next evening, on Yalbury Hill, Boldwood pleads with Bathsheba and worries her by threatening violence against the absent Troy (Chapter XXXI). That night, Bathsheba's servant Maryann sees someone take Bathsheba's horse and gig. Gabriel and Coggan give chase and find that the horse has been taken by Bathsheba, who is driving to Bath to end her relationship with Troy and warn him about Boldwood (Chapter XXXII).

Activity 3.2

Allow around 1 hour to complete this activity

Reread the passage from the final section of Chapter XXXII, from 'Bathsheba's perturbed meditations …' (p. 212) to the end of Chapter XXXIII (p. 221). You have now read the final section of the part for July. Then look at Figure 3.5: these are the pages a reader of the *Cornhill* serialisation would have seen when they began to read the August part.

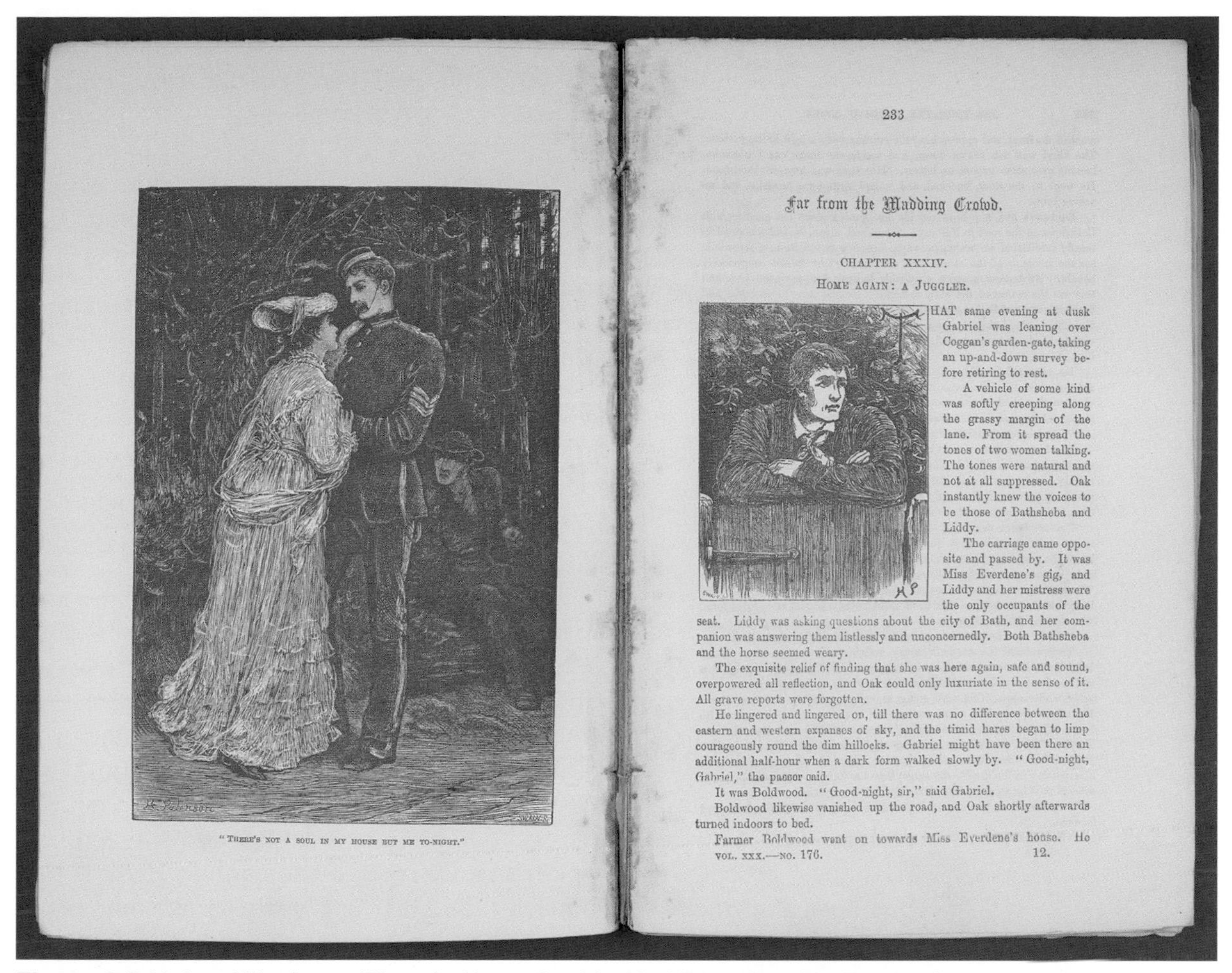

"THERE'S NOT A SOUL IN MY HOUSE BUT ME TO-NIGHT."

233

Far from the Madding Crowd.

CHAPTER XXXIV.

HOME AGAIN: A JUGGLER.

THAT same evening at dusk Gabriel was leaning over Coggan's garden-gate, taking an up-and-down survey before retiring to rest.

A vehicle of some kind was softly creeping along the grassy margin of the lane. From it spread the tones of two women talking. The tones were natural and not at all suppressed. Oak instantly knew the voices to be those of Bathsheba and Liddy.

The carriage came opposite and passed by. It was Miss Everdene's gig, and Liddy and her mistress were the only occupants of the seat. Liddy was asking questions about the city of Bath, and her companion was answering them listlessly and unconcernedly. Both Bathsheba and the horse seemed weary.

The exquisite relief of finding that she was here again, safe and sound, overpowered all reflection, and Oak could only luxuriate in the sense of it. All grave reports were forgotten.

He lingered and lingered on, till there was no difference between the eastern and western expanses of sky, and the timid hares began to limp courageously round the dim hillocks. Gabriel might have been there an additional half-hour when a dark form walked slowly by. "Good-night, Gabriel," the passer said.

It was Boldwood. "Good-night, sir," said Gabriel.

Boldwood likewise vanished up the road, and Oak shortly afterwards turned indoors to bed.

Farmer Boldwood went on towards Miss Everdene's house. He

VOL. XXX.—NO. 176. 12.

Figure 3.5 Helen Allingham, 'There's Not a Soul in My House But Me To-night' and initial letter vignette "T" (Gabriel leaning over Coggan's garden gate) from *The Cornhill Magazine*, August 1874. British Library, London, Shelfmark no. RB.23.a.15320. Photo: © British Library Board. All Rights Reserved/ Bridgeman Images. The opening of the August 1874 part of *Far from the Madding Crowd*.

Now read the first section of the August part, Chapter XXXIV (pp. 222–31), and write down your answer to the following question:

How do Hardy and his illustrator use both suspense and surprise to draw in the *Cornhill* reader over these chapters and the break between July and August?

Discussion

Here are my thoughts.

At the end of Chapter XXXII, we are left in suspense about what will happen to Bathsheba. There are several possibilities. Will she reach Bath? If she does, will she be successful in her attempt to renounce Troy? Or will she be unable to resist him? Hardy's narrator suggests that the latter is most likely:

> Was Bathsheba altogether blind to the obvious fact that the support of a lover's arms is not of a kind best calculated to assist a resolve to renounce him?
>
> (p. 213)

The *Cornhill* reader is likely to have realised at this point that there is now only one chapter, Chapter XXXIII, to go before the end of the July instalment – and therefore not much time left to resolve the suspense. Hardy plays with this remorselessly. Chapter XXXIII begins with the words 'A week passed, and there was no tidings of Bathsheba' (p. 215). Something must have happened to her, but what? In the rest of the chapter, the reader begins to find out, but this is an agonising – and hilarious – process. It transpires that Cainy Ball has been to Bath, and has seen Bathsheba with a soldier (p. 216). One possible outcome of Bathsheba's night ride – that she didn't get to her destination – has been removed, and suspense has been intensified: has Bathsheba managed to remove Troy from her life, or not? The reader has to wait until Cainy recovers from sending a breadcrumb down the wrong way, swallowing a gnat, and getting cider up his nose, and then while Poorgrass and Moon talk about Cainy's family. Finally, the news comes: Bathsheba and the soldier sat in a park talking, at the end of which 'they looked as far-gone friendly as a man and woman can be' (p. 218). It sounds, therefore, as if Troy and Bathsheba have not parted company. The reader's initial suspense has been resolved. Gabriel, however, unlike the reader, is unaware of Bathsheba's motivation for going to Bath, so the suspense he feels is different. Having heard that Bathsheba has been seen in Bath with a soldier, he wants to know more (is he worried that they have gone off together?). Gabriel is kept in suspense, along with the reader, while Cainy describes the rest of his visit to Bath in excruciating detail. At the end of the chapter – and the July part as a whole – we are left none the wiser, and under Joseph Poorgrass's stern interrogation, Cainy begins to doubt his own memory: 'All I mane is that in common truth 'twas Miss

Figure 3.6 Still from *Far from the Madding Crowd*, Terence Stamp as Sergeant Troy and Julie Christie as Bathsheba, dir. John Schlesinger (Metro-Goldwyn-Mayer, 1967). Photo: Vic/Appia/Kobal/Shutterstock.

Everdene and Sergeant Troy, but in the horrible so-help-me truth that ye want to make of it perhaps 'twas somebody else' (p. 221).

Chapter XXXIII, in other words, has resolved suspense about one thing but created new suspense about something else – leaving the reader in a state of uncertainty at the end of the July number. The opening of the August part, Chapter XXXIV, seems to suggest that Bathsheba has in fact, despite Cainy Ball's report, been able to leave Troy; Gabriel sees Bathsheba arrive home alone, safe and sound. The frontispiece (Figure 3.5), however, would seem to contradict this, showing Troy and Bathsheba together, watched by a skulking, jealous Boldwood. The scene illustrated is one that feels parallel in some ways to the scene at the end of the July part, Chapter XXXIII: in that chapter, one of Bathsheba's would-be lovers, Gabriel, finds out something about Bathsheba and Troy from Cainy Ball, after a suspenseful delay. In Chapter XXXIV another admirer, Boldwood, finds out something else about Bathsheba and Troy from Troy himself, in an even more agonisingly suspenseful way. (The difference is, however, that Cainy does not delay giving his information maliciously as Troy does – but, of course, Hardy is cunningly manipulating the reader in both cases.) In his conversation with Troy, Boldwood (and perhaps also the reader) is led to believe, first, that Troy wants to marry Fanny and has come to say goodbye to Bathsheba (pp. 225–7), and next that he is about to spend a night with Bathsheba as her illicit lover (pp. 227–9), before, finally, he has the truth: that Bathsheba and Troy were married in Bath (p. 230). Where Cainy told Gabriel too little at the end of the July part, at the beginning of the August one, there are too many resolutions. The news of the marriage comes as a surprise to Boldwood because of how it violates his expectations about the way Troy might have behaved – expectations Troy has been sadistically stoking across the course of the chapter.

Whether the *Cornhill* reader is surprised or not will depend on whether they share Boldwood's expectations about Troy. At least one reader – Hardy's friend the 'interesting and well-known woman' Anne Benson Procter (Hardy, 1984, p. 103) – did share those expectations, as she admitted in a letter to him written while *Far from the Madding Crowd* was still being serialised: 'You would be gratified to know what a shock the Marriage of Bathsheba was. I resembled Mr Boldwood—and to deceive such an old novel-reader as myself is a triumph. We are always looking out for traps, and scent a long way off a surprise …' (Hardy, 1984, p. 103).

Serialisation and the role of Gabriel

To conclude this exploration into the way in which serialisation split the novel into parts, we will now look at the endings of those parts. If you read the last few paragraphs of the final chapter of each month's part (Chapters V, VIII, XIV, XX, XXIV, XXIX, XXXIII, XXXVIII, XLII, XLVII, LI and LVII), you will notice a striking pattern: each instalment – except two – ends with a scene featuring Gabriel, often in a moment marking a milestone in his life (for example, the sheep disaster at the end of the first instalment, or his sacking at the end of the fourth part). Gabriel's competence in a wide range of agricultural jobs anchors the book anyway, of course, and he seems to earn his marriage to Bathsheba through sheer staying power as much as anything else. This is an impression many modern readers will have when reading the book: the sense that the story is being mediated largely through Gabriel, and that we constantly return throughout the novel to Gabriel's sturdy, 'Oak'-like presence to sum things up. That impression would, however, have been even more marked for the original readers of the serialised version in the *Cornhill*, as they closed the pages on each issue.

I mentioned two exceptions to this pattern, when Gabriel does not close an instalment – but I'll leave you find out what those are.

Illustrating *Far from the Madding Crowd*

While Hardy's name did not appear in the newspaper advertisements for *The Cornhill Magazine*, the name of his illustrator, Helen Allingham (*née* Paterson), did. Illustrations were a crucial part of the appeal of Victorian magazines, and the advertisement for the January 1874 issue (the issue in which the first section of Hardy's text was published), which appeared in *The Illustrated London News*, highlighted Allingham's contribution (*The Illustrated London News*, 1873). Hardy himself clearly did not read this advertisement, for when he first saw the published version of the part for January – after buying a copy of *The Cornhill Magazine* at Plymouth railway station on New Year's Day 1874 – he was pleasantly surprised to see that it was illustrated at all (Hardy, 1984, p. 100). He seems to have had some contact with Allingham during the publication of the rest of the text and, indeed, confessed afterwards to having had romantic feelings for her. But the two do not seem to have collaborated closely on the illustrations. Pamela Dalziel has argued that Allingham – who went on to become a popular watercolourist famous for producing picturesque and consoling images of country life – underplayed the more dramatic elements in the narrative (Dalziel, 1998).

You will now compare the full-page illustration produced by Helen Allingham for the October part of *Far from the Madding Crowd* with the text it illustrated in *The Cornhill Magazine* for that month. As the *Cornhill* text for October differs in a number of ways from the equivalent passage in your set text (incorporating cuts suggested by Stephen as described earlier in this chapter), the *Cornhill* text has been provided for you within the following activity.

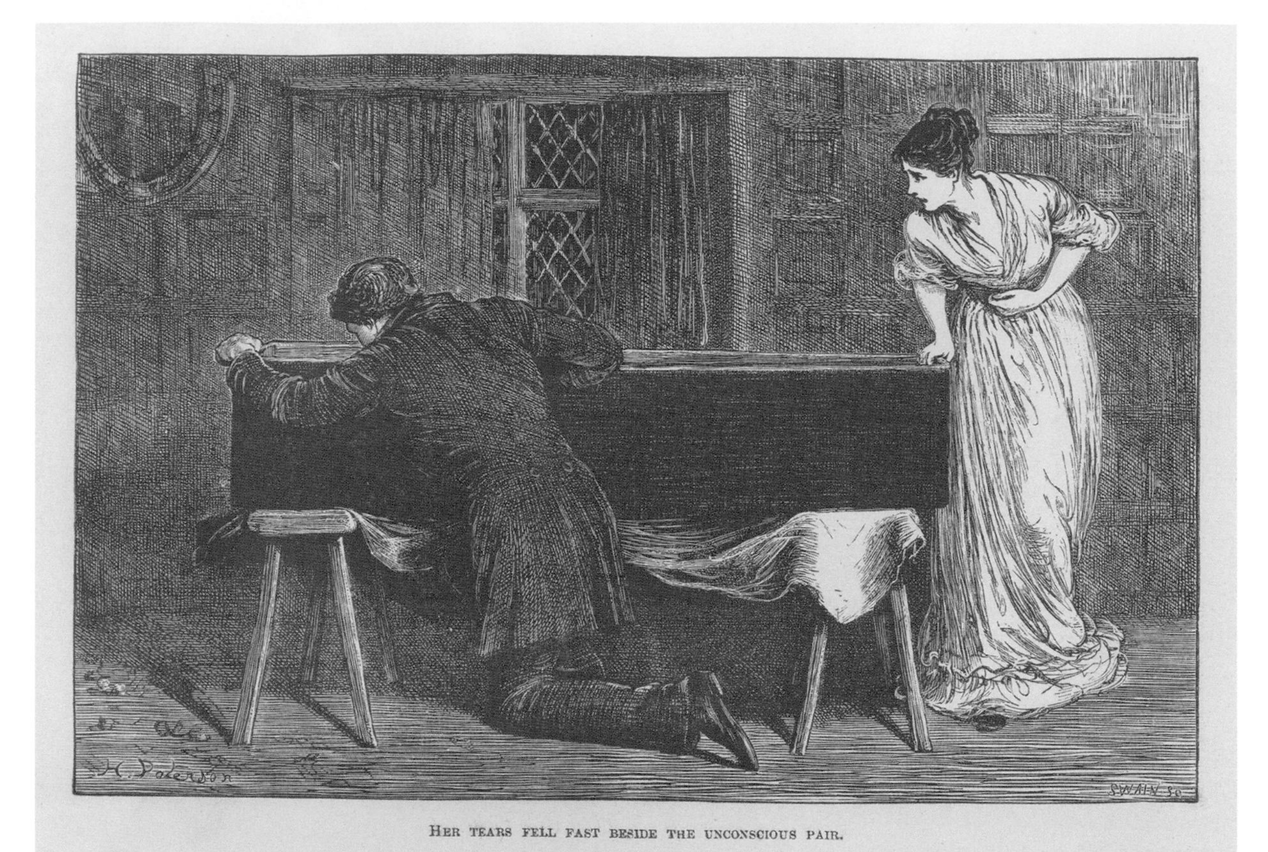

HER TEARS FELL FAST BESIDE THE UNCONSCIOUS PAIR.

Figure 3.7 Helen Allingham, 'Her Tears Fell Fast Beside the Unconscious Pair' in *The Cornhill Magazine*, October 1874. Cambridge University Library, classmark: P900.c.68.30. Photo: Reproduced by kind permission of the Syndics of Cambridge University Library.

Activity 3.3

Allow around 30 minutes to complete this activity

First, look at the illustration (Figure 3.7) and its title, a quotation from the text. Next, read the excerpt from *The Cornhill Magazine* printed here, and then answer the following questions:

1 At what point in the passage does the quotation in the title of the illustration appear?

2 Does the illustration depict this part of the passage? If not, which part of the passage does it show?

Excerpt from *The Cornhill Magazine*

More fevered now by a reaction from the first feelings which Oak's example had raised in her, she paused in the hall, looking at the door of the room wherein Fanny lay. She locked her fingers, threw back her head, and strained her hot hands rigidly across her forehead, saying, with a hysterical sob, "Would to God you would speak and tell me your secret, Fanny! .... Oh, I hope, hope it is not true! .... If I could only look in upon you for one little minute I should know all!"

A few moments passed, and she added, slowly, *"And I will."*

Bathsheba in after times could never gauge the mood which carried her through the actions following this murmured resolution on this memorable evening of her life. At the end of a short though undefined time she found herself in the small room, quivering with emotion, a mist before her eyes, and an excruciating pulsation in her brain, standing beside the uncovered coffin of the girl whose conjectured end had so entirely engrossed her, and saying to herself in a husky voice as she gazed within—

"It was best to know the worst, and I know it now!"

She was conscious of having brought about this situation by a series of actions done as by one in an extravagant dream; of following that idea as to method, which had burst upon her in the hall with glaring obviousness, by gliding to the top of the stairs, assuring herself by listening to the heavy breathing of her maids that they were asleep, gliding down again, turning the handle of the door within which the young girl lay, and deliberately setting herself to do what, if she had anticipated any such undertaking at night and alone, would have horrified her, but which, when done, was not so dreadful as was the conclusive proof which came with knowing beyond doubt the last chapter of Fanny's story.

Bathsheba's head sank upon her bosom, and the breath which had been bated in suspense, curiosity, and interest, was exhaled now in the form of a whispered wail: "Oh-h-h!" she said, and the silent room added length to her moan.

Her tears fell fast beside the unconscious pair: tears of a complicated origin, of a nature indescribable, almost indefinable except as other than those of simple sorrow. Assuredly their wonted fires must have lived in Fanny's ashes when events were so shaped as to chariot her hither in this natural, unobtrusive, yet effectual manner. The one feat alone—that of dying—by which a mean condition could be resolved into a grand one, Fanny had achieved. And to that had destiny subjoined this rencounter to-night, which had, in Bathsheba's wild imagining, turned her companion's failure to success, her humiliation to triumph, her lucklessness to ascendency; it had thrown over herself a garish light of mockery, and set upon all things about her an ironical smile. Fanny's face was framed in by that yellow hair of hers; and there was no longer much room for doubt as to the origin of the curl owned by Troy. In Bathsheba's heated fancy the innocent white countenance expressed a dim triumphant consciousness of the pain she was retaliating for her pain with all the merciless rigour of the Mosaic law: "Burning for burning; wound for wound; strife for strife."

Bathsheba indulged in contemplations of escape from her position by immediate death, which, thought she, though it was an inconvenient and awful way, had limits to its inconvenience and awfulness that could not be overpassed; whilst the shames of life were measureless. Yet even this scheme of extinction by death was but tamely copying her rival's method without the reasons which had glorified it in her rival's case. She glided rapidly up and down the room, as was mostly her habit when excited, her hands hanging clasped in front of her, as she thought and in part expressed in broken words: "Oh, I hate her, yet I don't mean that I hate her, for it is grievous and wicked; and yet I hate her a little! Yes, my flesh insists upon hating her, whether my spirit is willing or no. .... If she had only lived I could have been angry and cruel towards her with some justification; but to be vindictive towards a poor dead woman recoils upon myself. O God, have mercy! I am miserable at all this!"

Bathsheba became at this moment so terrified at her own state of mind that she looked around for some sort of refuge from herself. The vision of Oak kneeling down that night recurred to her, and with the imitative instinct which animates women she seized upon the idea, resolved to kneel, and if possible, pray. Gabriel had prayed; so would she.

She knelt beside the coffin, covered her face with her hands, and for a time the room was silent as a tomb. Whether from a purely mechanical, or from any other cause, when Bathsheba arose it was with a quieted spirit, and a regret for the antagonistic instincts which had seized upon her just before.

In her desire to make atonement she took flowers from a vase by the window, and began laying them around the dead girl's head. Bathsheba knew no other way of showing kindness to persons departed than by giving them flowers. She knew not how long she remained engaged thus. She forgot time, life, where she was, what she was doing. A slamming together of the coach-house doors in the yard brought her to herself again. An instant after, the front door opened and closed, steps crossed the hall, and her husband appeared at the entrance to the room, looking in upon her.

He beheld it all by degrees, stared in stupefaction at the scene, as if he thought it an illusion raised by some fiendish incantation. Bathsheba, pallid as a corpse on end, gazed back at him in the same wild way.

So little are instinctive guesses the fruit of a legitimate induction that at this moment as he stood with the door in his hand Troy never once thought of Fanny in connection with what he saw. His first confused idea was that somebody in the house had died.

"Well—what?" said Troy, blankly.

"I must go! I must go!" said Bathsheba, to herself more than to him. She came with a dilated eye towards the door, to push past him.

"What's the matter, in God's name? who's dead?" said Troy.

"I cannot say; let me go out. I want air!" she continued.

"But no; stay, I insist!" He seized her hand, and then volition seemed to leave her, and she went off into a state of passivity. He, still holding her, came up the room, and thus, hand in hand, Troy and Bathsheba approached the coffin's side.

The candle was standing on a bureau close by them, and the light slanted down, distinctly enkindling the cold features within. Troy looked in, dropped his wife's hand, knowledge of it all came over him in a lurid sheen, and he stood still.

So still he remained that he could be imagined to have left in him no motive power whatever. The clashes of feeling in all directions confounded one another, produced a neutrality, and there was motion in none.

"Do you know her?" said Bathsheba, in a small enclosed echo, as from the interior of a cell.

"I do," said Troy.

"Is it she?"

"It is."

He had originally stood perfectly erect. And now, in the well-nigh congealed immobility of his frame could be discerned an incipient movement, as in the darkest night may be discerned light after a while. He was gradually sinking forwards. The lines of his features softened, and dismay modulated to illimitable sadness. Bathsheba was regarding him from the other side, still with parted lips and distracted eyes. Capacity for intense feeling is proportionate to the general intensity of the nature, and perhaps in all Fanny's sufferings, much greater relatively to her strength, there never was a time when she suffered in an absolute sense what Bathsheba suffered now.

This is what Troy did. He sank upon his knees with an indefinable union of remorse and reverence upon his face, and, bending over Fanny Robin, gently kissed her, as one would kiss an infant asleep to avoid awakening it.

At the sight and sound of that, to her, unendurable act, Bathsheba sprang towards him. All the strong feelings which had been scattered over her existence since she knew what feeling was seemed gathered together into one pulsation now. The revulsion from her indignant mood a little earlier, when she had meditated upon compromised honour, forestalment, eclipse by another, was violent and entire. All that was forgotten in the simple and still strong attachment of wife to husband. She had sighed for her self-completeness then, and now she cried aloud against the severance of the union she had deplored. She flung her arms round Troy's neck, exclaiming wildly from the deepest deep of her heart—

"Don't—don't kiss them! Oh, Frank, I can't bear it—I can't! I love you better than she did: kiss me too, Frank—kiss me! *You will, Frank, kiss me too!*"

There was something so abnormal and startling in the childlike pain and simplicity of this appeal from a woman of Bathsheba's calibre and independence that Troy, loosening her tightly clasped arms from his neck, looked at her in bewilderment. It was such an unexpected revelation of all women being alike at heart, even those so different in their accessories as Fanny and this one beside him, that Troy could hardly seem to believe her to be his proud wife Bathsheba. Fanny's own spirit seemed to be animating her frame. But this was the mood of a few instants only. When the momentary surprise had passed, his expression changed to a silencing imperious gaze.

"I will not kiss you," he said, pushing her away.

Had the wife now but gone no further. Yet, perhaps, under the harrowing circumstances, to speak out was the one wrong act which can be better understood, if not forgiven in her, than the right and politic one. All the feeling she had been betrayed into showing she drew back to herself again by a strenuous effort of self-command.

"What have you to say as your reason?" she asked, her bitter voice being strangely low – quite that of another woman now.

"I have to say that I have been a bad, black-hearted man," he answered.

"And that this woman is your victim; and I not less than she."

"Ah! don't taunt me, madam. This woman is more to me, dead as she is, than ever you were, or are, or can be. If Satan had not tempted me with that face of yours, and those cursed coquetries, I should have married her. I never had another thought till you came in my way. Would to God that I had; but it is all too late! I deserve to live in torment for this!" He turned to Fanny then. "But never mind, darling," he said; "in the sight of Heaven you are my very, very wife."

At these words there arose from Bathsheba's lips a long low cry of measureless despair and indignation, such a wail of anguish as

> had never before been heard within those old-inhabited walls. It was the Τετέλεσται of her union with Troy.
>
> "If she's—that,—what—am I?" she added, as a continuation of the same cry, and sobbing fearfully: and the rarity with her of such abandonment only made the condition more terrible.
>
> "You are nothing to me—nothing," said Troy, heartlessly. "A ceremony before a priest doesn't make a marriage. I am not morally yours."
>
> A vehement impulse to flee from him, to run from this place, hide, and escape humiliation at any price, not stopping short of death itself, mastered Bathsheba now. She waited not an instant, but turned to the door and ran out.
>
> (Hardy, 1874, pp. 493–7)

Discussion

1. The quotation, 'Her tears fell fast beside the unconscious pair', comes from early on in the passage, just after Bathsheba has opened the coffin and seen Fanny and the baby.
2. No, Allingham does not actually illustrate this part of the passage. Troy has not even entered at the point at which the quotation comes. In the illustration, however, he is bent over the coffin, having presumably just kissed the dead Fanny. At this juncture in the text, Bathsheba springs across to Troy, demanding that he kiss her. Troy pushes her away and Bathsheba rushes out of the house. The illustration does not reflect the energy in this part of the text: in effect, it pastes the melancholy attitude of Bathsheba from earlier in the passage into the end of the scene.

Why did Allingham illustrate the scene in this way? One answer could be to avoid giving too much away to the reader about what would happen in the story they were about to read. (Remember that the illustrations appeared at the beginning of each part.) Another answer might be a reluctance to show Bathsheba behaving in too vigorous and 'unladylike' a way. The mismatch between illustration and caption, meanwhile, might be connected to Stephen's unwillingness to offend his subscribers. Significantly, when the illustration was reprinted in the two-volume edition of the whole text, which appeared towards the end of the serialisation, a more accurate quotation was used: 'Bending over Fanny Robin, he gently kissed her' (Dalziel, 1998, p. 21).

In this section, we have explored the effects of serialisation on the text of *Far from the Madding Crowd* from a number of different angles: Stephen's advice to Hardy; the structure of the plot; the use of suspense to engage readers' attention; and the role of illustration. In doing so, we have highlighted the role played by people other than Hardy in the production (in a broad sense) of *Far from the Madding Crowd*. Stephen's anxieties – and, at a remove, the prurience and desire for exciting action of the readership he was struggling to please – had an important effect on the kind of text *Far from the Madding Crowd* turned out to be. Meanwhile, Allingham's rather prim and proper illustrations mediated the text to its first readers, just as paperback cover designers mediate the experience of reading *Far from the Madding Crowd* to twenty-first-century readers. We now turn to consider the role of a different set of people: the critics.

Criticism and *Far from the Madding Crowd*

Literary criticism starts by asking questions. In the case of *Far from the Madding Crowd*, these questions might include the following: What is the book 'about'? Are there are important things that the novel is telling us other than the events of the plot? Are there general ideas of some kind in it – about, perhaps, the relationship between people and nature, the different ways in which Victorian men and women thought about each other, and/or about the place of coincidence in human life? Do any of the generalisations it is possible to make about what happens in *Far from the Madding Crowd* contradict each other? Or do any go together particularly well? Is there a 'message' of some sort in the novel? Or 'messages'? Thinking about these sorts of general questions, and then going back to the book and trying to find out how its details can be linked to them, is a 'critical' activity – 'critical' not in the everyday sense of having a negative opinion about something, but in the more limited 'literary critical' sense of starting a 'reasoned discussion' (Baldick, 2015b) of a poem, novel or play – an attempt to interpret and analyse it.

The author and the critics

Hardy read widely and was interested in a number of philosophical and scientific theories, which critics have found to have been influential on his novels. Early on in Hardy's adulthood, he seems to have lost his Christian faith, and his interest in the ideas of non-fiction writers such as the naturalist Charles Darwin (1809–1882) and the philosopher John Stuart Mill (1806–1873) appears to have been connected with this. It is clear that there are connections of some sort between these ideas and Hardy's novels (Mallett, 2009). It also seems that, as was discussed in Chapter 2, Hardy's anomalous class status – the clash between his relatively humble Dorset origins and the middle-class London world he later mixed in – affected his fiction. Hardy himself, interestingly, is not the best guide to these connections between his life and ideas and his literary works. Throughout his career, he made very clear public statements rejecting the idea that his works were written to put forth any coherent theory about the world: he stated 'no harmonious philosophy is attempted in these pages – or in any bygone pages of mine, for that matter' (Hardy, 1967, p. 61).

These statements have not, as you may have guessed, stopped later critics attempting to find just such a 'harmonious philosophy' in Hardy's novels. It's tempting, out of respect for Hardy, to dismiss such attempts out of hand. I think this would be a mistake, however. I would argue, instead, that authors are not always the most reliable commentators on what is going on in their own writing. In a book as rich and complicated as *Far from the Madding Crowd*, there are inevitably many things that aren't really within the author's control: images, ideas, patterns and so on that an author won't have anticipated or even have been aware of while they were writing or afterwards.

Whenever I think about this topic, I always remember something said by the famous playwright Tom Stoppard (1937–), in a talk I once saw him give at my school. He compared his feelings when reading criticism of his work to the experience of a traveller whose suitcase was being examined by customs officers: as the officials (or critics) pulled out more and more incriminating items, he could only stand by and protest that he hadn't known they were there! The significance of the analogy seems to me now (as it didn't then) to be this: that, whether or not packed knowingly by the author, those objects nevertheless most certainly *were* in the case.

Hardy himself, towards the end of his career, in 1912, lightheartedly addressed this very point: 'no doubt,' he wrote, 'there can be more in a book than the author consciously puts there' (Hardy, 1967, p. 36). He was referring to the idea that had been put to him that Sue Bridehead, a character in his final novel, *Jude the Obscure* (1895), was 'the first delineation in fiction' of a new kind of 'feminist', 'bachelor girl' kind of woman (Hardy, 1967, p. 35).

Assessing the critics

One of the most important things to do when you read criticism of a text is to return constantly to your own thoughts and feelings (and notes!) about that text – to compare what a critic is saying with your own experience and knowledge of the novel, poem or play. You will probably find that you will agree with some things the critic says and disagree with others. This is an exciting process, and it will provide you with a starting point for developing critical ideas of your own.

Here is a brief example of my own disagreement with a critic.

Lord David Cecil (1902–1986) – a critic of Hardy writing less than twenty years after Hardy's death – argued that Hardy's 'theme' was 'mankind's predicament in the universe' (Cecil, 1943, p. 19). This theme was, Cecil said, specifically a 'conflict … not, as in most novels, between one man [or woman] and another, or between man and an institution,' but '[a] struggle between man on the one hand and, on the other, an omnipotent and indifferent Fate' (Cecil, 1943, p. 26). In *Far from the Madding Crowd* in particular, this means that, for Cecil, 'Bathsheba looks at Troy as the author of her misfortunes. But from the point of vantage from which Hardy surveys [her story] Bathsheba [is] seen to be under a delusion' (Cecil, 1943, pp. 26–7). When I first read this argument, I found it interesting, but when I thought about it more, and compared it to my own experience and memory of *Far from the Madding Crowd*, I realised that I disagreed with it. It's true, of course, that Troy is at fault. But equally, there isn't any reference to anything like 'Fate' in the book that would seem to support Cecil's argument. Almost ten years after writing *Far from the Madding Crowd*, Hardy did read books by the philosopher Arthur Schopenhauer (1788–1860), arguing that everything that happens in the world is predetermined by an impersonal force, or 'Immanent Will', and this idea does seem to have had some kind of influence on Hardy's later work (Mallett, 2009). But in Cecil's application of this idea to *Far from the Madding Crowd*, he seems to me to be forcing it on to a text where it doesn't belong.

The point of this example is not to suggest that you should agree with me rather than Cecil. It is, rather, to stress the fact that you should not feel bound to agree with critical work that seems to go against your own knowledge and experience of the text. You may feel that Cecil's interpretation of *Far from the Madding Crowd* is more compelling than mine. Critical differences of this kind, whether between the published works of critics, or within this module between members of an online forum, are one of the things that makes the study of literature so rewarding and exciting.

Conclusion

In this chapter, we have looked at two ways in which *Far from the Madding Crowd* has been affected by factors beyond Hardy's control: the demands of serialisation and the work of critics. We have also thought more broadly about the extent to which *Far from the Madding Crowd* can be considered a 'realist' novel. As the Introduction to this book has argued, realism can take many different forms. As you continue to study this module, you will find that the other set texts on it are realist in a variety of ways, some of them very different from the realism of *Far from the Madding Crowd*.

References

Set text

Hardy, T. (2002) *Far from the madding crowd*. Edited by Suzanne B. Falck-Yi, introduction by Linda M. Shires. Oxford: Oxford University Press. Oxford World's Classics.

Other references

Baldick, C. (2015a) 'Realism', in *The Oxford dictionary of literary terms*. 4th edn. Oxford: Oxford University Press. Available online via the OU Library.

Baldick, C. (2015b) 'Criticism', in *The Oxford dictionary of literary terms*. 4th edn. Oxford: Oxford University Press. Available online via the OU Library.

Bell, A. (2012) 'Stephen, Sir Leslie (1832–1904)', in *Oxford dictionary of national biography* (2004). Available at: http://www.oxforddnb.com.libezproxy.open.ac.uk/view/10.1093/ref:odnb/9780198614128.001.0001/odnb-9780198614128-e-36271 (Accessed: 30 April 2019).

Cecil, D. (1943) *Hardy the novelist: an essay in criticism*. London: Constable.

Cooke, S. (2016) '"The kindly fruits of the earth": the materiality of the *Cornhill Magazine* (1860)', *Cahiers victoriens et édouardiens*, 84. Available at: https://journals.openedition.org/cve/2940 (Accessed: 8 May 2019).

Cox, R.G. (ed.) (1979) *Thomas Hardy: the critical heritage*. London: Routledge.

Dalziel, P. (1998) '"She matched his violence with her own wild passion": illustrating *Far from the madding crowd*', in Pettit, C.P.C. (ed.) *Reading Thomas Hardy*. Basingstoke: Macmillan, pp. 1–31.

Frawley, M. (2017) 'The Victorian age', in Poplawski, P. (ed.) *English literature in context*. Cambridge: Cambridge University Press, pp. 364–469.

Hardy, T. (1874) 'Far from the Madding Crowd', *The Cornhill Magazine*, 30(178), pp. 490–512. Available online via the OU Library.

Hardy, T. (1967) *Thomas Hardy's personal writings.* Edited by Harold Orel. London: Macmillan.

Hardy, T. (1984) *The life and work of Thomas Hardy.* Edited by Michael Millgate. Basingstoke: Palgrave Macmillan.

Hardy, T. (1986) *Far from the madding crowd.* Edited by Robert C. Schweik. New York: Norton.

Higginbotham, A. R. (1989) '"Sin of the age": infanticide and illegitimacy in Victorian London', *Victorian Studies*, 32(3), pp. 319–37. Available online via the OU Library.

Hughes, L.K. and Lund, M. (1991) *The Victorian serial.* Charlottesville, Va.: University Press of Virginia.

Hughes, L.K. and Lund, M. (2010) 'Serial reading', in Maunder, A. and Phegley, J. (ed.) *Teaching nineteenth-century fiction.* Basingstoke: Palgrave Macmillan, pp. 148–67.

Mallett, P. (2009) 'Hardy and philosophy', in Wilson, K. (ed.) *A companion to Thomas Hardy.* Oxford: Wiley-Blackwell, pp. 19–35. Available online via the OU Library.

Morgan, R. (1992) *Cancelled words: rediscovering Thomas Hardy.* London: Routledge. Available online via the OU Library.

Pite, R. (2009) '"His country": Hardy in the rural', in Wilson, K. (ed.) *A companion to Thomas Hardy.* Oxford: Wiley-Blackwell, pp. 131–45. Available online via the OU Library.

Pyrhönen, H. (2005) 'Suspense and surprise', in Herman, D., Jahn, M. and Ryan, M-L. (eds), *Routledge encyclopedia of narrative theory.* Abingdon: Routledge, pp. 578–80.

Shires, L.M. (2002) 'Introduction' in Hardy, T., *Far from the madding crowd.* Edited by Suzanne B. Falck-Yi, introduction by Linda M. Shires. Oxford: Oxford University Press. Oxford World's Classics, pp. xi–xxx.

The Illustrated London News (1873), 'New books and publications', *The Illustrated London News* historical archive, 1842–2003. 20 December, p. 606. Available online via the OU Library.

The Illustrated London News (1874a) 'The magazines for January', *The Illustrated London News* historical archive, 1842–2003. 3 January, pp. 10–11. Available online via the OU Library.

The Illustrated London News (1874b) 'The magazines for July', *The Illustrated London News* historical archive, 1842–2003. 3 July, p. 42. Available online via the OU Library.

The Illustrated London News (1874c) 'The magazines for November', *The Illustrated London News* historical archive, 1842–2003. 14 November, pp. 474–5. Available online via the OU Library.

Chapter 4 Edith Wharton, *The Custom of the Country*: Reading the novel

Sue Asbee

Contents

Introduction

The Custom of the Country (1913) by Edith Wharton (1862–1937) begins with a fascinating line of dialogue which delivers us immediately into the middle of conflict: 'Undine Spragg – how *can* you?' (Wharton, 2008, p. 3). We don't know who Undine is or what outrage she has committed, but with this cry of protest we are introduced to the novel's **protagonist** by her mother; it is a cry we are likely to echo ourselves, time and again, as we follow Undine's progress in her naked ambition to be accepted by New York society. The novel recounts her flirtations, courtship, marriages and divorces, and we discover that Undine Spragg always seems to get what she wants – whatever that may be; however, once she has secured it, there is always something on the horizon that she wants even more. Undine is rarely satisfied for long.

The Custom of the Country was published nearly forty years after Hardy's *Far from the Madding Crowd* (1874). Hardy lived in and wrote about his native Dorset, whereas Wharton, an American, was living in France by 1913. The societies they wrote about are quite different – Hardy's is rural whereas Wharton's is metropolitan – but both use a third-person narrator, with all the flexibility and possibilities that offers. Both give internal views of their major characters. Like Hardy, Wharton will present an episode from a particular character's point of view, juxtaposing it with a different one, or a more general perspective altogether. But whereas Hardy's narrator has, ultimately, an affectionate, sympathetic attitude towards his characters, Wharton writes **satire**. That is, she is critical of her characters without explicitly condemning them. The key aspects of a realist novel, characterisation, settings, locations and duration – the time covered by the action of the novel – are all present in *The Custom of the Country*, as we saw they were in *Far from the Madding Crowd*.

Figure 4.1 Edith Wharton as a young woman around the time of her engagement to her future husband, Edward Wharton, *c.*1884, unknown photographer. Photo: Granger/Bridgeman Images.

Context in focus: serialisation

Wharton was a great admirer of Hardy's novels – indeed, her title *The Custom of the Country* is the title of a chapter in Hardy's *The Return of the Native* (1878). Wharton's novel was serialised in the New York-based *Scribner's Magazine* in monthly numbers from January to October 1913, and it had colour illustrations. Like Hardy, whose *Far from the Madding Crowd* was serialised in *The Cornhill Magazine*, Wharton hadn't finished writing her novel when the serialisation started, and in fact she only finished writing it in August 1913 (with just three numbers to go). The serialisation was in ten monthly instalments. Like Hardy, Wharton revised the serial text slightly for volume publication. When *The Custom of the Country* was published as a single volume after serialisation, it was divided into the five-book structure you will find in the set text edition.

Scribner's Magazine was a very popular literary magazine – it had a circulation of about 200,000 when *The Custom of the Country* was serialised (some ten times larger than *The Cornhill Magazine*'s circulation). For the volume publication in October 1913 (which actually came out in November), the initial print run in the USA was for 30,000 copies – again, a significantly substantial sale.

Introducing Undine and her family

As the novel begins, Mrs Spragg is indignant because Undine has whipped a letter from her grasp, exclaiming 'how *can* you?' (p. 3). Reading in general – and reading newspapers and letters in particular – is of great importance in this novel, so it is significant that the receipt of a letter begins the story. Undine characteristically but wrongly assumes it must addressed to her, but the hotel bell-boy very properly delivers it to her mother. Undine is unmoved and unapologetic at Mrs Spragg's protest: '"I guess it's meant for me," she merely threw over her shoulder at her mother' (p. 3). With the pretence of being annoyed at this dismissive and unmannerly response, Mrs Spragg appeals to the other character in the room: 'Did you *ever*, Mrs Heeny?', a question she delivers not with annoyance, but with a rather incongruous 'deprecating pride' in her daughter's disobedience. This brief and otherwise insignificant exchange is important simply because it sounds a key note which will effectively become a pattern, repeated time and again in different situations with different characters throughout the novel. The constant is Undine, who in this case demonstrates complete lack of deference to her mother in order to get what she wants.

The first chapter introduces readers to the nuanced manners of New York fashionable society, from the perspective of the Spraggs – the outsiders. Mrs Heeny, the 'stout professional woman' engaged to manicure Mrs Spragg's nails, knows everybody: the Marvells, Fairfords, Dagonets, the 'Old' New York families, as well as the nouveau riche Van Degens and Driscolls. These represent distinctions of class and standing of which the Spraggs are as yet unaware. As we follow Undine's misunderstandings and misreading of social situations, as well as Mrs Spragg's isolation, we begin to learn, as they do, about the ways in which the complex world they have entered works.

The Spraggs – father, mother and daughter – live in a New York hotel because 'all the fashionable people' Undine knows of 'either boarded or lived in hotels' (p. 11); this is not a parental or even family choice, but evidence of the influence Undine has over her parents. In spite of their accommodation, we discover that although the Spraggs have been in the city for two years, they are still outsiders. The first demonstration of this comes with Undine's response to the letter she was so eager to read, crumpling it she tosses it 'with a contemptuous gesture' (p. 4) into her mother's lap. It is not from Claude Walsingham

Popple, the fashionable portrait painter, as she had hoped and expected, but merely someone's sister inviting her to dine. It is Mrs Heeny who explains this particular 'custom of the country': 'When a young man in society wants to meet a girl again, he gets his sister to ask her' (p. 6), adding to an incredulous Undine that she must never accept an invitation from a gentleman without saying that she must ask her mother first.

Narrative and narrator

The following short passage from the end of Chapter I makes it clear that the family moved from Apex to New York for Undine's benefit, but the third-person, omniscient narrator suggests that there is more than one reason for their relocation:

> They had lived in New York for two years without any social benefit to their daughter; and it was of course for that purpose that they had come. If, at the time, there had been other and more pressing reasons, they were such as Mrs Spragg and her husband never touched on, even in the gilded privacy of their bedroom at the Stentorian; and so completely had silence closed in on the subject that to Mrs Spragg it had become non-existent: she really believed that, as Abner put it, they had left Apex because Undine was too big for the place.
>
> (p. 9)

We have already seen that Undine is an indulged, admired and wayward daughter, and this short passage confirms it. However, it also hints at something else: the narrative tone of voice both reveals and conceals information. It was 'of course' for Undine's social benefit that they had come, yet the suggestion that there was something more is suggested by the conditional 'If, at the time, there had been other and more pressing reasons'. Wharton's narrator, rather like Hardy's does, sets up expectations and then withholds information. Something that happened in the past is never 'touched on', with the result that 'silence closed in on the subject' to the extent that for Mrs Spragg, whatever it was is now 'non-existent'. The silence is eloquent, but when Mr Spragg announces later that he saw 'Elmer Moffatt down town to-day' (p. 11), Mrs Spragg's 'physical apprehension' and the way the 'pulpy curves of her face collapsed' like a 'pricked balloon' (p. 12) suggest that what is not spoken of may need to be confronted. Undine also meets Moffatt, but the conspiracy of silence endures and she conceals the meeting from her parents. The real significance of Moffatt is not fully explained until the end of the novel, although he appears at various points. The narrator, then, both conceals and reveals information. This is a time-honoured storytelling technique, involving both plot and development of characterisation, which results in tension and suspense for readers.

Activity 4.1

Allow around 15 minutes to complete this activity

Read the following passage and assess the way the narrative reveals Undine's efforts to 'read' New York society:

> She had read in the 'Boudoir Chat' of one of the Sunday papers that the smartest women were using the new pigeon-blood note-paper with white ink; and rather against her mother's advice she had ordered a large supply, with her monogram in silver. It was a disappointment, therefore, to find that Mrs Fairford wrote on the old-fashioned white sheet, without even a monogram – simply her address and telephone number. It gave Undine rather a poor opinion of Mrs Fairford's social standing, and for a moment she thought with considerable satisfaction of answering the note on her pigeon-blood paper. Then she remembered Mrs Heeny's emphatic commendation of Mrs Fairford, and her pen wavered. What if white paper were really newer than pigeon-blood? It might be more stylish, anyhow. Well, she didn't care if Mrs Fairford didn't like red paper – *she* did! And she wasn't going to truckle to any woman who lived in a small house down beyond Park Avenue …
>
> Undine was fiercely independent and yet passionately imitative. She wanted to surprise every one by her dash and originality, but she could not help modelling herself on the last person she met, and the confusion of ideals thus produced caused her much perturbation when she had to choose between two courses. She hesitated a moment longer, and then took from the drawer a plain sheet of paper with the hotel address.
>
> (pp. 12–13)

Discussion

Undine's inability to recognise style and social status is revealed in this passage through narrative description. Her indecision over how to reply to Laura Fairford's dinner invitation is described in comic terms, as she decides to write with white ink on her silver monogrammed pigeon-blood notepaper, certain of its stylish superiority over Mrs Fairford's plain white paper – then, doubting her judgement, she changes her mind and uses instead 'a plain sheet with the hotel address'. The passage begins with straightforward description: there is no derogatory comment from the narrator about the value of 'Boudoir Chat', or why red notepaper might be considered stylish, nor is there a comment about Undine's purchase of a 'large supply'. But then, again without comment, the narrative shifts to report Undine's thoughts: she has 'rather a poor opinion' of Mrs Fairford's social standing, based on her choice of writing material. It is up to readers to notice the superficial nature of the judgement. The narrative focuses on Undine's thoughts so that the sentences that follow are written in language she, not the narrator, would use. They are still part of the narrative. In Undine's thought, 'What if white paper were really newer than pigeon-blood?', the use of the word 'newer' is especially telling: her concerns only ever focus on trends and fashion, and she is attracted by whatever is new and novel. The next sentence, 'And she wasn't going to truckle to any woman who lived in a small house down beyond Park Avenue…' again gives us direct access to her thoughts: the use of the word 'truckle' is particularly telling, as it is part of Undine's **register** rather than the narrator's. The narrator, of course, is fully aware that families like the Fairfords are considered to have superior social standing, even though they may live in smaller, less fashionable houses in Washington Square, beyond Park Avenue. Wharton's narrator expects the readers to recognise the satire at Undine's expense – although, as we shall see eventually, 'Old New York' families are not exempt from criticism in their turn.

The narrative shifts again in the second paragraph, explaining exactly what Undine is like, rather than using the more subtle technique of allowing readers to find out for themselves from observing her motives and actions. The narrator tells us that Undine was 'fiercely independent and yet passionately imitative. She wanted to surprise everyone by her dash and originality, but she could not help modelling herself on the last person she met' (p. 13). Later in the text, we discover that she learns by 'adapting herself to whatever company she was in' (p. 100), and in her own words, she wants 'what others want' (p. 64). Her so-called 'fierce independence' then is of a very different nature from Bathsheba Everdene's.

A key question to ask yourself, as you continue reading and reflecting on the narrative point of view, is not just what is the narrator's attitude to Undine, but also what is the narrator's attitude to Mr and Mrs Spragg and the way they have brought up their daughter? To what extent are they responsible for indulging her? Does their history of

Figure 4.2 *New York City street scenes – 5th Avenue*, 1913, unknown photographer. Library of Congress, Washington DC, repro no. LC-USZ62-107837. Photo: George Grantham Bain Collection/Library of Congress.

bereavement excuse them – if we even notice the brief, passing reference to Mr Spragg's vow 'on his children's graves' (p. 52)? Another important question to consider is how is Mrs Heeny presented, the '"society" manicure and masseuse' (p. 4) servicing the wealthy and feeding on their gossip, yet also able to do more for Mrs Spragg's 'spirit than her body' as she peoples 'the solitude' of Mrs Spragg's 'long ghostly days with lively anecdotes' (p. 8)? Mrs Heeny's anecdotes relate to the Old New York families as well as the new up-and-coming stylish wealthy individuals – but is the narrative voice as uncritical of New York society as Mrs Heeny appears to be? You should think about this question and the ones above as you read and reread passages in the novel.

Figure 4.3 Women reading, April 30, 1910, Siegel-Cooper Company. Photographed by Lewis Wickes Hine. The New York Public Library Archives, Shelf no. MssArc RG10 5928. Photo: The New York Public Library Archives, The New York Public Library.

If Undine has 'rather a poor opinion' of Mrs Fairford's style, this opinion is not mended when she attends the dinner. Undine is critical of the Fairford house, which she thinks is 'small and rather shabby' while the dinner too is 'disappointing' (p. 21).

> There was no gilding, no lavish diffusion of light: the room they sat in after dinner, with its green-shaded lamps making faint pools of brightness, and its rows of books from floor to ceiling, reminded Undine of the old circulating library at Apex, before the new marble building was put up. Then, instead of a gas-log, or a new polished grate with electric bulbs behind ruby glass, there was an old-fashioned wood-fire, like pictures of 'Back to the farm for Christmas'; and when the logs fell forward Mrs Fairford or

> her brother had to jump up to push them in place, and the ashes scattered over the hearth untidily.
>
> (p. 21)

The details in this paragraph bring out the difference between Undine's taste for everything that is bright, new and artificial – summed up by those 'electric bulbs behind ruby glass' – and the world of old-fashioned wood fires which the Fairfords inhabit. The floor-to-ceiling books, which suggest reading, culture, education and the leisure time to spend reading them, merely remind Undine of the 'old circulating library' in Apex; this implies that her own home was devoid of reading material. Knowing no one, Undine judges the other guests by age and appearance: a woman with white hair and a bald man with a grey moustache are of no interest, while she dismisses 'at a glance' a girl of her own age as 'plain and wearing last year's "model"' (p. 22). But a lingering mistrust prevents Undine at first from taking part in the conversation; again she has only her experience of 'voluble' Apex City ladies to compare with Mrs Fairford's graceful effort to ensure that conversation is a 'concert and not a solo'. She draws the guests in, 'giving each a turn, beating time for them with her smile, and somehow harmonizing and linking together what they said' (p. 23). Undine recognises the skill involved, and is astute enough to resist it. She has just enough self-awareness to realise that she risks exposing her ignorance and will fail to show herself to advantage. Instead she listens, taking note 'of all that was said' (p. 23). The narrator comments that 'All was blurred and puzzling to the girl in this world of half-lights, half-tones, eliminations and abbreviations; and she felt a violent longing to brush away the cobwebs and assert herself as the dominant figure of the scene' (p. 24). She is puzzled by talk of exhibitions, unaware that 'there were any pictures to be seen, much less that "people" went to see them' (pp. 24–5). If 'Back to the farm for Christmas' is the extent of her experience of visual arts, it is no wonder that she feels out of place.

Pamela Knights sums up her sense of Undine as seeming to be 'a being without a centre – self-created, in a series of improvised personalities made up of floating resources from the passing moment: she mimics the pose and costume for looking at pictures in a gallery, constructs her lady's manners from the tips in *Boudoir Chat*' (Knights, 2009, p. 91).

Figure 4.4 John Singer Sargent, *Portrait of Lady Helen Vincent, Viscountess D'Abernon*, 1904, oil on canvas, 159 × 108 cm. Photo: Private collection © Christie's Images/Bridgeman Images. Wharton had Singer Sargent's portraits of society women in mind as the kind her character Popple produced.

As Knights suggests, the imagery associated with Undine is dazzling but superficial: Undine's hair is 'starred with a hard glitter of diamonds' and she wears a 'shimmering' dress (p. 118) when she sits for her portrait with Popple; at the theatre she sees the 'culminating blaze of the central chandelier' and herself as 'the core of that vast illumination, the sentient throbbing surface which gathered all the shafts of light into a centre' (p. 39). She shines and reflects wherever she goes, but has little or no substance.

Narrative techniques

Third-person narratives like this one can be very subtle, swiftly changing focus from a detached account of events, into the point of view and language of one particular character; as with the inner view of Undine's thoughts when she writes her letter, and when she unwittingly exposes her ignorance of theatre and about plays at the dinner party. The author Jane Austen (1775–1817) is credited with the first sustained and developed use of what is called free indirect speech. The term – sometimes also known as **free indirect style** or free indirect discourse – is a more nuanced version of **focalisation**, which is when the narrative more generally presents the point of view of a particular character. We will use 'free indirect style' in this chapter, for the simple reason that 'free indirect speech' can be confusing if the narrative shifts into a character's thoughts, rather than what they say. So, for example, when Undine visits the theatre and is seated in her exclusive box, the narrator explains that rather than feeling that she had achieved a social triumph, Undine simply felt as tired and helpless as she had done back in Apex: '*Was it going to be as dreary here as there*?' (p. 44, my italics). This is free indirect style. If Wharton had written '*She wondered if it was going to be as dreary here as there*', or '*She asked herself if it was going to be as dreary*', that would have been reported speech, or indirect style, because of the narrator's explanatory words '*She wondered*' or '*She asked herself*'. Without the narrator's 'she said' or 'she thought' tags, we slip directly into Undine's thoughts – we read her mind. The technical terms 'reported speech', 'focalisation' and 'free indirect style' are very useful for analysing narrative: they help us to describe moments in passages of narrative where we have an interior view of a character's consciousness.

The questions to ask yourself, then, as you read a passage of narrative, are: whose words are these? Who do these thoughts belong to? Is this the narrator's perception, or have we drifted into a particular character's point of view? Wharton's narrator manages to maintain an ironic distance from Undine as she dithers about choosing paper and pen in the paragraph analysed in Activity 4.1, without explicitly commenting on her. Later in the novel, there is explicit comment, but it comes after readers have already experienced Undine's thoughts unmediated.

Whose words are these?

In academic essays, we are always careful to put quotation marks around passages, words or phrases that are not our own but which we have taken from elsewhere. In this way we avoid plagiarising; it is a way of distancing or separating ourselves from other people's ideas, even if we find them useful to develop or argue against. You may have already noticed how often Wharton's narrator puts scare quotes around particular words; it is something that Stephen Orgel points out in the introduction to the set text edition of *The Custom of the Country*: 'through the persistent use of inverted commas [Wharton] seems almost to be writing in a foreign language' (p. x). If you had not noticed this stylistic technique before, you certainly will now. It functions in an oddly opposite way from free indirect style, in which readers are imperceptibly drawn into a character's consciousness; instead, by picking out and drawing attention to words by putting them in inverted commas, Wharton's narrator manages to maintain an ironic distance from the society that they describe and the kind of language that society and those characters use. These words are not the narrator's words. According to Orgel, 'Wharton's very punctuation establishes her distance from her characters, insists that this is not her language; the decorum of her style in the novel not only does not admit slang, but even undertakes to insulate itself from the natural changes of the language' (p. xi).

So, for example, the portrait painter Popple 'was the only man who could "do pearls"', while 'the "messy" element of production' was not visible in his studio (p. 117). Undine and Ralph 'had decided to be married "right off", instead of waiting till June' (p. 80); and at an exhibition, 'some of the ladies and gentlemen wedged before the pictures had the "look" which signified social consecration' (p. 31). In each of these examples, the narrator uses expressions which are in general use as common parlance, but which the narrator makes clear she (supposing the narrator to be female) would never use herself. Try reading out loud any of the sentences you find that use quotation marks around particular words. To indicate the quoted words as you read, you need to use a different tone of voice. This exercise makes it clear that the technique Wharton uses implies a certain distaste for the characters at the very basic level of storytelling.

Ralph's point of view

Figure 4.5 Tuscan hills near San Gimignano, Tuscany, Italy, 2009. Photo: Christian Mueringer/Alamy.

Wharton's use of free indirect style is fundamental to the way her narrative works. One way in which the novel is structured and dramatised is by focusing on different characters as the story unfolds, so that alternative 'realities' are juxtaposed. Chapter XI provides an example of different points of view being brought sharply into relief.

Activity 4.2

Allow around 20 minutes to complete this activity

Reread Chapter XI (pp. 87–97), thinking about how the narrative point of view shifts.

Discussion

Undine, still not fully understanding the society or the family she has married into, or indeed the man that she has married himself, is in Italy on her honeymoon with Ralph. The chapter begins with a lengthy section, focalised through Ralph as he lies in the sunshine in the hills outside Siena, on his honeymoon. The setting is idyllic:

> Ralph loved the heavy Italian summer, as he had loved the light spring days leading up to it: the long line of dancing days that had drawn them on and on ever since they had left their ship at Naples four months earlier. Four months of beauty, changeful, inexhaustible, weaving itself about him in shapes of softness and strength; and beside him, hand in hand with him, embodying that spirit of shifting magic, the radiant creature through whose eyes he saw it.
>
> (p. 87)

There is, then, a discrepancy between what readers have seen of Undine in the opening chapters, and Ralph's sense of her as the 'radiant creature' who embodies the 'spirit of the shifting magic' he believes in. This is free indirect style: the narrator uses the kind of fanciful language that Ralph would use to describe his new wife. Can they really be metaphorically and blissfully 'hand in hand'? As we shall see, that is only true in Ralph's imagination, in his interior world. If we haven't already perceived the gap between his reality and his fantasy, the narrator swiftly makes it clear. Ralph's sense of well-being and contentment expands as he experiences a 'mysterious confusion of beauty', and blissful moments of understanding when he 'thrilled with a sharper sense of individuality than can be known within the mere bounds of the actual'. Gazing up through the branches of trees, he imagines words 'flashing like brilliant birds…so beautiful … weaving their fantastic flights against the blue'. The language is extravagant, hyperbolic, and represents his thoughts, not the narrator's. The narrator is fully conscious that Ralph is deluded in his belief that everything he perceives is from the point of view of 'the radiant creature through whose eyes he saw it' (p. 87). Ralph watches till his eyes ache, and then 'he changed his position and looked at his wife' (p. 88). With that half sentence the narrator signals an alternative reality, counter to his ecstatic mood. Undine is not comfortable with her back against a gnarled tree, neither is she cool, though Ralph had told her there would be a breeze.

This ironic discrepancy between the loving details the narrator lavishes in transcribing Ralph's expanded and joyful state of mind is marked by the dialogue that follows. Undine's replies are peevish: it is too hot, she is bored from sitting in the cathedral every evening, and the food in the hotel is disgusting. It is not until Ralph mentions a 'good-looking cavalry-officer' that Undine's face 'brightened' (p. 90): 'You know he's not a Count; he's a Marquis. His name's Roviano; his palace in Rome is in the guide-books' (p. 90). She is very well aware of this gentleman and she is clearly attracted by his status. Undine has no interest in her husband's abstract ideas of supporting himself and her extravagancies by writing. It then comes to him 'with the sharpness of a knife-thrust, that a crowd was what she wanted – that she was sick to death of being alone with him' (p. 92). In the space of an afternoon he confronts the knowledge which has been on 'the edge of [his] consciousness' for some time: the difference between his imaginary wife's 'spirit of shifting magic' (p. 88) and the impossibility of picturing 'the bareness of the small half-lit place in which his wife's spirit fluttered' (p. 92).

There are no interior views of Undine's thoughts or feelings in this chapter; they are represented only through her speech – a kind of realism in the form of the words that Ralph hears his wife utter. We only have a superficial view of her, which you may feel is entirely appropriate: are there any inner depths to Undine at all?

Activity 4.3

Allow around 15 minutes to complete this activity

Chapter XI focuses on Ralph throughout, but do you think that the narrator is entirely sympathetic to him at Undine's expense? Reread the following passage, making notes on any evidence you find to support or refute the narrator's empathy with Ralph:

> Even now a hundred qualifying reasons rushed to his aid. They told him it was not of himself that Undine had wearied, but only of their present way of life. He had said a moment before, without conscious exaggeration, that her presence made any place the one place; yet how willingly would he have consented to share in such a life as she was leading before their marriage? And he had to acknowledge their months of desultory wandering from one remote Italian hill-top to another must have seemed as purposeless to her as balls and dinners would have been to him. An imagination like his, peopled with such varied images and associations, fed by so many currents from the long stream of human experience, could hardly picture the bareness of the small half-lit place in which his wife's spirit fluttered. Her mind was as destitute of beauty and mystery as the prairie school-house in which she had been educated; and her ideals seemed to Ralph as pathetic as the ornaments made of corks and cigar-bands with

> which her infant hands had been taught to adorn it. He was beginning to understand this, and learning to adapt himself to the narrow compass of her experience.
>
> (p. 92)

Discussion

At the beginning of the passage, Ralph tries to persuade himself that, in spite of his moment of understanding – the 'knife-thrust' that his wife was bored with being alone with him – she is actually only bored with their 'present way of life'. Creditably and very reasonably, he works at seeing their situation from her point of view, and does so with some imaginative engagement: the word 'desultory', which he uses for their travels, does not describe the way he has experienced them – travelling in Italy has made him feel ecstatic. He compares 'wandering from one remote Italian hill top to another' – which he planned as the ideal honeymoon – with the 'purposeless' feelings he would have had, had he been forced to attend the balls and dinners Undine revels in. Ralph's thoughts are undeniably presented as fair-minded as he tries to reassure himself that she has not wearied of him, merely of their travels. But the next sentence seems to have a different tone: 'An imagination like his, peopled with such varied images and associations, fed by so many currents from the long stream of human experience…' has a self-regarding ring. It is an example of free indirect style, representing Ralph's somewhat lofty thoughts about himself; unless we stop to question what exactly his experience of life has been, and what varied images and associations he can possibly have encountered, we can be carried along with his eloquent thoughts and seduced into agreeing with him. Instead, if we read closely enough, we may recognise that Ralph is not quite as even-minded as we may have been teased into believing. The narrator, then, is not entirely sympathetic to the way Ralph has idealised Undine. He has allowed himself to be blind to her faults, to focus on her stunning appearance rather than recognising her lack of substance. Ralph's next thoughts about his wife's education and background may be accurate, but you might also think that they sound rather patronising: it is important that this is an opinion filtered through his now jaded view of Undine.

Figure 4.6 *Tuscan hills*, Chianti, Italy, 2008. Photo: Domenico Farone/Alamy.

At times, the narrator subjects Ralph to gently comic moments, like the one below which takes place earlier in the afternoon (before the 'knife-thrust') when his sense of happiness is at its peak:

> But now he knew the sensation in its fullness, and with it came the releasing power of language. Words were flashing like brilliant birds through the boughs overhead; he had but to wave his magic wand to have them flutter down to him. Only they were so beautiful up there, weaving their fantastic flights against the blue, that it was pleasanter, for the moment, to watch them and let the wand lie.
>
> (p. 88)

Ralph finds it 'pleasanter' to think about the power language has to convey his glorious sensations than to apply himself to actually writing it down. He either fails to understand that writing is hard work and consists of a great deal more than waving a wand, or is too lazy to do anything about it. A little later, playing with her hand, 'Ralph had never felt more convinced of his power to write a great poem; but now it was Undine's hand which held the magic wand of expression' (p. 89). The poem is never written. In spite of recognising that he must earn a living on their return to New York, Ralph 'still secretly hoped that, in the interval, his real vocation might declare itself in some work which would justify his adopting the life of letters' (p. 93). Ralph is a dreamer, incompatible with the materialistic Undine. He also could not be more different from his author, Wharton herself, who was critically acclaimed, commercially successful, and fully aware of the hard work entailed in writing fiction. Making that comparison suggests a particularly damning moral critique of Ralph.

Comparing characters in Hardy and Wharton

Comparing and contrasting two very different texts can be productive in helping to distinguish distinctive features about each one. While there are many different kinds of comparisons that could be made between Hardy's and Wharton's novels, we are going to focus on just one: the ways in which two untrustworthy men, Frank Troy and Peter Van Degen, are presented. These male characters throw into relief the female protagonists, Bathsheba Everdene and Undine Spragg. Undoubtedly, Troy is more significant in the plot of *Far from the Madding Crowd* than Van Degen is in *The Custom of the Country*, but both are essential in helping to illustrate moral values in the societies in which they operate.

Troy is introduced in Hardy's novel in Chapter XI, but we don't actually see him until Chapter XVI, when the sound of his 'smart footstep' and the clink of his spurs announce the 'intense vigour' of his walk up the aisle at All Saints' church to the altar rail, where he waits to marry Fanny (p. 115). Embarrassment and determination are equally evident in his demeanour, while embarrassment becomes his dominant emotion as Fanny fails to appear and the interested congregation begin to enjoy his plight. When she does arrive, Troy calls her a fool for going to the wrong church and then for expecting that her mistake can be easily rectified; he walks away from her coldly, leaving the situation unresolved. It is significant that the narrator does not specifically condemn Troy in this episode, but merely reports, leaving readers to infer for themselves that he is both self-regarding and unkind. This, then, is the man that later fascinates and attracts Bathsheba, who marries him, ignorant (unlike readers) of his past with Fanny.

Van Degen does not merit a chapter to himself, but his name occurs frequently before Undine meets him early in the novel (Chapter IV), when she ventures to the exhibition on Fifth Avenue. He is part of the hedonistic society she is desperate to belong to; significantly, she first meets him at the opera.

Activity 4.4

Allow around 20 minutes to complete this activity

Read the following passages from *The Custom of the Country* and *Far from the Madding Crowd*. The first describes the first time Undine meets Van Degen, the second Bathsheba's first meeting Frank Troy.

The Custom of the Country

Undine's heart was beating excitedly, for as he turned away she had identified him. Peter Van Degen – who could he be but young Peter Van Degen, the son of the great banker, Thurber Van Degen, the husband of Ralph Marvell's cousin, the hero of 'Sunday Supplements', the captor of Blue Ribbons at Horse-Shows, of Gold Cups at Motor Races, the owner of winning race-horses and 'crack' sloops: the supreme exponent, in short, of those crowning arts that made all life seem stale and unprofitable outside the magic ring of the Society Column?

Undine smiled as she recalled the look with which his pale protruding eyes had rested on her – it almost consoled her for his wife's indifference!

(Wharton, 2008, p. 33)

Far from the Madding Crowd

The man to whom she was hooked was brilliant in brass and scarlet. He was a soldier. His sudden appearance was to darkness what the sound of a trumpet is to silence. Gloom, the *genius loci* at all times hitherto, was now totally overthrown, less by the lantern light than by what the lantern lighted. The contrast of this revelation with her anticipations of some sinister figure in sombre garb was so great that it had upon her the effect of a fairy transformation.

It was immediately apparent that the military man's spur had become entangled in the gimp which decorated the skirt of her dress. He caught a view of her face.

> 'I'll unfasten you in one moment miss,' he said with new-born gallantry.
>
> 'O no – I can do it thank you,' she hastily replied, and stooped for the performance.
>
> (Hardy, 2002, p. 162)

Now compare and contrast the narrative points of view in the passages, and identify any other literary techniques and their effects that you notice. You may find it useful to look up the passages in the novels to remind yourself of the context.

Discussion

Both passages are written in third-person narrative, as both novels are throughout. However, in the Wharton extract where Undine first sees Van Degen, we see from her point of view and the narrative is focalised, whereas we are onlookers at the scene where Bathsheba and Troy first see each other. Undine's excitement is conveyed first by the narrator, who tells us that her 'heart was beating excitedly', but then it is as if Undine herself takes over, listing all the reasons why she is so excited by 'Peter Van Degen – who could he be but young Peter Van Degen'. Notice that this is a statement, not a question, and that his name is repeated – quite unnecessarily – except for the pleasure we might assume Undine feels in mentally saying it to herself. He is 'son of the great banker', 'husband of Ralph Marvell's cousin', he is 'hero', 'captor', 'owner' and 'supreme exponent' of everything that Undine finds desirable in the unfamiliar society she is so keen to become part of. **Clause** is piled upon clause, and the whole paragraph is made up of a single sentence – a breathtaking stylistic device that conveys Undine's excitement at this encounter.

By contrast, the encounter between Bathsheba and Troy is awkward. The Wharton passage is set in a public place at the opera, whereas Hardy's characters meet, and become literally entangled, when they are alone, out of doors and in the dark. The description of the scene has a theatrical quality. It is the narrator who tells us that the man is 'brilliant in brass and scarlet', while the arresting comparison of Troy's 'sudden appearance', vividly described as being 'to darkness what the sound of a trumpet is to silence', is the narrator's too. Like the readers, the narrator is detached, presenting what happens. The 'sound of the trumpet' image suggests that a herald has announced Troy on stage: the light the lantern sheds is overshadowed 'by what the lantern lighted' – that is, the brilliance of Troy's appearance. This is described as a 'revelation'. The light, the sound and the use of that particular word 'revelation' might suggest a religious experience; for Bathsheba it represents 'a fairy transformation' after her fearful encounter in the dark.

The next brief lines of dialogue show that Troy now addresses her respectfully, referring to her as 'miss', while the narrator draws our attention to his 'new-born gallantry'. However fearful or embarrassed Bathsheba is during the encounter, she cannot fail to be fascinated once she has seen him. Unlike Undine, who knows of Van Degen by reputation and is anxious to meet him, Bathsheba has never heard of Troy. Readers who remember the way Troy's spurs ring out in the church when he abandons Fanny may notice that it is those same spurs that have tangled him up with Bathsheba, but she knows nothing of him and is unaware of his history.

The final two short sentences in the Wharton passage continue to focus on Undine's perception of Van Degen, as she recalls 'the look with which his pale protruding eyes had rested on her' which almost 'consoled' her for his wife's indifference to her. Two things are significant: unlike Troy, Van Degen's protruding eyes imply that he is not a physically attractive man. In fact in the paragraph before this extract, he is described as being 'so unpleasant-looking' that had Undine not recognised something in his 'eye-lids as thick as lips and lips as thick as ear-lobes', she would have shunned him. His looks alert her to a Van Degen family resemblance, and it is quite clear that it is his social position, not his looks, that attract her. There is also a certain one-upmanship evident in Undine's smile as she recalled 'the look' he gave her: she craves attention. That he is married is of no consequence to her at all, although much earlier in the story the narrator said that in Undine's opinion 'married men were intrinsically uninteresting' (p. 22). Bathsheba's response, on the other hand, is one of relief when Troy is revealed as other than the 'sinister figure in sombre garb' she imagined in the dark.

In this activity you have focused on two brief passages from novels by different authors, compared the techniques of their uses of third-person narrative when introducing a new encounter, and noticed some effects of stylistic techniques like imagery, repetition and sentence structure. However, if you reminded yourself of the context of those passages, you may have realised how this close analysis exercise could form part of much wider thematic comparisons. How, for instance, do these relationships develop? Focusing now just on *The Custom of the Country*, it is not long before Ralph thinks of Van Degen as 'unspeakable' (p. 52) – that is, so contemptible that he is not fit to be spoken of – a potent word echoed throughout the novel by the repeated use of other words like 'silence' and 'mute', indicating secrets or events that are sometimes known about, but are not acknowledged or spoken of. We are left, for example, to ponder whether Undine actually has an affair with Van Degen after she is married to Ralph, or if she merely flirts extensively with him – and is not that as bad, from Ralph's point of view? That question also remains unspoken between husband and wife (Chapter XVI, pp. 138–43), and represents one of the many silences about Undine's history, a topic which was raised near the beginning of this chapter in the 'Narrative and narrator' section.

Conclusion

In this chapter you have gained a greater understanding of third-person narrative techniques – focalisation and free indirect style – which present views of characters' inner thoughts and consciousnesses. You will have noticed how the narrative point of view shifts between characters and contributes to the novel's structure. You have also begun to think about comparative work between the two novels that you have studied so far, noting similarities as well as differences.

References

Set text

Wharton, E. (2008) *The custom of the country*. Edited by Stephen Orgel. Oxford: Oxford University Press. Oxford World's Classics.

Other references

Hardy, T. (2002) *Far from the madding crowd*. Edited by Suzanne B. Falck-Yi, introduction by Linda M. Shires. Oxford: Oxford University Press. Oxford World's Classics.

Knights, P. (2009) *The Cambridge introduction to Edith Wharton*. Cambridge: Cambridge University Press. Available online via the OU Library.

Chapter 5 Edith Wharton, *The Custom of the Country*: Understanding the social realist novel

Shafquat Towheed

Contents

Introduction

By now, you should have a good understanding of the main themes and narrative techniques in Wharton's novel *The Custom of the Country*. In your study of the guided close reading in Chapter 4, you will have begun to develop your capacity to identify and understand some of Wharton's key narrative techniques, as well as learned to look out for the different points of view in the novel; the guided close reading and activities in this chapter will develop those skills even further.

The Custom of the Country is a **social realist novel** par excellence – it is both a novel about society, and one that depicts society in fictional form, through the conventions of realism. There are no elements of the supernatural or the Gothic, no improbable extensions of narrative plausibility, and no concerted pressures on our suspension of disbelief. Unlike Hardy, Wharton does not make excessive use of coincidences, mistaken identity or unopened/unread letters, nor does she focus entirely on the resolution of the plot – the novel finishes with a characteristically open ending and we are left wondering what Undine will do next (based on her track record, she is sure to do something). From your study of Hardy's *Far from the Madding Crowd*, you will already be aware that careful structuring of time is a key feature of the realist novel and *The Custom of the Country* is a great example of this. The narrative unwinds in linear, chronological fashion and – despite there being gaps in the telling and backstories that are only implied (such as Undine's childhood in Apex) – this is not a modernist narrative, so we don't have to scramble around to put together a fractured story, told by multiple narrators or from different points of view. Instead, under the unwavering control of the omniscient narrator, *The Custom of the Country* is an exercise in **verisimilitude**, with plausibly life-like characters, occupations, activities and trajectories, as well as a highly consistent narrative voice – Wharton's only exercises in the fanciful are in the names of places, people and things, and even these imaginary names often relate to real world equivalents. Wharton also includes realistic dialogue in the novel, faithfully transmitting the accents, expressions, verbal ticks and **malapropisms** of her characters, who are often minutely differentiated by class, gender, education and social standing.

Wharton's novel is a contemporary, rather than a **historical novel**. It is set in the first decade of the twentieth century – roughly the same time as when Wharton was writing it – and was first serialised in the pages of the highly popular society journal *Scribner's Magazine* (January–October 1913); many of the places, social events and practices described in the novel would have been familiar to her readers. All the while, Wharton writes with an undercutting tone of sustained narrative **irony**, which is often used to develop the elements of satire in the novel. Wharton's bitingly satirical novel dissects contemporary elite New York society, while inviting members of that very society (and a wider American audience) to read about it and (by extension) see themselves fictionalised. Like many social realist novels, *The Custom of the Country* acts like a satirical mirror, in which society is seen reflected back to the viewer (reader). Because of Wharton's accomplished use of free indirect style, focalisation and dialogue, as readers we are often required to reconcile more than one point of view when reading the novel. For example, what a character is thinking – their point of view – might be subtly undercut by the ironic tone of the omniscient narrator. In Activity 4.2 in Chapter 4, Sue Asbee talked you through such an example, with Ralph Marvell's lofty romantic idealism being gently mocked and undermined by the omniscient narrator. This complexity of perspectives is everywhere in Wharton's novel, and you will encounter some more examples through the close reading exercises in this chapter. The discussion in this chapter assumes that you have finished reading the novel.

Irony in the novel

Irony is one of the most common literary devices you will encounter in literature, especially in social realist novels. Stated simply, irony is where the surface meaning and the underlying meaning of a statement are not the same; for irony to be effective, it must state the contrary of what is meant. Irony can take many forms, including: **dramatic irony**, where the reader (or viewer) is aware of some information of which one character is unaware; **tragic irony**, where the audience is aware of the likely tragic outcome of the plot before one or more of the participants in the action; and most commonly, **verbal irony**, where a speaker intentionally states the opposite of what they mean, instead conveying the actual meaning largely through their tone of voice (in spoken conversation) or use of qualifiers, such as speech marks, italics, exclamation marks, gestures or laughter (in written narrative).

An extended form of dramatic and tragic irony in *The Custom of the Country* is Ralph Marvell's discovery of his wife's previous marriage when he confronts Elmer Moffatt; we as readers, party to the information offered early on in the novel by the omniscient narrator, figure out that Undine Spragg and Elmer Moffatt had been married long before Ralph does. In *The Custom of the Country*, you will find many instances of verbal irony through dialogue and Wharton's use of free indirect style, where a character says or thinks something quite different from what they actually mean. Often, irony is demonstrated through the tone of speech in dialogue. For example, when Undine forgets her son's birthday party, Laura Fairford makes an ironic comment to Charles Bowen: 'I haven't noticed that she follows Ralph's movements so closely' (p. 128). What she actually means here is almost entirely the opposite of what she says: that she *has* noticed that Undine doesn't pay much attention to her husband's interests, therefore in her opinion, the marriage is already in very serious trouble. To make sure that the readers understand that Laura Fairford is being ironic, the narrator adds contextual information ('Laura laughed') just before this bit of dialogue. Laura's laughter, and her comment on Undine's lack of wifely devotion, is therefore clearly intended to be ironic. You will find similar instances of verbal irony throughout the novel. Look out for how dialogue in the novel works to generate irony, and how Wharton uses speech marks, exclamation marks, italics, gestures or laughter. Are these used to reinforce the point being made? Or are they used to generate ironic distance between what is being said, and what is actually meant?

As well as conveying irony through speech acts and the tone of the omniscient narrator, Wharton makes good use of irony in the names of people, places and things, where terms are often the exact opposite of what they should mean. The Spragg family and Moffatt are from a small, insignificant and financially struggling midwestern town called Apex, which from all the information we have, is anything but the 'apex' of twentieth-century America. Similarly, after Undine and Moffatt elope together, they run away to the small town of Opake where, as Moffatt says towards the end of the novel, Abner Spragg 'came out to Opake after us and pulled you back' (p. 358). The irony in the place name is evident, for 'Opake' is a **homophone** (a word sounding the same as another but with a different meaning) of opaque – i.e. not transparent – but it is in the not too transparent setting of Opake that Moffatt and Undine's elopement is publicly brought to light and made transparent for all to see. There are many more similar instances throughout *The Custom of the Country.* As you reread parts of the novel through the activities in this chapter, you might want to note when you think Wharton's omniscient narrator is using irony to specifically undermine or undercut the social pretentions, aspirations or values of the characters in the novel.

Undine at the opera: 'reading' society

An example of how Wharton uses the classic narrative techniques of the realist novel is in Chapter V of *The Custom of the Country*, which features the first meeting between Undine and her (next) ex-husband to be, Ralph Marvell. Undine's greatest ambition – and indeed that of her parents – is for her to make a clean break from her past in Apex and find a suitable match, ideally with a rich, highly connected and respectable husband from 'Old Wealth' New York. Undine, the narrator observes, is relentless and strategic in her ambition and she is prone to sulky tantrums in the rare instances when she doesn't get her way. Lacking a season ticket to the opera, Undine is 'plunged in one of the moods of bitter retrospection when all her past seemed like a long struggle for something she could not have, from a trip to Europe to an opera-box' (p. 34).

Figure 5.1 Metropolitan Opera House New York, ticket, 1911. New York Historical Society. Photo: Collection of the New-York Historical Society/Bridgeman Images.

Undine's relentless ambition and energy are couched in the language of personal self-improvement: 'as she had often told her parents, all she sought for was improvement: she honestly wanted the best' (p. 34). You should already have noticed the ironic narrative tone here, because Undine's project of 'self-improvement' – as you can see through the course of the novel – is entirely material and financial, rather than moral, spiritual or cultural. The first requirement for the success of 'Project Undine' is an opera box, and not just for an evening, but ideally for the whole season. When her long-suffering father Abner Spragg finally presents her with a packet of tickets for the season, Undine's reaction is electrifying: her fingers are 'twitching for the tickets', her 'radiant eyes' glowing, she 'sprang up, all alight' and 'exulted' in her triumph (p. 38).

Figure 5.2 Metropolitan Opera House, New York, 1912, engraving. Photo: Antiqua Print Gallery/Alamy.

Activity 5.1

Allow around 30 minutes to complete this activity

Quickly reread the account of Undine at the opera in Chapter V of *The Custom of the Country* (pp. 39–48). As you read, make notes about the narrative techniques that Wharton uses in this chapter, such as omniscient narration, free indirect style, focalisation, point of view, dialogue and description. Then answer the following questions:

1 What does a night at the opera mean for Undine?
2 What insights into Undine's character and interior consciousness are afforded by the use of this realist device?
3 What does Wharton intend the readers to think and feel about the major characters (Undine and Ralph) focused on in this chapter?

Figure 5.3 Crowd of opera goers in the lobby of the Metropolitan Opera House, New York, 1913. Photo: Chronicle/Alamy.

Discussion

1 Now that her father has paid for an opera box, Undine's rise in social standing (and therefore her value in the marriage marketplace) is alluded to right at the beginning of the chapter: 'She had looked down at them, enviously, from the balcony – she had looked up at them, reverentially, from the stalls; but now at last she was on a line with them, among them, she was part of the sacred semicircle whose privilege it is, between the acts, to make the mere public forget that the curtain has fallen' (p. 39). Narrative focalisation here means that we see the opera through Undine's eyes – gazing across at the glittering New York elite who are the real 'between the acts' social spectacle. The proud owner of an opera box, her 'crimson niche' for the night, Undine sees herself as the ultimate spectacle: 'she herself was the core of that vast illumination, the sentient throbbing surface which gathered all the shafts of light into a centre' (p. 39).

2 The use of focalisation and free indirect style provides insight into Undine's self-absorption and unstinting sense of self-worth; she is conscious of being on show and sees herself as a diamond, gathering in and reflecting out all the shards of light in the opera

house, moving the focus from the chandelier to herself. Wharton's use of irony in the narration is also evident when Undine scopes the audience for familiar faces: 'Undine, for the moment unconscious of herself, swept the house with her opera-glass, searching for familiar faces' (p. 39). The words here that generate irony are 'for the moment', because Undine is almost always conscious of herself in public as an object permanently on display; apart from when she is in the presence of her parents or Moffatt, she hardly ever betrays an unconscious reaction.

Finding no one recognising her and the opera box opposite her empty, Undine consults her programme, which lists the names of the subscribers (in this case the empty box belongs to the Van Degens). Undine consulting her programme for this information is the kind of seemingly insignificant detail that is a standard feature of realist novels; you will notice that Wharton often carefully includes this sort of detail in the narrative, to provide the texture of everyday life.

Undine panics, realising the objective of her evening might be jeopardised, and the narrative cleverly uses free indirect style so that we have access to Undine's overheated imagination: 'Undine had a sharp vision of the Van Degen dining-room – and she pictured it as oak-carved and sumptuous with gilding – with a small table in the centre, and rosy lights and flowers, and Ralph Marvell, across the hot-house grapes and champagne, leaning to take a light from his hostess's cigarette' (p. 40). Free indirect style means that we 'hear' an imagined conversation in Undine's mind, in this case, Clare Van Degen speaking to her cousin, Ralph: '*Peter will be at one of his club dinners*' (p. 40). However, the narrator undercuts Undine's understanding of the world with a sustained ironic tone, reminding the readers of the limitations of Undine's experience. In imagining Ralph at the Van Degen's, 'Undine had seen such scenes on the stage, she had come upon them in the glowing pages of fiction, and it seemed to her that every detail was before her now' (p. 40). The irony here comes from the fact that Undine only has examples from fiction and drama to draw upon, rather than real life – this is, after all, her first outing in New York high society. The irony is further compounded when, soon after that, we learn that Ralph and Peter Van Degen are at the opera. Free indirect style shows some of Undine's inner thoughts, but also the limitations of her thinking. Chapter V of *The Custom of the Country* is not solely focused on Undine; at the end of the chapter, the focus is firmly on Ralph and his society, rather than Undine's first venture into high society. We arrive at the opera with Undine, but leave it with Ralph; he walks back to Washington Square, accompanied by Claud Walsingham Popple up to their club, and then returns home alone.

3 In Chapter V of *The Custom of the Country*, Wharton skilfully demonstrates the full range of narrative techniques available to the realist novelist. By using focalisation and free indirect style, she gives us access to the inner thoughts of Undine and Ralph, while at the same time through the subtle use of irony, Wharton demonstrates their limited and flawed understanding of the world around them. Dialogue is used to comic effect, for example through Mabel Lipscomb's overblown and wildly inaccurate pronouncements, but is also used to moral effect, for example, by damning Popple's misogyny and sexual hypocrisy through his own words: he refers to Undine as a 'mere bit of flesh and blood' and tells Ralph that he prefers 'Mrs Van Degen's type – personally, I *must* have breeding' (p. 46). By splitting the chapter between the earlier, dominant focalisation on Undine in society, and the later focalisation on a solitary Ralph, Wharton demonstrates the relative weight and competing trajectories of these two characters, pivoting around their meeting at the opera. It is clear at the end of Chapter V that Undine and Ralph are fundamentally incompatible – they have different needs and desires, and their life trajectories are in opposite directions. Ralph is only too content, as an 'aboriginal' of Washington Square, to hold on to what he has – a privileged, secure and stable, albeit severely circumscribed, world. Undine, on the other hand, is a disrupter, and the night at the opera offers merely a glimpse into her insatiable ambition and ruthless will to power.

Wharton and New York society

When describing in such detail the social practices of young, marriageable women in New York high society, Wharton was drawing upon her own life experiences. As a debutante a generation earlier in the 1880s, Edith Newbold Jones (as she was then) would have attended parties and balls. She also would have been aware of the newly built New York Metropolitan Opera House on 1411 Broadway, which opened on 22 October 1883 (when she was 21) with a performance of *Faust*, an opera that she knew well and loved. This venue was demolished in 1966. Like Undine, Wharton would have known that for young women with aspirations to marry well, it would always be '*better to watch than to ask questions*' (p. 42). Unlike Undine, however, she maintained a genuine lifetime interest in opera. She spoke French, Italian and German with ease, and spent much of her teenage years in Europe, unlike her fictional creation Undine, who – despite being named after a German novella, Friedrich de la Motte Fouqué's *Undine* (1811) and its German opera adaptation, *Undine* (1814) by E. T. A. Hoffmann – was denied all these opportunities in her materially and culturally deprived childhood in Apex. For Wharton, going to the opera was a cultural event; for Undine, it is simply a tactical marketing move, a public space to glitter like a diamond, a first step on the ladder to marrying and moving up in the world.

By the time of the publication of *The Custom of the Country*, divorce was becoming commonplace in America, with some 945,625 divorces being granted in the USA and one in nine marriages ending in divorce by 1916 (Knights, 2012, p. 230); Wharton became a divorcee herself in 1913, the same year as the novel's publication. The exponential rise in the divorce rate did nothing to quell the appetite for marriage; Pamela Knights notes that the median age for marriage for women in America at this time was 22, and by the age of 29, 'nearly three-quarters of all women could expect to be, or have been, married' (Knights, 2012, p. 224). Marriage was the primary 'route to economic security' (Knights, 2012, p. 224), and effectively the most important business transaction most women would ever make in their lives. For Undine, essentially an economic migrant to New York City, marriage (repeatedly if necessary) was her only vehicle for upward social

Figure 5.4 Edith Wharton as a young woman, *c.*1885, unknown photographer. Photo: Granger/Bridgeman Images.

mobility; she is in New York to sell herself and thereby further her (and her family's) social standing. Such a strategy, however, brings with it a series of moral and ethical decisions and compromises.

Undine's reading and the morality of fiction

Social realist novels often have at their core a set of moral or ethical dilemmas that the main characters must try to negotiate. In Hardy's *Far from the Madding Crowd*, for example, Gabriel Oak's knowledge that Troy is responsible for Fanny Robin's pregnancy places him in a moral dilemma: should he or should he not tell Bathsheba about this? Either course of action for Gabriel would lead to a potentially disastrous outcome, as it would cause great pain to Bathsheba, the woman he steadfastly loves and admires. Hardy uses this dilemma both as a plot device, to keep us reading to the end of the novel, and also to further deepen characterisation by demonstrating the inner consciousness of his characters (in this case, Gabriel). The fact that Gabriel is prepared to carefully consider the potential outcomes of any course of action demonstrates his moral worth. In this way, the social realist novel both articulates moral and ethical dilemmas, explored through the predicament of individual fictional characters, and also contributes to the wider debate about the morality of fiction.

Activity 5.2

Allow around 30 minutes to complete this activity

Quickly reread the account of Undine at the Malibran and the episode of the Van Degen necklace in Chapter XXVI of *The Custom of the Country* (pp. 231–40). Make notes about the narrative techniques that you can identify Wharton using in this chapter, and see if you can determine what Wharton intends us to think and feel about the major characters (Undine and her father) who are in focus in the chapter. Pay close attention to two interlinked themes: references to (or accounts of) reading; and examples of moral or ethical dilemmas.

Then answer the following questions:

1. How does the narrative convey Undine's disappointment at finding her parents in the Malibran?
2. How are free indirect style and irony used to demonstrate the moral and ethical dilemmas in this chapter?
3. Can you identify a moral or ethical dilemma in this chapter that is used by Wharton as a satirical critique of the hypocrisy of wider society?

Discussion

1 Chapter XXVI opens with Undine returning to New York from the divorce courts in Dakota, momentarily with her tail between her legs, having been passed over by 'the gentleman from Little Rock' (p. 231) at the end of Chapter XXV, who instead proposed marriage to Mabel Lipscomb. Mabel's unexpected success in the marriage market (one of many by the minor female characters in the novel) provokes Undine's unbridled rage and anger; seeing Mabel's 'hand on which her new engagement-ring blazed, Undine hated her as she hated everything else connected with her vain exile in the wilderness' (p. 231). The omniscient narrator reminds us that this is not the triumphal return to the city that Undine had anticipated: her parents are now living at another hotel, the Malibran, rather than on Fifth Avenue, and the narrative focalisation and free indirect style is used to full effect to show Undine's outrage and disappointment: 'it was another thorn in her pride that her parents could not – for the meanest of material reasons – transfer themselves at her coming to one of the big Fifth Avenue hotels' (p. 232). When she challenges her father about their accommodation choice, Wharton uses the ironic tone of the omniscient narrator to full advantage: 'Mr Spragg had briefly replied that, owing to the heavy expenses of her divorce suit, he couldn't for the moment afford anything better; and this announcement cast a deeper gloom over the future' (p. 232). Free indirect style here uses reported speech (Mr Spragg's answer) and focalisation through interior consciousness (Undine's disappointment). One word, however, is clearly deployed in an ironic sense – the use of the definite article 'the' – for the future under discussion is not that of Mr and Mrs Spragg, but of 'Project Undine' who, despite the social stigma of divorce, now needs to be remarried to advantage, and as quickly as possible.

2 The narrative tone is consistently ironic in this chapter, with careful understatement and qualification deliberately designed to demonstrate Undine's almost total lack of ethical and moral scruples. An example of this is the conversation between Undine and her parents about Paul Marvell's future, which is entirely conveyed through reported speech by the narrator, but from Undine's point of view (achieved through focalisation). First of all, Wharton uses the free indirect style to allow us to glimpse the conversation from Undine's point of view without using dialogue. Undine and her parents bear their 'common failure in a common silence', a silence which is only broken by Mrs Spragg's 'tentative allusions to her grandson', which only 'left a deeper silence behind

them' (p. 232). 'Undine', the narrator tells us in no uncertain terms, 'did not want to talk of her boy' (p. 232). Free indirect style allows Wharton to convey this awkward, stilted and uncomfortable episode without the use of voiced dialogue. Wharton uses speech marks to gives us small snatches of spoken conversation, without reproducing the dialogue, such as Mrs Spragg's phrase 'bring him round'. The only direct speech act is Undine's full-fronted (and fully vocalised) assault on the Marvells: 'I wouldn't ask them a favour for the world – they're just waiting for a chance to be hateful to me' (p. 232). The biting irony of the narrative tone is everywhere; we are told that 'it had not occurred' to Undine to 'try to gain possession of the child' (p. 232), and she 'quieted her scruples by thinking of him as "better off" with Ralph's family, and of herself as rather touchingly disinterested in putting his welfare before her own' (p. 232). The key word here that conveys the irony of the narrative tone is 'disinterested', which carries two different meanings or senses. If you wish to, look up the different senses of 'disinterested' in Stevenson, A. (2015) *Oxford Dictionary of English*, which is the dictionary recommended in Chapter 1. The first sense is the one that Undine wishes us to believe, that she is 'disinterested' as in impartial, thereby unselfishly putting Paul's welfare before anyone else's. The second sense is of course is the actual one – she is disinterested in the sense that she is lacking in any kind of genuine maternal interest in the welfare of her son.

3 This issue of Paul Marvell's parenting is a clear example of a moral and ethical dilemma dissected in the novel: Undine has been awarded custody of her son, which she evidently doesn't want to take up. What would appear to Undine's parents – and indeed most of the readers of the novel – to be an ethical dilemma is brushed aside by Undine. Ever the centre of attention, she consoles herself by blaming circumstances for her abandonment of Paul Marvell, rather than taking any moral responsibility for her actions: 'poverty, and the relentless animosity of his family … put an end to so perfect a union' (p. 233). Indeed, Undine claims that society as a whole is to blame by fancifully rewriting her own marital history: 'everything might have been different if "people" had not "come between" them' (p. 233). Wharton's clever use of free indirect style gives us sufficient insight into Undine's thinking to show us how radically different it might be from our own.

Undine displays a systemic lack of empathy, with a stunted moral development and resolute will to power at any price. But what might one of the causes for Undine's mindset be? Perhaps Undine was affected by her reading, for while she is no intellectual, she does read (chiefly magazines, newspapers and romantic fiction). Unfortunately, Undine reads uncritically and often accepts what she reads as literally true – this often leads to errors and social faux pas, but more importantly, it fuels her material greed and social ambition. Undine arrives back in New York in 'midseason' (the traditional summer social season ran from late March/early April to July), but owing to her now stigmatised social status, she cannot easily flaunt herself in public, and instead she resorts to shutting herself in her 'room at the Malibran, reading novels, and brooding over possibilities of escape' (p. 233). Despite trying to shun the daily papers, the narrator describes how Undine 'could not help taking one up and turning to the "Society Column"' where she follows Van Degen's 'tour around the world' (p. 233) with keen interest.

Addicted to Mrs Heeny's clippings which 'supplied her with such items as her own reading missed' (p. 233), Undine becomes increasingly obsessed with how success is represented in the news media. Reading one of Mrs Heeny's clippings, 'a long article from the leading journal of Little Rock' about the 'brilliant nuptials of Mabel Lipscomb – now Mrs Homer Branney – and her departure for "the Coast" in the bridegroom's private car' (p. 234), adds the 'last touch to Undine's irritation' and provokes her into a potentially disastrous course of action: she asks her father to take her to the opera, in a concerted bid to show her face in New York high society. Faced with the prospect of being 'merely part of the invisible crowd out of range of the exploring opera glasses', Undine 'felt a defiant desire to make herself seen' (p. 234). Again, Wharton uses focalisation so that the evening at the opera is seen entirely through Undine's point of view, and free indirect style offers us glimpses into her thinking (including thinking aloud). Seeing her potential nemesis and erstwhile rival, Clare Van Degen, Undine ponders whether to approach her – 'Shall I go up and speak to her?' (p. 235) – before deciding against it. However, on her return to the Malibran from the opera, while yet again gazing at herself 'before the wardrobe mirror studying her reflection' (p. 235), her father catches her wearing the Van Degen pearls. Wharton's narrative moves from free indirect style to dialogue as Abner Spragg asks her about the provenance of the pearls. 'Did your husband give them to you?' he asks, provoking an exclamation and laughter from Undine: '"*Ralph*!"

THE NEW YORK HERALD.

NEW YORK, TUESDAY, OCTOBER 15, 1912.—TWENTY-SIX PAGES. PRICE THREE CENTS.

THEODORE ROOSEVELT SHOT BY CRANK IN MILWAUKEE STREET

Man Who Gives Name as John Schrank, of 370 East Tenth Street, New York, and Who Styles Himself an "Avenger," is Put Under Arrest.

PHYSICIANS PROBE FOR BULLET; WOUND IN VICTIM'S RIGHT BREAST

Nominee, Who Was on Speaking Tour, Insists on Delivering Speech at Auditorium When Injury Was Pronounced Not Serious.

NOT SERIOUS, IS MESSAGE SENT TO MRS. ROOSEVELT

Roll of Manuscript in Pocket Is Declared To Be All That Saved Life of the Erstwhile President.

RAMBLING DOCUMENT IS FOUND IN POCKET OF WOULD BE ASSASSIN'S CLOTHES

Wounded Nominee Speaks for Twenty-Five Minutes in Auditorium Before Consenting to Go to a Hospital for Examination and There Quickly Recovers from Shock.

WHAT HIS OPPONENTS SAY OF ATTACK ON MR. ROOSEVELT

THEODORE ROOSEVELT

"AVENGER," ASSAILANT CALLS HIMSELF

NATIONAL SECRETARY DESCRIBES SHOOTING

HENRY S. COCHEMS

SHOOTING DEPLORED AT BUFFET BANQUET

LEADERS HEAR OF SHOOTING AT HOTEL

MR. STRAUS SHOCKED BY THE SHOOTING

ATTACK LIKE THAT ON MAYOR GAYNOR

Figure 5.5 *The New York Herald*, 15 October 1912. Everett Collection. Photo: Everett Collection Historical/Alamy. The front page of the newspaper shows the assassination attempt on the prominent politician Theodore Roosevelt. *The New York Herald* was one of the highest circulating newspapers in New York at the time and often featured news about high society. As such, it would be the object of Mrs Heeny's (and Undine's) regular attention.

She could not restrain a laugh' (p. 235). Abner Spragg's order to his daughter 'You better send 'em back to Peter Van Degen the first thing to-morrow morning' (p. 236) only provokes defiance, despite the fact that this was 'the first time in her life that he had ever ordered her to do anything' (p. 236).

Instead of introspection or moral reflection, Undine's response is one of anger, outrage and defiance, and free indirect style provides access to her emotions: 'The humiliation her father had inflicted on her was merged with the humiliation to which she had subjected herself in going to the opera, and she had never before hated her life as she hated it then' (p. 236). While moral and ethical scruples effectively lead Ralph to death by suicide, Undine's lack of a moral education means that her response is exactly the opposite: defiance, followed by escape. Indeed, Undine's self-education has largely been through reading society magazines, newspapers and romantic fiction, and it is the latter in particular that has formed her understanding of the world: 'Her novel-reading had filled her mind with the vocabulary of outraged virtue, and with pathetic allusions to woman's frailty, and while she pitied herself she thought her father heroic' (p. 236). Rather than Undine seeing herself as a person who has broken an unspoken moral contract, free indirect style shows us that she instead sees herself in the light of romance novels, as a wronged and frail woman and victim, despite being perhaps the least frail character in the novel.

Under the pretext of having the Van Degen pearls restrung, Undine asks Mrs Heeny to sell them for her and thereby fund her planned escape to Europe. Free indirect style allows Wharton once again to demonstrate that what might appear to be a moral or ethical dilemma to us (returning the Van Degen pearls) is, however, not the case for Undine, because for her, money and the visible social esteem it buys conquers even the slightest ethical concerns; when a 'bundle of banknotes considerable enough to quiet Undine's last scruples' emerges from Mrs Heeny's handbag, Undine 'no longer understood why she had hesitated' (p. 238). Mrs Heeny's handbag, and the endless source of society news clippings, now becomes the means to facilitate Undine's next big adventure: crossing the Atlantic again in the hope of another foray into the marriage market.

Being shaped by the unrealistic expectations and social hypocrisy evident in so much romantic fiction – novels which Undine has uncritically accepted as true to life – means that Undine lacks an ethical compass and has had no moral education. Despite the fact that

Figure 5.6 *RMS Olympic, c.*1911, postcard. Photo: Mary Evans/Grenville Collins Postcard Collection.

The Custom of the Country was serialised in *Scribner's Magazine* and was aimed squarely at middle-class and middlebrow readers of light fiction, Wharton here makes a potent criticism of the moral worth of novel reading – and, in doing so, she again reminds us of the need to read carefully, closely and thoughtfully, therefore to consider and reflect on our own actions. Reading is in fact 'everywhere in *The Custom of the Country* and almost all the interlocutors in the narrative are also explicitly or implicitly represented as readers' (Towheed, 2010, p. 31). Through the course of the novel, there are 'some seventy acts of reading either directly represented or alluded to', and these range from 'magazine reading, to the purposive reading of temperance writing, from reading to gather social intelligence in the society columns of the popular press, to novel reading as a form of personal seclusion, and from borrowing novels through the public circulating library system, to the private circulation and reading of correspondence' (Towheed, 2010, p. 31).

The novel opens and ends with acts of reading. In the opening scene, it is Undine's interception of the bell boy's letter (from Laura Fairford and intended for Mrs Spragg) that provokes her mother's exclamation; observant readers will also note that on the gilt-topped table of their private drawing room at the Hotel Stentorian sits a copy of Arthur Conan Doyle's *The Hound of the Baskervilles* (1902), which the narrator notes is one of the few 'traces of human use' (p. 3) in their heavily

Figure 5.7 Poster advertising the White Star Line, 1911. Cauer Collection, Germany, article no. SFP409459. Photo: Cauer Collection, Germany/ Bridgeman Images. Undine takes a liner like this (the *Semantic*) to cross the Atlantic in Chapter 24 of the novel.

Figure 5.8 *National Biscuit Company: women reading*, 1910. Photographed by Lewis Wickes Hine. The New York Public Library Archives, Shelf no. MssArc RG10 5928. Photo: The New York Public Library Archives, The New York Public Library. Undine would have made use of a library reading room like this to while away the boredom of her teenage years in Apex, as suggested in Chapter XVI.

over-furnished accommodation. Undine's first social faux pas – writing her dinner acceptance to Mrs Fairford on 'pigeon-blood note-paper with white ink' (p. 13) – is inspired by her reading, for she has read about this in the 'Boudoir Chat' section of 'one of the Sunday papers' (p. 12), and so she decides to act upon this advice to the letter. The novel closes with another act of reading, for Moffatt brings Undine a newspaper covering Jim Driscoll's appointment as the US Ambassador to England; Undine 'caught up the paper and stared at the paragraph he pointed to' (p. 371). Throughout the novel, Undine's reading is almost always for a purpose – she reads newspapers to find out about high society, the social columns of 'Boudoir Chat' to know how to behave, the opera programme to mug up on operatic productions that she doesn't know about, and romantic fiction to understand the ins and outs of flirting and marriage – but there is a major flaw in Undine's method: she is an uncritical, unreflective reader, and while her reading informs her actions, it does not result in any kind of moral education or improvement. You might want to compare how Undine's reading informs her actions with that of Ralph; there is a discussion of

Figure 5.9 Edith Wharton, *c.*1900, unknown photographer. Photo: Bridgeman Images. Wharton is seated at her desk.

this in Towheed, 'When the reading had to stop' (2010, pp. 35–9). Chapter XXVI ends with Undine heading to Paris, having said goodbye to her parents, but her next social encounter, at the start of Chapter XXVII, is also mediated and predicated by her reading of the press. Loitering on the terrace of her Parisian hotel, Undine meets an 'untidy-looking young woman' who introduces herself as the Princess Estradina: 'No one figured more largely in the Parisian chronicle than the Princess Estradina' (p. 241). Once again, newspaper reading propels Undine uncritically forward, for the Princess Estradina becomes the means by which she is introduced to her next (ex-) husband, the French Marquis, Raymond de Chelles.

Throughout this chapter, Wharton uses focalisation (primarily through Undine's point of view) and free indirect style (through a partial insight into Undine's thinking) to present Undine's perspective, and then cleverly and consistently undercuts it through the deployment of irony in the omniscient narrator's tone. This brings into sharp focus the gap between Undine's sometimes unrealistic expectations and her actual circumstances. In doing so, Wharton challenges us to consider whether in fact Undine sees the same moral dilemmas that we (as readers of the novel) see, and also to consider the moral role of the social realist novel. Undine has clearly learned social hypocrisy (if nothing else) from her reading of romantic fiction, and her frantic scanning of the press for news demonstrates her approach to reading as an instrumental skill, rather than part of a moral or ethical education. *The Custom of the Country* is an acutely observed satire on greed, ambition and social hypocrisy, but it is not simply a **didactic** novel or a piece of moral advocacy: Wharton is not telling us how to live, nor is American society the only target of her acute and relentless critical gaze.

Undine in France

By Book Five of *The Custom of the Country*, Undine has a new social position, as the wife of a French aristocrat, Marquis Raymond de Chelles, at the medieval Château Saint Désert in Burgundy. In Chapters XXXVII and XXXVIII, which you will return to now, Wharton continues to use free indirect style and narrative tone to convey Undine's growing disenchantment with French aristocratic (and provincial) life. Wharton also, however, uses two other main narrative devices – narrative description and dialogue between characters – to convey the growing gulf between Undine's unrealistic expectations of married life in France and her increasingly constrained reality. At this point, after having completed guided close reading activities, you should now be fairly confident in conducting close reading and analysis of sections of the novel.

Figure 5.10 La Clayette château. Photo: Andrew Cowin/Alamy. French château in Burgundy, representing Saint Désert. The fictional Saint Désert in Chapter 38 is a similar medieval château.

Activity 5.3

Allow around 45 minutes to complete this activity

Quickly reread the first two chapters (XXXVII and XXXVIII) in Book Five of *The Custom of the Country* (pp. 299–315). Make notes about the narrative techniques that you can identify being used in these chapters, paying close attention to the following: the narrative depiction of buildings and landscape; and misunderstandings conveyed through dialogue in these chapters. Then answer the following questions:

1. How does Wharton use extended narrative descriptions of landscape and the interiors of buildings to convey Undine's changing mental state?
2. How does Wharton use dialogue to engage in a satirical or moral criticism of her characters – for example, to what extent are the characters damned by their own words?
3. How does Wharton use narrative techniques to convey the differences between expectations and reality?

Discussion

1. Chapter XXXVII opens with an extended description of the interior of a building – a drawing room in the Hötel de Chelles, the de Chelles family's Parisian residence – from the perspective of the omniscient narrator (rather than from Undine's), and the desired effect is very specific: the drawing room is 'hung with portraits of high-nosed personages in perukes and orders', but beneath them sit an audience 'looking not unlike every-day versions of the official figures above their heads' (p. 299). This cleverly ironic observation by the omniscient narrator is designed to make the readers immediately aware of something that Undine de Chelles finds out the hard way: that the French aristocratic family she has married into is traditional to a fault, and despite massive upheavals such as the French Revolution, the family is inflexible in its centuries-old adherence to the custom of the country. Similarly, Chapter XXXVIII opens in the de Chelles' family château, the ironically named Saint Désert. Wharton again uses a lengthy narrative description of an interior (the long gallery of Saint Désert) and an exterior landscape (the view looking down the avenue of poplars), from Undine's point of view, to demonstrate her less than fulfilled emotional state. It has been raining relentlessly for months, and Undine is exiled in Saint Désert – a wet, rather than a dry, wilderness. The description of the interior, 'the great empty house smelt of dampness: the stuffing of the chairs, the threadbare folds of the faded curtains, the splendid tapestries, that were fading too' (p. 307) is focalised

through Undine's point of view, and encapsulates her sense of entrapment in an old, wet, crumbling and isolated château, a world away from the social whirl of Paris. Ominously, the narrator comments on Undine's realisation of the fundamental incompatibility in their marriage, for Raymond does not prove to be a compliant and subservient husband: 'she was gradually to learn that it was as natural to Raymond de Chelles to adore her and resist her as it had been to Ralph Marvell to adore her and let her have her way' (p. 310).

2 As well as using narrative description to set the scene and provide context, Wharton brilliantly uses dialogue to satirical effect. In the mouth of the innocent Paul Marvell, Wharton places one of the most devastating moral judgements of Undine's mercenary and negligent parenting. When asked to kiss his 'new granny' – Raymond's mother, the older Marquise de Chelles – Paul asks 'How many more do you think there'll be?' (p. 299), a question that causes Undine to blush to 'the ripples of her brilliant hair' (p. 299). Another example is in Chapter XXXVIII. The increasingly heated conversational exchange between Undine and Raymond in the library of Saint Désert results in one of the greatest ironic statements from Undine in the entire novel; responding to Raymond's explanation about how renting the *premier* to the Arlingtons for 12 years makes good financial sense, Undine's retort is bitterly ironic, and she is effectively damned by her own words: 'I daresay – but I'm not always thinking about money, as you are' (p. 315). Chapter XXXVIII ends with a bitter quarrel, with Undine refusing to countenance providing Raymond with an heir, and issuing a threat to leave; the fact that Raymond does not rise to the argument or raise his voice – he merely says 'Ah' in a 'low voice' (p. 315) – shows how completely unaccustomed he is to Undine's often unreasonable demands. The dialogue that degenerates into a monologue at the end of Chapter XXXVIII demonstrates the gulf in values and expectations between Undine and Raymond and the evident misunderstandings between them. It also shows the fact that, in this case, Undine has singularly failed to understand and negotiate the 'custom of the country', i.e. the expectations of French aristocratic, provincial society of her role as the new Marquise de Chelles. By the end of the library scene in Chapter XXXVIII, it is clear that this marriage, like Undine's previous one to Ralph, is doomed.

3 In these two chapters, Wharton cleverly uses narrative description to convey Undine's inability to adapt to her new circumstances, while the omniscient narrator provides us with ironic commentary about the difference between Undine's expectations and reality. Dialogue

is used not just to convey misunderstandings between characters (most notably between Undine and Raymond), but also to provide a moral critique of them – Undine is, on more than one occasion, damned by her own words in these chapters, and Raymond's lack of understanding of his wife's thinking is made painfully clear, denoting once again a moral critique of his choice of bride (she is, after all, a glittering trophy wife). Despite the mirrored interiors on display, especially in the long gallery of Saint Désert, this is one of the only episodes in the novel where Undine does not spend time gazing in the mirror admiring herself, or even catching her reflection in passing.

Wharton's critique of Undine's new life in France is even-handed: Wharton is as pointed in her criticism of crass 'New Money' American materialism as she is of the hidebound, hypocritical patriarchy of the French aristocracy, which is prepared to sell itself and its titles (as in the case of Hubert de Chelles) to the highest bidder. In Chapters XXXVII and XXXVIII, we see Wharton negotiate one of the great themes of the late nineteenth- and early twentieth-century realist novel: the potential clash between European and American social, cultural and economic values. Chapter XXXVIII ends with an ultimatum from Undine that she does not carry out, but for any close reader of the novel, by this point, it should be evident that Undine's third marriage is doomed, for the Marquis Raymond de Chelles is an unreliable vehicle, unable or unwilling to fulfil Undine's aspirations for fame and fortune. While Wharton's novel provides a detailed dissection of the transatlantic theme in relation to high society, there is much that she does not give space to in the novel, for Wharton was writing in a period of tremendous economic and social change.

Conclusion

In this chapter, we have explored how Wharton uses key narrative techniques – especially focalisation, point of view, free indirect style and dialogue – to develop characterisation and individual interior consciousness in *The Custom of the Country*. The guided close readings of specific chapters of the novel also demonstrate Wharton's frequent and consistent use of irony, often indicated through the use of speech and exclamation marks, italics and gestures. Contextual information in this chapter shows how Wharton's social realist novel engages with some of the most important issues of the time (such as divorce and upward mobility), while also commenting on the rapidly changing values of early twentieth-century American (and European) society. Finally, we have also reflected on the ethical and moral dilemmas in the social realist novel and considered the extent to which reading fiction might (or might not) lead to the moral development of its readers.

References

Set text

Wharton, E. (2008) *The custom of the country*. Edited by Stephen Orgel. Oxford: Oxford University Press. Oxford World's Classics.

Other references

Knights, P. (2012) 'The marriage market', in Rattray, L. (ed.) *Edith Wharton in context*. Cambridge: Cambridge University Press, pp. 223–33.

Stevenson, A. (ed.) (2015) 'Disinterested', *Oxford dictionary of English* (2010). Available at http://www.oxfordreference.com.libezproxy.open.ac.uk/view/10.1093/acref/9780199571123.001.0001/acref-9780199571123 (Accessed: 11 April 2019).

Towheed, S. (2010) 'When the reading had to stop: reading and the circulation of texts in *The custom of the country*', in Rattray, L. (ed.) *Edith Wharton's* The custom of the country*: a reassessment*. London: Pickering & Chatto, pp. 29–42. Available online via the OU Library.

Chapter 6 Ali Smith, *Hotel World*: A close reading

Fiona Doloughan

Contents

Introduction

So far you have been reading and studying a late nineteenth-century British novel, Hardy's *Far from the Madding Crowd* (1874), and an early twentieth-century American work, Wharton's *The Custom of the Country* (1913). We are now going to take a leap in time to the beginning of the twenty-first century and examine a work by Scottish novelist and short story writer, Ali Smith (1962–). *Hotel World*, first published in 2001 and shortlisted for the Booker Prize and the Orange Prize for Fiction, may strike you as a rather different kind of storytelling, with perhaps a less conventional and more experimental narrative structure. Its treatment of the sequencing and narration of events, its use of multiple voices and perspectives, its adoption of innovative narrative forms and its artful deployment of language can make it a demanding read. Yet it is the kind of book that rewards patience and sustained attention. In addition, the fact that the language used in Smith's novel is by and large very accessible contemporary English is likely to make things easier. Nevertheless, some of you may experience the first section of the book, in particular, as a little disorientating, since it may not be immediately clear to you what is happening. It should become apparent that this is not a consequence of poor writing on Smith's part, nor an attempt simply to dazzle the reader, but rather a conscious act designed for stylistic and emotional effect in the context of the unfolding story. As you work your way through *Hotel World*, you will begin to 'get your bearings' and settle in for the ride!

This chapter will help you build on what you've already learned about the art and craft of storytelling, and will guide you through a work which asks further questions about notions of realism in the novel and what they might mean at the beginning of the twenty-first century. This chapter will focus on a close reading of the novel itself and on understanding its narrative construction. The next chapter, Chapter 7, will locate the novel more broadly within Smith's work and determine the extent to which it fits within or subverts a novelistic tradition that seeks to reflect aspects of social reality. In addition to a brief overview of the novel, Chapter 6 provides a detailed section-by-section guide to the book. Do bear in mind, however, that these sections make up a whole, even if they initially appear to be quite different from each other in register, **style** and **tone**. This chapter will look at different aspects of storytelling and we will consider, among other things, the difference it makes when a character tells their own story (first-person

Figure 6.1 The Thunder Dolphin rollercoaster in Korakuen amusement park, Tokyo. Photo: David Kleyn/Alamy.

narrative), and when their story is told by someone else (third-person narrative). We will also think about how point of view is encoded in a novel, examining the narrative techniques that writers use to present to the reader the world as seen through the eyes of a particular character or characters.

In the context of a close reading of *Hotel World* we will also consider the role of the hotel as the site where much of the 'action' in the novel takes place, and the extent to which it is simply a backdrop or point of orientation or whether it serves other purposes as well. As you read, you may wish to bear in mind whether hotels in the early twenty-first century look and feel different from those represented in fiction of the late nineteenth/early twentieth centuries, and ask yourself whether they have a similar or different narrative function. More specifically, you might think of the Hotel Stentorian and its description at the beginning of *The Custom of the Country*, comparing it with what you learn about the Global Hotel in *Hotel World* and the people who work there and stay there. We will return to this later in the chapter but for now, before working systematically through each section of the novel, let us start with an overview.

An overview of *Hotel World*

Hotel World is divided into six sections: each section is preceded by a title relating to time and, as you will see, time is important in the novel. These sections each focus on and tell the story of a particular character. Each character has some kind of connection to the hotel, for example, as a guest or as an employee. The way in which each section is narrated – either by the character whose story we are witnessing or by someone else (e.g. an **authorial narrator**) – has consequences for the manner in which we as readers tend to 'hear' or understand it. This is one of the things we will focus on in more detail later. For now, look at Table 6.1, which outlines the various characters and the mode of narration for each section. The table is intended to help you see at a glance something of the structure and sequencing of the novel and to alert you to the fact that the sections are narrated in different ways, with a different character being the focus of interest in each section.

Table 6.1 Time, mode of narration, point of view and tense in *Hotel World*

Section details	Section title	Mode of narration	Principal character focalised, i.e. perspective from which the reader 'sees' events	Main tense/s
Section 1 (pp. 3–31)	Past	First person	The ghost of Sara Wilby	Simple past; present
Section 2 (pp. 35–78)	Present historic	Third person	Elspeth Freeman ('Else'), a homeless woman	Present
Section 3 (pp. 81–122)	Future conditional	Third person	Lise O'Brien, hotel receptionist	Future conditional ('would/might/could'); past; present
Section 4 (pp. 125–181)	Perfect	Third person	Penny Warner, journalist/reviewer	Simple past

Section details	Section title	Mode of narration	Principal character focalised, i.e. perspective from which reader 'sees' events	Main tense/s
Section 5 (pp. 185–221)	Future in the past	Interior monologue	Clare Wilby, grieving sister of Sara	Past and present (verbs of cognition and likelihood)
Section 6 (pp. 225–236)	Present	Omniscient narrator	Ghosts from past and present; assorted people from fringes of the story in 'the rough rainy northern town' (p. 134)	Present

As you can see, Table 6.1 also notes the tenses that predominate in each section, since there is often a connection between time and tense in the novel. While initially it may seem complicated, given the changes of focus and the different modes of narration in each section, working through each section will allow you not just to understand the detail of each but also to get a handle on the design of the novel as a whole.

In terms of understanding the relationship between time and tense and how actions and events can be represented in fiction, let's take an example from real life. For instance, you might talk with a friend about what you did yesterday: 'I went for my first driving lesson yesterday, and it was nerve-racking, though whether it was more nerve-racking for me or for the instructor is a moot point!' This mini-narrative, recounted orally, situates the action in the past relative to the present of narration: we know that the action took place the previous day ('yesterday') and that the speaker ('I') had their first driving lesson. We also learn that the speaker found the experience nerve-racking and was aware of its potentially anxiety-inducing effects on the instructor as well. The manner in which the story is told suggests that the speaker is seeking to amuse or entertain as well as tell their listener about what happened the previous day. In the light of discussion of this invented example, as you work through *Hotel World*, you may wish to think not just about when something is said to have happened, but also to consider how it is narrated in the novel, by whom, and to what effect.

Context in focus: Tenses (in relation to time)

Unless you have studied the grammatical system of English or have learned English as a second language, you may not be familiar with how English marks temporality and locates events in time. Time in the English language can be expressed in terms of past, present and future location; it can also refer to events, actions and states that are complete or still in process. So, for example, English has a *past simple* (e.g. 'she spoke') and a *past progressive* or *continuous* (e.g. 'she was speaking'), where the former indicates a completed event and the latter refers to one in process. You might also consider the difference between '*he walks* to work every day' (*present simple*) and '*he is walking* round the block' (*present progressive*), where the first suggests a regular activity and the second focuses on an unfolding action taking place now.

Stories are essentially sequences of events and actions located in time and space. These events and actions are usually presented after the fact but sometimes they can be narrated as they unfold – think of Sara falling to her death. It is also possible to imagine what would have happened in a situation had things been different (**disnarration**), and to consider from a vantage point in the future the effects of what is happening now. You can look forward in time (**prolepsis**) or backwards (**analepsis**). In other words, how time is articulated depends on the location of the narrator and/or the character in relation to the events projected or recalled.

Hotel World uses section titles to flag up both issues of temporality and sequencing (when and in what time frame did/will something happen/have happened?) and narrative stance (from what location or position is something relayed and evaluated?). Location can be both temporal and spatial at the same time. The book also asks questions about **frequency** (how often?), duration (for how long?) and **narrative impact** (what are the consequences of particular actions both 'real' and 'speculative'?) on the agents and antagonists involved in the **storyworld**.

At a glance, you can see from Table 6.1 that there are only two sections in which the principal character gets to tell their own story, namely Section 1 – narrated by Sara, as she plummets to her death in the dumb waiter (which is a kind of lift for dishes), and Section 5 – where Clare, Sara's grieving sister, comes to terms with the loss of Sara. The other sections, which focus on the stories of Else, Lise and Penny, are told in the third person by someone else (not the character). It is natural to assume this someone else to be the person responsible for constructing the novel as a whole (hence the term authorial narrator). However, as we will see, within these sections there are moments when the reader comes very close to occupying the mind of the character on which the section focuses. In other words, rather than just seeing a character from the outside, we appear to follow them from the inside and have the impression of merging with their consciousness at times when the narrator seems to disappear. You will recall the discussion of free indirect style from Chapter 4.

Section 6 is different again. It is narrated by an all-seeing, all-knowing consciousness which moves across space and time with impunity, recording and evaluating whatever presents itself. The focus is not on a particular individual, what they see and feel and how they behave; rather, it is like a camera eye which records at a distance and close up whatever comes into view. This might suggest that Section 6 is entirely **objective**; as we will see, however, there is a generalising but also an evaluative tone about it. This is how things are, it seems to say, and this is what is happening now. Section 6 draws together much of what has been set in motion in the course of the novel and brings it to a poetic close.

Modes of narration and their effects

As you have just read, the person on whom a particular section focuses does not always get to tell their own story. Sometimes their story is told by a narrator, who may or may not be involved in the events that they record. The question then is: what difference, if any, does that make to the way in which we, as readers, process and understand the story? As you work your way through the different sections of *Hotel World*, think carefully about who is telling the story and consider the extent to which as readers we identify with the character whose actions, behaviour and thoughts are the focus of the narrative. As you know already, stories can be told by a narrator who is not a participant in the action but constitutes a kind of observer and commentator. One of the things to keep in mind is the difference between various modes of narration, in terms of the 'distance' between you as a reader and the protagonist whose story and/or point of view you are inhabiting.

Reading and analysis: first-person narration

Unlike in previous chapters, you will be working through this novel section by section and responding to questions designed to help you with this process. You will start by reading the novel's opening in the following activity.

Activity 6.1

Allow around 1 hour and 30 minutes to complete this activity

Read Section 1 of *Hotel World* (pp. 3–31) and answer the following questions:

1. Who is speaking and from what location?
2. How would you briefly summarise the overall story of this section?
3. What happens in this section and within what time frame?
4. Why, do you think, is there a change of tense at the end of Section 1, from pages 29 to 31?

Discussion

1 While to begin with you may have felt a little disoriented, you will perhaps have begun to realise that the person telling this story in the first person is Sara, who has plunged to her death in a dumb waiter.

2 The story, as is indicated, starts at the end with Sara's demise, and continues with the aftermath of her death, including her funeral and her family's reactions to their loss.

3 What is perhaps strange, and unsettling – or oddly humorous depending on your perspective – is the fact that Sara's ghost 'hangs around' from summer to winter, gradually losing her ability to distinguish sights, sounds and colours, to speak and to be heard, to move and to feel. As well as spending her time post-death repeating her fall in the dumb waiter (until the shaft is sealed off), she enters the coffin of her own corpse and tries, through dialogue and by insisting that the dead body tell its story, to establish what happened on the day of her death and how long she took to fall.

4 While most of Section 1 is recounted in the simple past ('I told them all', p. 28), the final pages switch to the present as Sara's ghost is in the process of disappearing, losing her bearings and her language.

You may be wondering what Sara was doing in a dumb waiter and how she came to fall to her death, whether it was accidental or deliberate. If you don't know or you're not sure early on, don't worry; like all good books, there's a certain amount of suspense in Smith's work and sometimes the questions are as important as, if not more so than, the answers. The story that Sara has to tell is summed up in three lines, each line a deformation and transformation of the preceding line: 'Remember you must live. Remember you most love. Remainder you mist leaf' (p. 30). These three lines are doing quite a bit of work: the first line stands in opposition to 'Remember you must die', which is one of the epigraphs or quotations that are printed before the beginning of the main text. While reflections on and reminders of mortality have a long history, the reference here is to the title of the 1959 novel by Muriel Spark (1918–2006), *Memento Mori* (a well-known Latin phrase meaning 'Remember death'). The plot of Spark's *Memento Mori* revolves around various protagonists receiving phone calls from an unknown caller who tells them, 'Remember you must die'. The three lines in *Hotel World* also provide a kind of refrain throughout the work, thereby becoming an **intertext**, or reference within the text to another work, sending a message to the reader to enjoy life while they can. This message is repeated at the very end of the novel, beyond the final page in increasingly small type, suggestive of the diminishing power of Sara's ghost. Section 1 finishes with a rather insistent direct address from the ghost to her sister or possibly to the reader: 'Time me, would you? You. Yes, you. It's you I'm talking to' (p. 31).

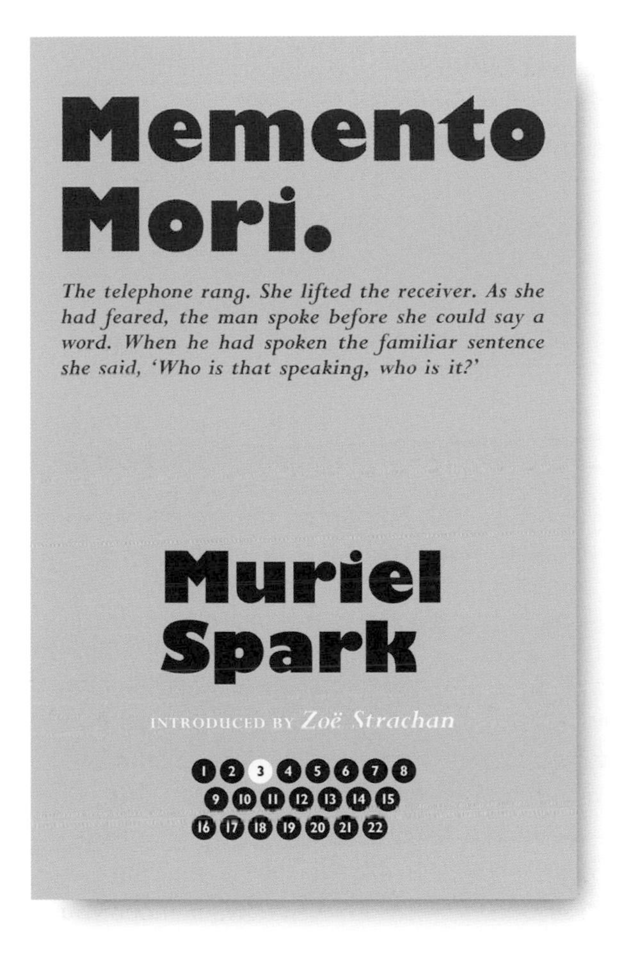

Figure 6.2 Front cover of Muriel Spark, *Memento Mori*, 2017. Birlinn Ltd, Edinburgh. Reproduced with permission of the Licensor through PLSclear. Photo: ©PLSclear.

Reading and analysis: third-person narration

You will now read and answer questions on the second section of the novel.

Activity 6.2

Allow around 2 hours and 15 minutes to complete this activity

Read Section 2 of *Hotel World* (pp. 35–78) now and reflect on the difference between the notion of 'who speaks' (or who is responsible for the narrative) and 'who sees' (or from whose perspective the action is conveyed). Considering the following questions will help you:

1 Who is the main character in this section and how does the reader learn about their situation?
2 How does the reader know what kind of person the main character is?
3 What kind of reaction do you, as a reader, have to the main character's predicament and what might explain this reaction, from a narrative point of view?

Discussion

1 The focus of Section 2 is on Else and her life on the streets, as well as on her memories of the past. Her situation is recounted by a third-person unnamed narrator. One of the things that you may have found the most striking in this section is the fact that although Else's story is being told by someone else, the reader does in fact 'hear' Else's voice, as well as at moments 'see' what is happening from her perspective. We begin by viewing Else from the outside: she is sitting outside the hotel, 'near a grating through which some warmth rises' (p. 35). We are told about and observe her movements: 'She leans forward … She looks up … She drops her gaze down the side of the building' (pp. 35–6). Yet we also get a sense of her voice, in more ways than one. First, her voice is represented by the sentences in brackets that contain no vowels – for example, '(Spr sm chn?)' (p. 35), which the reader imagines to be spoken by Else each time someone passes to encourage them to give her some spare change. Second, we appear to enter her consciousness at various points, moving, so to speak, from an outside to an inside view. For example, within the first paragraph, we are told by a third-person narrator that 'Else is outside' (p. 35), but has only managed to collect small change so far. Then the reader begins to occupy Else's consciousness, as the grammar

and tenor of the text reflect what are likely to be Else's thoughts, rather than those of the narrator.

2 The reader learns who Else is through observing her actions and behaviours, as well as through the stretches of speech that externalise her thoughts. In the following extract, the italicised sentences (the italics are mine) reflect Else's **idiolect** (or way of speaking), while the surrounding sentences reveal the presence of a narrator ('There's one there, just to the side of Else's foot') or are more ambivalent, in that they could be either the narrator or the character or both ('Nobody ever misses it, do they, a penny that's fallen out of the hand or the pocket on to the street?').

> Nobody ever misses it, do they, a penny, that's fallen out of the hand or the pocket on to the street? There's one there, just to the side of Else's foot. *Who needs one pence? Fucking nobody who is anybody. That's quite funny, the idea of fucking a nobody, just a space there where a body might be, and yourself flailing backwards and forwards against the thin air.*
>
> (p. 35; my italics)

What, in essence, is being negotiated here is an ability to present both an exterior and an interior view of a character. In terms of voice – although Else's story is being reported to us by a third-person narrator – the reader has at times the illusion of unmediated access to Else's consciousness, conveyed through what looks like her inner speech and thoughts. The narrator, who is otherwise controlling the flow of information to the reader, seems to disappear at these points; it is as if the reader is inside Else's head, looking at the world through her eyes and hearing her private thoughts. (You may remember Sue Asbee's discussion of free indirect style in Chapter 4.) There are also some brief stretches of dialogue – for example, between Else and the hotel receptionist, Lise – which again give the reader a sense of how Else speaks, though of course the representation of this speech is conveyed by the narrator: 'Fck sk, Else says' (p. 70). Inside the hotel room, the reader is again aware of moving between a report by a narrator of what Else is doing and thinking and getting a sense of Else's unmediated voice through representation of her consciousness. So, for example, when she is lying in the bath and considers what a terrible coughing fit she has had, the reader moves once more from external to internal view, and registers to varying degrees the presence or absence of a narrator (pp. 71–2). The sentences 'Giving birth to a cough. Congratulations! Proud parent of snot and gob, twins, she hacks out a laugh' (p. 72) move from Else's imaginings to a report of her laughing with a strong sense of her inner voice in between. The punctuation – the presence of an exclamation mark after 'congratulations' – is evidence of this.

3 It could be argued that in some ways the reader gets as close to Else as to Sara, even though Sara is telling her own story and Else is not. So perhaps it's less a grammatical question – first-person versus third-person narration – and more a question of the extent to which the reader gets to know a character and/or feels empathetic towards them. Tense can make a difference here. The present tense, particularly the present continuous or present progressive, tends to give us a sense of things unfolding before our eyes: 'She is lying in the bath and looking at the taps' (p. 70). The reader is placed in Else's position and is therefore more likely to be able to see things from her perspective.

The role of the social in *Hotel World*

Another important feature of *Hotel World* is the fact that many of the sections incorporate different **sociolects** (socially shaped ways of communicating, and different registers and types of **discourse** within them). By this I mean to point to language that is normally associated with particular social and professional contexts. For example, in Section 3 (pp. 81–122), Lise, the former hotel receptionist, is lying sick in bed, trying to fill out a form in order to be able to claim sickness benefit; in Section 4 (pp. 125–81), Penny, a journalist, is writing a review of the Global Hotel. To receive sickness benefit, for instance, you need to satisfy the authorities that you are unable to function in a work environment, explaining the symptoms of your illness and their consequences for your health and well-being. Likewise, writing a review of a hotel for a newspaper or hotel guide requires that you follow a particular format determined by convention as well as by the purpose(s) of the review. In both cases, the social world enters the world of the characters in the novel via the discourses and registers (formal or informal; professional or familiar) and genres (e.g. forms, reviews, etc.) associated with each context.

Activity 6.3

Allow around 2 hours to complete this activity

As you read Section 3 of *Hotel World* (pp. 81–122), make a note of other discourses or ways of talking and writing about the world which permeate the text, and reflect on their function.

Discussion

One of the things that you may have noticed is the way in which advertising jingles come into Lise's head as she lies in her sick bed. There's the Mazola oil jingle, the Kellogg's Country Store song, and the singing bottle of bubble bath shaped like a sailor. While Lise has difficulty focusing on anything serious or functional and struggles to remember events leading up to her illness, she is able to access in her memory TV adverts and commercial jingles with relative ease. Her mother, Deirdre, seems to have been at one time a well-known TV personality who wrote little poems and sang commercial ditties for a living, but whose moment in the spotlight has passed, leaving her miserable. So at one level, it may be that in sickness, Lise returns to the world of her childhood. At the same time, however, the fact that Lise's mind is imbued with the rhythms of advertising jingles and commercially successful songs may also constitute a kind of indirect social commentary, in so far as it points to the subliminal power of advertising. Lise has repressed conscious knowledge of what happened on the night that she invited Else, the homeless woman, into the hotel, when damage was caused to the room and adjoining corridor by the water from the overflowing bath; an innocent person, the chambermaid, lost her job as a consequence, since Lise and her co-worker, Duncan, denied that the room had been occupied. So Lise's inability to remember events from the past indicates the trauma associated with them. Her failure to take responsibility for her actions on the night in question and the subsequent guilt connected with the dismissal of the chambermaid has impacted upon Lise's sense of well-being.

Figure 6.3 Homeless person sitting on the street.
Photo: photospower/Getty.

So far, the focus in this chapter has been on how a story is told, by whom, and the extent to which the presence of a narrator is made visible to the reader. We have also looked at the impact of ways of speaking which help the reader distinguish narrator from character and permit us to build up a picture of who that character is – socially, professionally and psychologically. In addition, we have reflected to a certain extent on relationships between events represented in the narrative and their location in time, as reflected in the choice of tense used to situate them relative to the narrative present. We will return shortly to questions of narration when discussing Section 6, since it draws on a different mode – omniscient narration – but for now let us focus on representation of Penny, the journalist writing a review of the hotel.

Representation and evaluation

Characters may be presented positively, negatively or ambivalently within the pages of a novel by the narrator responsible for telling their story. Sometimes the very act of describing can indicate or imply an evaluation of a character. It is, therefore, always useful to be alert to the language used to discuss a character's behaviour and interactions.

Activity 6.4 gives you an opportunity to consider further links between how a character is presented and the kind of view that you, as a reader, are invited to form.

Activity 6.4

Allow around 2 hours and 30 minutes to complete this activity

As you read Section 4 of *Hotel World* (pp. 125–181), make notes on Penny's character as it appears to you, providing evidence for your view.

Do you think the narrator approves of her? Give reasons for your answer.

Discussion

Penny is presented as a not particularly likeable character. She appears to be bored easily, is rather self-satisfied and is always looking for a story or an angle, regardless of the human consequences. In addition, she doesn't seem to be very perceptive when it comes to working out people's situations, nor very responsive to human emotion. The gulf between what she supposes to be the case and the reality is huge and would be laughable, were it not at the same time extremely distressing and concerning. For example, it takes her forever to work out that Else is in fact homeless, rather than someone who is wandering around neighbourhoods at night looking to buy a house. When we first encounter Penny, she's typing up a review and trying to watch pornography on TV at the same time. She laughs at her own jokes – she says 'Remember you must diet' (p. 129), in one of the book's many references to '*Memento mori*' – and imagines scenarios in which she is the heroine (pp. 132–3). She abandons Clare when the latter begins to cry, since she doesn't know how to respond (p. 152), and she cancels a cheque that she has written to Else (p. 173) as soon as she gets back to her hotel room, and the sense of adventure recedes alongside her moment of 'mad' generosity: 'For a minute there she thought she'd gone soft. For a minute there, the universe had shifted' (p. 178).

There are a number of indications that the narrator is critical of Penny. It's partly conveyed through the over-the-top way in which Penny is presented, that is to say, her presentation is such that the reader is unlikely to find her sympathetic. The tone is also sardonic. When, for example, we read that: 'She [Penny] was firing on all cylinders' (p. 179), it is in a context that emphasises Penny's poor judgement, poor taste and lack of empathy. Penny's thoughts – rendered in the section beginning 'If you were poor, you were poor' down to 'It was no accident that the words poor and pure were so alike' (p. 178) – are so out of place and anachronistic, like those of another era, that it is made clear to the reader that the narrator is appalled and expects the reader to be so as well. At the same time, however, there is a suggestion that Penny's lack of warmth and ability to identify with human emotions may stem from a childhood trauma.

This chapter began by noting that you were likely to find *Hotel World* more demanding than the novels you have studied so far, in terms of the range and variety of its modes of narration. You have already seen that it is possible, narratively speaking, to move from an outer view of a character to the semblance of an inner view, even within a third-person narrative, via free indirect style. In Else's section the reader has the impression of inhabiting her consciousness and of knowing her inner thoughts, despite the presence of a narrator. We've also spent some time analysing first-person narration in Section 1 where Sara tells her story in her own words as a ghost. Section 5 will introduce another variation on modes of narration, since what we have here is a kind of **interior monologue**: an extended stretch of text in which Clare, Sara's grieving sister, returns from the hotel where she has timed the fall and talks – in an explanatory and associative way – ostensibly to her dead sister, but really to herself, in a kind of coming to terms with her sister's death.

Representing inner speech

The following activity focuses on the kind of techniques novelists may use to convey a character's inner thoughts when, strictly speaking, we have no direct access to them. Yet it is possible to give a sense of what is going on in the mind of a character through the use of carefully chosen and skilfully organised bits of language which are reflective of how that character feels and thinks.

Activity 6.5

Allow around 1 hour and 45 minutes to complete this activity

As you read Section 5 of *Hotel World* (pp. 185–221), note down at least three features that strike you about the way in which it is written.

Discussion

There are many things that may have drawn your attention here. One feature is the systematic repetition of the '& since' structure present throughout the section: the **main clause** is often deferred and the reader has multiple subordinate clauses beginning with '& since' – clauses that seem to present reasons for something without completing the sentence and saying what that something is. For example, you could say, 'And since (or because) I counted, I know you were fast', where the main clause, 'I know you were fast' depends on the action of counting. In other words, there is normally a relationship (of dependence) between the two clauses.

Another feature that may have struck you is the fact that the verb 'count' is used across this section in two senses: one a literal sense, since Clare counts the seconds it takes for her shoe to fall down the shaft – she literally timed it; at the same time, there is the sense of 'counting' as in 'being important'. 'I know I counted for you' (p. 221) refers to the actual counting (of seconds), but may also be read as the final and most important piece of information in this long sequence: Clare has assured herself that she was important to her sister and that her sister did not commit suicide. She now knows that the fall was an accident.

A further feature of the text that you may have noticed relates to **voice**: the repetition of words such as 'lobotomic', and using various swear words, have the effect of reminding the reader that the speaker is an adolescent with a particular idiolect or characteristic way of speaking.

Finally, something you can see at a glance: there is no punctuation in the section – just a series of clauses and some white space. The whole is delivered as one long monologue which follows the internal logic of Clare's mind.

Omniscient narration

An omniscient narrator is one that seems to know everything that is happening, and can even see inside people's heads! Unlike the previous five sections, which focus on a particular character, Section 6 operates in a different way. As seen in Table 6.1, this section is narrated in the third person in the present tense, and to begin with, it appears to be without a narrator, in that it is simply a series of descriptions of an early morning winter's day and of a town and some of the townsfolk as they awaken. Yet as you read on, you may perhaps pick up on some signals that there is in fact a narrator present: a narrator who has the power to roam the country from top to bottom, from the Highlands of Scotland to the Globe Theatre or the Millennium Dome (now called the O2 Arena) in London, for example. This same narrator seems to know the history of the sweet shop owned by Mrs Reid in the Highlands of Scotland and is able to pass on the gossip about her. Much of what the narrator recounts relates to a distant past: think, for example, of the child actor Solomon Pavy and the former executioners' block on the site of what would become the Millennium Dome. This narrator, therefore, seems to know everything and be able to see across time and space.

Activity 6.6

Allow around 45 minutes to complete this activity

Read Section 6 of *Hotel World* (pp. 225–36), and note down any indications you find of the explicit presence of a narrator.

Discussion

You may have noticed that there are moments in Section 6 when we, as readers, are made explicitly aware of a narrator's presence: think, for example, of the text in brackets on page 229 – ('for neatness' sake let's say the town where the heft and the scant of this book have been so tenuously anchored'). That 'let's say' is an intervention by the narrator responsible for constructing the entire story – a story characterised in terms of its location as having been 'tenuously anchored' in a particular place. In other words, the narrator is signalling that this story might just as easily have taken place elsewhere in another town, since to a certain extent and despite indications to the contrary – like the names of specific streets (Short Street) and particular houses within those streets (number 14 Short Street) – many towns are alike. Also, of course, ghosts are free to roam: the ghost of Dusty Springfield, a singer from the 1960s, is resurrected in the shape of her song, 'The Look of Love', which blares out of a terraced house in Short Street.

Figure 6.4 Dusty Springfield, glamorous and talented singer, record producer and TV personality, at the London Palladium, 1965. Photo: ITV/Shutterstock.

At this point the narrator appears close to being identical with the author of *Hotel World*, in that those familiar with Smith's preferences will know that she often includes references to popular music and art in her work. Smith grew up at a time when the songs of Dusty Springfield were popular. There is also potentially a coded message here, in so far as Dusty Springfield lived for a time with another woman and part of what *Hotel World* is concerned with is same-sex desire: Sara is attracted to the girl in the jeweller's shop; that interest is reciprocated but too late. The girl from the watch shop has taken to wearing Sara's watch and it seems to fit perfectly. In this sense, there is a symmetry between Sections 1 and 6: Section 1 recounts Sara's fall and her falling in love (the two 'falls' are linked); the final section returns to the object of her desire, the girl in the watch shop, and to the latter's recognition of her own attraction to Sara – 'The timing was wrong. It was embarrassing. It's embarrassing now, when she thinks about it, and when she does she can feel small wings moving against the inside of her chest, or something in there anyway, turning, tightened, working' (p. 235).

Earlier in this chapter, Section 6 was characterised as poetic in places. This is because of the descriptions of 'morning', particularly at the end of the section with its almost **haiku**-like quality: the birds landing, the tree shaking, the rainwater which 'jolts off the branches and falls, a miniature parody of rain' (p. 236). In addition, repetition is used throughout the section to structure it and provide a kind of internal rhythm, just like the effect of the seasons which give way to and follow on from one another, returning in an endless cycle.

Now that you have read all six sections of *Hotel World* and given some thought to how the story is told and how the characters are presented, we will return to the question of time and space.

Figure 6.5 (Left) Ladies' watch. Photo: Mouse in the House/Alamy. (Right) Goods lift (dumb waiter). Photo: GeoPic/Alamy.

Time and space in *Hotel World*

As a genre, the novel has always been concerned with time and what happens in and over time. Some novels take place over years, even decades (e.g. Leo Tolstoy's *War and Peace* (1867)), while others focus on events on a single day (e.g. James Joyce's *Ulysses* (1922)). *Far from the Madding Crowd* and *The Custom of the Country* both, as you know, take place over a number of years. We have noted already in relation to *Hotel World* that time is important in multiple senses. For example, it takes time to come to terms with grief or loss after a death in the family, and part of what the novel is doing is showing us how Clare comes to accept her sister's untimely death. We also see how events in the past can impact on the present: Lise becomes ill and is bed-ridden for some time following a particularly eventful night at the hotel, during which a homeless person, Else, occupies one of the rooms and leaves a tap running in the bathroom. Time is also represented in the novel in relation to the spirits or ghosts that roam the earth: Sara's ghost is in limbo for a while; other spirits haunt the novel, as the omniscient narrator roams the length and breadth of Britain and points to changes in the landscape and cityscape that reflect the passage of time. Time and place are of course both essential parts of our sense of the here and now, or serve to disclose aspects of the past at a particular point. So, for example, the dumb waiter in the Global Hotel is the site of Sara's breath-taking plunge to her (it turns out, accidental) death: this plunge takes place in finite time – a few seconds – and can be relived in imagination/re-experienced from beyond the grave by both Sara's ghost and her grieving family. The space of the novel is a real space encountered in and over time, in the sense that the reader takes time to read it, whether in chunks or at one sitting. At the same time, it is also an imaginational space or fictional world brought to life in each reader's mind as they visualise the scenes depicted, dramatised and re-enacted.

Writers have narrative tools for representing time and for presenting the passage of time. Two contrasting tools are the **scene** and **summary**. In a scene, events and dialogue play out as if in real time: the reader has the impression of witnessing events and conversations as they happen. For example, as readers, we witness Penny in her hotel room as she types multiple 'Fs' on to her keyboard; later we see her follow Else around the houses. However, in a summary the passage of time is elided and simply summarised – an example would be something like 'Ten years passed in much the same way' or 'Spring followed winter as surely as night follows day'.

Arguably, there is a difference between treatment of time in nineteenth- and twentieth/twenty-first century novels. It could be said that in nineteenth-century novels time is largely linear – events generally proceed in chronological order – and characters are often seen to develop over time, moulded perhaps by experience. By the time twentieth-century novelists such as Virginia Woolf (1882–1941) come along, time begins to be inflected differently in the novel, perhaps due to a different understanding of both the experience and effects of time. Time, for writers such as Woolf, can be and often is **subjective**: inner experience of time is often at odds with the passage of time demarcated by the clock. This approach to time has been an important influence on Smith's work.

Activity 6.7

Allow around 30 minutes to complete this activity

Return to Section 2 in *Hotel World*, pages 77–8, and consider how time is represented here. Begin with the sentence starting 'Else sits on the bed naked …' (p. 77), down to 'the sensitive shutters of cameras' (p. 78).

Discussion

One of the things you may have noticed is that Else's inner life is vibrant. She recalls events, feelings and sensations from her past: 'Inside her head she can still see the things the photographer took the picture of …' (p. 77). This of course is a representation of memory, but it also sets up a move from an outside view of Else and a sequencing of her present actions reported by the narrator – 'Else sits … She lies back … She closes her eyes…' (p. 77) – to an interior view as if we are occupying Else's thoughts and getting access to her inner being. The list of objects Else had presented to the photographer are at one level mere objects, yet at another, they can be seen as evidence of a life – a life that could have been otherwise. We learn, for example, that she has been to Venice and had sent her parents a postcard. **Exposition** of what is happening in the present continues, with anticipation of what will happen: 'The tap is still running … In a minute she will open her eyes … Her blood is pulsing …' (p. 78). Yet it's not just what is visible to the eye that is important: rather, it's Else's sensory memories and deep feelings which give the reader insight into her inner life – 'The taste of silver, metallic, rheumy' (p. 78) – and link her present back to the past. The set of almost surreal images in the final sentence: 'Her irises … bloom open …' (p. 78), alongside references to the action of cameras and the sensitivity of flowers in the simile, help emphasise Else's own sensitivity and innate humanity. Description of the actions and objects of the present reveal aspects of the deeper 'reality' and human subjectivity of an individual character.

We have already mentioned the space of the hotel. Hotels are places through which people pass, where they meet and stay temporarily either for professional reasons (e.g. working away from home) or for leisure purposes (e.g. holidays). There can be many factors determining where people stay, which may include price, value for money, rating, reputation, convenience and other factors. Hotels can differ in type (e.g. budget or luxury), size (boutique or corporate) and ranking in terms of both facilities and customer satisfaction. In some ways they represent a microcosm of society, since they include various kinds of staff (kitchen and restaurant staff; chambermaids, concierges, bell-boys/girls, cleaners, even gardeners perhaps and receptionists) as well as a range of guests. Hotels are designed and managed environments providing accommodation and a range of services to different types of people. The title of Smith's novel, *Hotel World*, is indicative of the way in which the hotel can be seen as a kind of self-contained, self-functioning world once you cross the threshold or go through the revolving doors! Yet at the same time, hotels exist within economic and social systems, both nationally and internationally, and can reflect the values and ethos of a kind of world where (some) people are mobile and get to travel. The entry of a homeless person into this site is therefore disruptive and in essence a critical and subversive gesture.

Moreover, as we have seen, space is encoded in other ways as well in the novel: there's the domestic space (the Wilby house and the girls' bedroom), residential and commercial spaces, enclosed and confined spaces such as the dumb waiter and the coffin, and outdoor spaces (e.g. gardens, the swimming pool). Space in Smith's novel is sometimes bounded and defined, yet sometimes unbounded and potentially liberatory, like the spaces of imagination.

To finish this section of the chapter, you may wish to return to the consideration raised at the beginning of the chapter of the role of hotels in different novels, and more specifically, the comparison of the Global Hotel with the Hotel Stentorian in Wharton's *The Custom of the*

Country. There is neither space nor time enough at this point to go into a history of the place of hotels in fiction, but consideration of the description of the Spragg rooms at the beginning of Wharton's novel is sufficient to indicate that hotels offered not just a bedroom, but also private drawing rooms, so that long-term residents might receive their guests. The description also gives the reader a sense of the social location of the Spragg family, their aspirations and sense of self.

Conclusion

This chapter has focused on getting to grips with the various sections of *Hotel World* – on the elements of story and character certainly, but more particularly on the different ways in which the elements of story are narrated from the perspective of particular characters. In other words, the *how* has been shown in some ways to be more important than the *what*; or, to put it differently, Smith is a writer for whom the manner in which a story is told and the language used to narrate it require a degree of attentiveness that may seem at odds with what, superficially, is very contemporary, accessible prose. The extent to which Smith pushes the novelistic envelope in terms of both language and formal innovation should now have become clear.

Chapter 7 will put Smith's work into a broader context, in terms of both her sources and her influences, and in relation to the evolution of the novel form as it navigates a series of pressures: how best to represent experience of the social world and aspects of reality at a time of continuing change; how to give voice to a multiplicity and diversity of stories; and how to bridge the gap between the world of imagination and that of reality.

References

Set text

Smith, A. (2002) *Hotel world*. London: Penguin Books.

Other references

Wharton, E. (2008) *The custom of the country*. Edited by Stephen Orgel. Oxford: Oxford University Press. Oxford World's Classics.

Chapter 7 Ali Smith, *Hotel World*: In critical context

Fiona Doloughan

Contents

Introduction

Now that systematic consideration has been given to the material substance and narrative structure of Ali Smith's *Hotel World*, Chapter 7 will seek to contextualise the novel in a number of ways. The chapter will briefly situate *Hotel World* in the context of Smith's life, work and interests as a whole and consider some critical reactions to her work. It will also engage with notions of realism and the extent to which Smith's work continues and/or subverts a broadly realist tradition. It will look at Smith's engagement with other writers and her contemporary critical position as a linguistically playful and formally innovative writer whose work stimulates critical reflection on social and political issues. In short, we will move beyond a narrow focus on the text of *Hotel World* and widen the lens to include broader contextual, critical and comparative perspectives.

Ali Smith: a brief biographical note and literary overview

The relationship between a writer's biography and their work is often fraught and may or may not shed meaningful light on their work; contextual factors can sometimes be helpful in situating aspects of a writer's trajectory, focus and interests. The fact, for example, that Smith was born in 1962 and grew up in Inverness, Scotland, is arguably important in locating and characterising her writing. The question of the extent to which she is a Scottish writer or simply a writer who happens to be from Scotland may seem to be splitting hairs, but it can result in viewing her work through a different critical and/or cultural lens. This is reflected in the work of academic and critic Monica Germanà (2010), who links Smith's work to the tradition of the Scottish Gothic. This is a somewhat contested term – usually applied to literature of the eighteenth and nineteenth centuries – which explores the supernatural and the uncanny, but which can be seen to manifest itself in later works by Scottish writers: they interrogate taken-for-granted histories and challenge single, unified narratives by introducing multiple and sometimes dissonant voices and perspectives. As Davison and Germanà (2017, p. 6) put it, in their introduction to Scottish Gothic: 'The critical interrogation of binary essentialism, particularly with regard to gender and sexuality, remains an important drive in contemporary Scottish Gothic'. The terminology here, 'critical interrogation of binary essentialism', simply means that we shouldn't always see things in terms of mutually exclusive categories, such as in black or white, and either male or female. Instead, we need to think along a continuum. Neither should we suppose that individual characteristics are innate rather than socially determined and influenced by circumstance. Rather than 'essential', they may be subject to change.

In relation to the question of what Smith's work owes to her Scottish origins, you might also consider the extent to which she incorporates in her writing Scottish words, expressions or references. Included in the opening passage of *Hotel World* is the word 'skirl', meaning a high-pitched wailing sound (commonly used to refer to the sound of bagpipes) – while originally a word of Scandinavian origin, it clearly reflects a very famous element in Scottish culture, as well as working within the novel to help create certain **onomatopoeic** sounds. We saw how the inclusion of a number of words can help to reflect both the speed of Sara's fall and potentially the sound of the dumb waiter as it hurtles to the ground. Think, too, of Smith's distortions and transformation of the legend, 'Remember you must die', which we noted was used in *Memento Mori* by Edinburgh-born writer Muriel Spark. Indeed, Spark is a writer that Smith has publicly recognised as being important to her development, and on whose work she spoke in Spark's centenary year (2018).

Figure 7.1 Author Ali Smith and the First Minister of Scotland, Nicola Sturgeon at the Edinburgh International Book Festival, 2018. Photo: Andrew O'Brien/Alamy.

Likewise, it can be argued that in some ways, Smith's novelistic practices and preferences – her attention to language, her playfulness, her (post)-modernist sensibility – are scarcely surprising given her academic background as an undergraduate student of English language and literature at the University of Aberdeen, who then began (but did not complete) a doctorate at the University of Cambridge on modernist writers. Her work extends beyond producing novels; she has also produced a play and is a consummate short-story writer, with a love of the work of New Zealand writer Katherine Mansfield (1888–1923) and American writer Lydia Davis (1947–), among others. Indeed, Smith's characterisation of the latter might stand in for a description of and commentary on her own work:

> What looks like a game will open to deep seriousness; what looks like philosophy will reveal playfulness, tragicomedy, ordinariness; what looks like ordinariness will ask you to look again at Davis's writing. In its acuteness, it always asks attentiveness, and it repays this by opening up to its reader like possibility, or like a bush covered in flowerheads.
>
> (Smith, 2013)

As you begin to consider further Smith's stylistic practices and narrative techniques, and how you might analyse them, both in relation to *Hotel World* and more broadly in relation to critical opinions about her work, you could revisit the terms in which Smith's assessment of Davis is expressed, with a view to applying them to Smith's own work. The mix of seriousness (of purpose) and playfulness (of language) is characteristic of Smith's work and evident in *Hotel World*, as has already been noted.

Another aspect of Smith's biography that is potentially relevant for her fiction is her sexuality. Many of Smith's works explore same-sex desire and relationships, some more centrally than others. So, for example, as we have seen in *Hotel World*, Sara is attracted to the girl in the watch shop, a feeling that is reciprocated with time but too late to act upon, given Sara's untimely death. Clearly *Hotel World* is about much more than sexual awakening or young love: it has to do with grief and loss and the effects of the passage of time; with human connectedness and interaction at the familial and societal levels; as well as the consequences for society of a politics of exclusion and marginalisation based on wealth and material values. Yet the strand of same-sex attraction crops up in much of Smith's fiction which deals more broadly with gender fluidity, doublings and reversals. Her 2007 book, *Girl Meets Boy*, for instance, is a modern-day rewriting of the myth of Iphis from the ancient Roman poet Ovid's *Metamorphoses*. In Ovid's version, a girl is raised as a boy (Iphis) and falls in love with another girl (Ianthe). Here the 'problem' of love between two girls is solved by the intervention of the goddess Isis to whose temple Iphis's mother, Telethusa, takes her daughter and prays for resolution. As Iphis leaves the temple, she is changed into a young man. In Smith's version of the story, Robin, a boyish-looking (female) anti-capitalist graffiti artist, falls in love with Anthea, who works for a company that bottles water. In Smith's book *How to be Both* (2014), a Renaissance painter, Francesco Del Cossa, is raised as a boy, but is imagined in fact to be a girl, while in the section dealing with teenager George (short for Georgia), we see her coming to terms with her mother's death and exploring her sexuality.

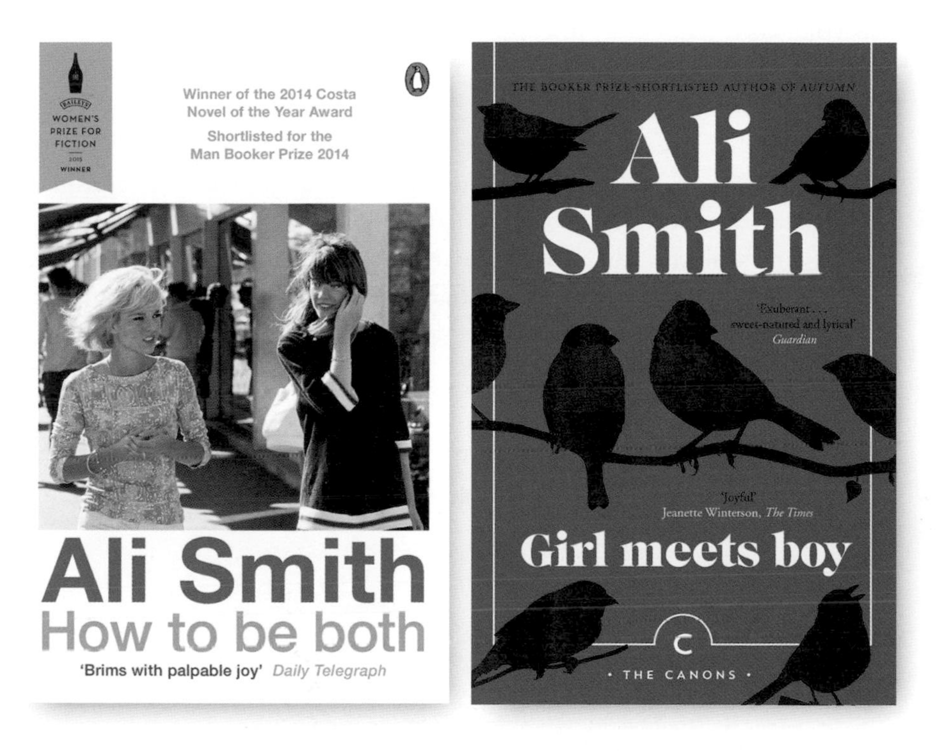

Figure 7.2 (Left) Front cover of Ali Smith, *How to be Both*, 2015, London, Penguin Books. Photo: © Penguin Books. (Right) Front cover of Ali Smith, *Girl Meets Boy*, 2018, Edinburgh, Canongate. Photo: Canongate.

Another important factor when considering Smith's work is the influence on it of physical book design and production. For example, we have already seen in relation to *Hotel World* how Smith uses typography in innovative ways to signal the disappearance of Sara's ghost, and to give voice to Else, the homeless woman. In the case of *How to be Both*, there are two editions available in the shops: in one edition, the Renaissance story of Francesco Del Cossa comes first, while the contemporary story of George comes second; in the other published edition, the reverse is the case. So while relatively speaking there are constants in Smith's work, such as her desire to innovate and to push the novelistic envelope, there are also differences in the ways the concerns that motivate and shape particular works are realised.

Even if you have not read *How to be Both*, you may wish to consider the possible impact on the reader of reading one edition rather than the other. As one reviewer of the novel put it: 'What is read cannot be unread' (Miller, 2014) – a statement suggesting that it is impossible for the same individual reader to test the differences in the experience of reading first one version, then the other, since inevitably you carry with you your knowledge and interpretive understanding from the first version you read and cannot undo that. However, it is possible to confer with a reader who has read a different version from yourself to discuss whether the experiences were similar or different. Of course, rereading any work, as will be discussed, is a qualitatively different experience from reading it for the first time, since you are no longer reading primarily for the story, but are more likely to look carefully at how the book is structured, how characters are drawn and the impact of the language used, as well as the role of metaphor and image.

Art, reality and the imagination

It might seem a given that a work of fiction depicts a textual world created from scratch, by the writer drawing largely, if not exclusively, on their own imagination. However, in actuality the picture is more complex: writers are also human beings born at particular social, political and cultural moments, who engage to varying degrees with the world around them. Their work may well reflect or refract aspects of the real social world, and indeed their very choice of subject and the way in which that subject is presented or treated can reflect a particular world view or politics, broadly speaking. At the same time, novelists are not sociologists or politicians per se and you would expect there to be a difference between a political tract or a sociological thesis and a novel! In addition, whether consciously or not, novelists work within novelistic traditions, adding their contribution to the genre through their particular 'take' on what is presented within the world of the novel in a style that they hope will be arresting, appropriate to the story they have to tell, and distinctive.

At one level, *Hotel World* is a mere fiction in the sense that Smith has created a medley of characters who exist within the pages of her novel and are part of that fictional world. At another level and at the same time, Smith's characters are drawn in such a way that they are largely relatable – for example, an adolescent girl grieving for her sister, and a bored hotel receptionist keen to disrupt the status quo – and they belong to a recognisable social world: one in which there are hotels, houses, shops, gardens and graveyards, and where some people have money and jobs (e.g. Penny) and others are homeless and jobless (e.g. Else). In other words, *Hotel World* creates a fictional space that is in many ways congruent with aspects of the social world of the late twentieth/early twenty-first century in the UK. Also, the more we know about the UK in the 1980s and 1990s, the more recognisable and congruent it seems. Yet – and this is where it gets interesting – there are other aspects of the novel that are rather more difficult to fit into the box of recognisable reality, such as Sara's wandering ghost or unquiet spirit: a character that seems to have come from another, less 'realistic', more 'fantastic' type of novel.

In some ways, this is what is distinctive about Smith's work – the way in which it draws on and combines different modes of writing (realism and the fantastic). She is a writer for whom boundaries between worlds (the real and the fictive; the living and the dead) are a spur to creativity. She disrupts assumptions and conventions, creating new possibilities – for example, the way in which she constantly undermines binaries or opposing terms, replacing notions of mutual exclusivity, of an 'either/or' mentality with a preference for narratives that focus on 'both/and'. This can be seen particularly in her treatment of gender and of social structures. She overturns the expected and the conventional (e.g. the homeless woman staying at a luxury hotel; the love of a girl for another girl). Fiction, for Smith, is not a world totally divorced from the world of reality; or, rather, it both is and isn't at the same time. For many writers, art is not a retreat, in the sense of escape from the world of reality, but rather a space for embodying a diversity of voices and viewpoints, and of creating alternative narratives which have the potential to change lives and ways of being in the world. When this happens, art can exercise a kind of transformative power on those who are open to it and reflect on its 'message'. It's not that all art is didactic, seeking to teach people a particular lesson or convey a social or political message; rather, art, at its best, imagines and thereby creates a new reality.

Figure 7.3 Afro-Brazilian man sleeps rough on a street with a mattress in front of a colourful mural depicting Ipanema Beach. Photo: Alexandre Rotenberg/Shutterstock.

The role of the reader in the construction of narrative

While writers work very hard to produce text that acts on readers in particular ways, once a novel or a story is 'out there', the writer cannot really control readers' and critics' reactions, nor would they wish to do so! It is also the case that individual readers can change their minds about a work with subsequent readings or when they return to it years later. A first reading is important in the sense that it is the only time you get to experience the work as it unfolds, without prior knowledge of what is coming next. A second reading is necessarily qualitatively different, since you already know the story, so to speak – that is, what happens next, who the characters are and what might motivate their behaviour. On a second reading, it is more likely that you will think more carefully about how the story is told and what might account for your initial reaction. You might also review and amend your initial reactions or make a more nuanced assessment of the work because of what you have read in the meantime. So it's always good to consider both your first, 'untutored' responses and your more considered reactions, and to reflect on what aspects of the text may have led to such a response or changing set of responses. So 'reading a text' is something that's not limited to a single act of reading: it's an ongoing and iterative process.

Activity 7.1

Allow around 30 minutes to complete this activity

Now that you have read and worked through each section of *Hotel World,* you may find that your view of the novel has changed. Write a couple of paragraphs indicating any differences in your understanding of the text upon completing it or upon rereading it.

Discussion

There is no right or wrong answer here, since not all readers have the same experience of a book and reactions will vary. It is more important to try to record any changes you may have noticed in your reactions to the book over time and to think about what might account for these changes.

The first time I read *Hotel World* was shortly after it had been published in paperback. I remember being struck by Smith's lively style; I particularly liked the multiplicity of voices and the mix of social and political critique and creativity in the book. I found the story of emerging same-sex love touching and the grief experienced by Clare upon her sister's death affecting.

One of the things that struck me on rereading the novel in 2018 was its timeliness in terms of some of the issues (such as homelessness) that it addresses. Perhaps because this is an issue that has become very visible again in our society, the novel feels very socially and politically relevant.

Reading *Hotel World* from a comparative perspective

In the previous section we compared different readings of the same book to see what, if anything, had changed over time. We will now focus on comparing treatment of a similar subject in two different books. Part of the reason for doing this is to increase awareness of how different writers may treat the same broad theme or subject, while at the same time recognising what is particular to an individual writer. Putting works (or sections of different works) side by side is a good way to highlight what is unique to each as well as pointing to any commonalities. Ideally it is good to have read two complete works in order to do this, but it can also be extremely valuable to look closely at just a section or sections in each. Such an exercise also demonstrates the fact that while in an absolute sense each work is separate – each can be read alone and on its own terms, so to speak – literature consists of a body of works that in different ways 'speak to' each other. Since writers are also readers, they do not write in a complete vacuum but often draw – either consciously or unconsciously – on what they have read. Readers, too, bring to bear on what they read prior knowledge and experience as they interact with and make sense of their reading. While it is important to read closely and carefully and to attend to the actual words on the page, it is equally important to acknowledge that the act of reading is not mechanical but interpretive. Reading obviously involves acts of consciousness directed to what we are reading; at the same time, however, our understanding and appreciation of what we read depends on our own knowledge, individual disposition, and the kind of frame, ideological or cultural, that we bring to what we read. As our literary repertoire increases, so too does our opportunity for comparing and contrasting works on broadly similar themes or subjects by different writers.

In order to experience what taking a comparative view feels like, the following activity asks you to read short extracts from another writer's work – as it happens, a work translated into English – and to view them in the light of an extract from Smith's *Hotel World*, a work with which you are now familiar. Do not worry if you have not read Kerstin Hensel's work, entitled *Tanz am Kanal* (1994) in the German original

Figure 7.4 Sacha Davison Lunt, front cover of Kerstin Hensel, *Dance by the Canal*, 2017, translated by Jen Calleja, London, Peirene Press. Photo: © Peirene Press.

and *Dance by the Canal* in Jen Calleja's 2017 translation. For the purposes of this activity, you do not need to do so. In fact, not having done so will enable you to understand the importance of context in helping you read, interpret and understand text. That said, you should be able to pick out some features of both narratives in the extracts, or at least know which questions to ask. A bit of context has been provided to help you out.

Activity 7.2

Allow around 45 minutes to complete this activity

Begin by reading the extracts printed here from Ali Smith and Kerstin Hensel separately and make notes on what you see as their significant narrative features.

Then reread them, focusing on any similarities and differences you have observed at the level of theme and the way in which that theme is realised. What contextual or other information might you need to know about the Hensel text that would enable you to be more confident about comparing these two texts?

Hotel World

[The first extract comes from Hotel World, *Section 2, on Else, the homeless woman.]*

She [Else] has been important before now. This is not the first time she has been it, and it is not just people in hotels who are it. There was the journalist last year, or the year before, in the spring, who brought a photographer with her who was photographing the things people on the streets have in their pockets. Else emptied her pockets on to the pavement and the man photographed the things. The photograph was for a Sunday paper. The insides of Else's pocket have maybe been seen by thousands of people. The journalist had written down Else's name; the people who read the paper would have read that as well as seeing the things in the picture; the word of her name and the photograph of what was hers would have passed through the eyes and into the brains and maybe the memories of what could be millions of people.

(Smith, 2002, pp. 74–5)

Dance by the Canal

[The main protagonist and first-person narrator in Dance by the Canal *is called Gabriela von Haßlau. The bearer of an aristocratic name (von Haßlau), she drops out of society and ends up living under a bridge by a canal. In the extract below, she discusses being prepared for interview by two women from a German magazine.]*

The big international women's magazine *Mammilia* awaits you in the café. They want an interview with you and to take your photo. I should have washed my jumper too, the filthy jeans should go straight in the bin, and these boots! I'm overheating from the confusion. Lilac Eva comes looking for me: I don't have to be embarrassed, people know too little about the women in need in the East. But this article in *Mammilia* will send a message. 'Women Having to Huddle under Kiosk Roofs' will be the title.

…

Don't smile for goodness' sake, look how you always look: aggrieved, dejected, tortured. Yes, that's great. And now like you're freezing. Yes! Yes! And now like you're hungry. Brutally hungry, great!

(Hensel, 2017, pp. 80–1)

Discussion

Starting with the Smith extract, you may have noted the contrast between Else's habitual invisibility to most of those who pass her by on the streets and the media exposure she – or rather the contents of her pockets – gets in the Sunday paper, in the context of a photographic spread on the homeless and what they carry or possess. In this sense her name and some of her possessions have been presented to what might be presumed to be a well-heeled public with leisure time for reading. At one level her 'reach' and exposure have increased dramatically; at the same time, however, she is presented as the sum of her possessions and to an extent objectified. Of course without a context it is difficult to determine the **meaning potential** of the photograph and the work done by the image(s) and name(s) of the homeless people photographed. While it represents a kind of mediated presence in print and brings Else to public attention, there is the danger that she has been ‘othered’ once again, even if in a different way: that is to say, given a measure of visibility but without **agency**, since it is the photographer and the newspaper who ‘frame’ her in the context of their particular story and concerns. As we saw previously, the contents of Else’s pockets, itemised on pp. 77–8, are indicative of her history and are suggestive of the fact that her life might have been otherwise (e.g. a postcard sent to her parents from Venice). The ten pence piece may be the one passed from mouth to mouth, a souvenir of a love affair on the streets. Other items, such as the teaspoon and box of matches, could be part of drugs paraphernalia. After all, as Else makes clear in dialogue with Penny: ‘Everyone takes them [drugs]. Everyone on the street takes stuff, we all do … You have to … Fucks with your brain. I mean really really fucks it’ (Smith, 2002, p. 170).

The mode of narration also impacts upon how, as readers, we ‘see’ and relate to Else. This is a third-person narrative focalised through Else. In other words, while Else is not telling her own story here – otherwise we would have a first-person narrative – we nevertheless remain quite close to her perspective and to her thoughts. Her story is told in this section by a narrator who is not an actor in the story. In this case, the choice of verb tenses is particularly interesting in so far as it helps situate the difference between a narrative recount of singular events in the past (e.g. ‘Else emptied her pockets’) and the use of the present perfect (e.g. ‘she has been important before now’), a way of linking what has happened in the past to the present moment. The shift to the present and the somewhat stilted but grammatical syntax in the second sentence (‘This is not the first time she has been it, and it is not just people in hotels who are it’) gets close to what we might imagine Else to be thinking/voicing, a kind of inner speech, even though use of the pronoun ‘she’ is a reminder of the presence of a narrator. You’ll remember the discussion of free indirect style in previous chapters.

In *Dance by the Canal*, you may have found it more difficult to work out who is being referred to when given so little context and the fact that ‘you’ and ‘I’ are **pronominal shifters**, that is to say that they are words whose meaning can only be determined in context by understanding who is speaking and who is being referred to. The ‘you’ in the first line in fact refers to Gabriela who has, in a sense, objectified or distanced herself as writer from herself as experiencing subject. In the third sentence, she changes from using ‘you’ to ‘I’ to refer to herself. Gabriela is being interviewed by two journalists from West Germany who are doing ‘a piece about women in need’ (Hensel, 2017, p. 79). They want to interview her and photograph her for a magazine called *Mammilia*. Embarrassed by her appearance, she tries to clean herself up and washes in the toilets of the hotel where they invite her for the interview. Again there is the sense of bringing to public attention a life or way of living that for the reader and viewer may be unfamiliar. Gabriela has become an example of an exotic species; her image and story are to be exploited by the journalists for their own professional and political purposes. As they photograph her, they make it plain that they need her to look a certain way, to fit the idea of a woman in need. What this extract makes clear is the way in which Gabriela is being exploited. It's as if she is a model in a photo shoot: her pose and image are being manipulated by the photographer for effect. Except that she is no fashion model but a homeless person who has been ill-treated and suffered abuse, albeit one who writes her life story on discarded paper and toilet paper, a feature that only serves to make her a more valuable commodity for the two journalists.

Without knowing more about the details of the novel, it may be difficult to gauge the satiric tone which permeates Hensel's novel, just as some general context in terms of how to read *Hotel World* is required. What may have struck you, however, in terms of similarities or parallels between these extracts, is that they both feature homeless characters and their interactions with the media. Why and how people end up on the streets may not be the same across cultures, nor indeed can we be certain that the journalists' motivation for bringing the issue of homelessness to public attention is the same in both cases. The politics of the two situations are certainly different. In the Hensel text, a West German magazine is highlighting the issue in East Germany, at a time when there are ideological differences between the two parts of what is now a unified state. Likewise, it is difficult to be certain about the exact motives of the journalist at the Sunday newspaper in England who did a feature on what 'people on the streets have in their pockets' (Smith, 2002, p. 74). However, in both cases there would appear to be a degree of voyeurism and exploitation involved.

The role of the artist

Figure 7.5 Edinburgh-born writer Muriel Spark, 1987. Photo: Sipa/Shutterstock.

In a lecture given on the occasion of Muriel Spark's centenary (2018) at the National Portrait Gallery in London, Smith talked, among other things, about the birth of the writer, the role of the artist and the power of art. Referring to Spark's 1970 address on 'The desegregation of art', Smith quotes Spark's view of the artist as 'a changer of actuality into something else' (Spark, 2014, p. 26). As a writer herself, Smith is very aware of the fact that, as she puts it in her lecture, 'What we make up has consequences' – a position which suggests that artists have a responsibility for what they create and the power to use their writing for good as well as for ill. As she goes on to say, fictions matter – the kind of fictions we tell ourselves, those that politicians spin, as well as the fictions we call history. In pointing to the similarities between and among different storytelling practices, and seeming to blur the boundaries between the representation and experience of reality, Smith is not dismissing the importance of engagement with pressing social issues, nor separating the artistic realm from everyday life; on the contrary, like Spark, Smith is suggesting that art has a role in holding reality to account, through the impetus to make people think as well as feel, and by means of satire and ridicule as well as entertainment.

The role of intertextuality and cultural allusions

The term **intertextuality** can be defined in various ways. For the purposes of this chapter, however, we will situate the notion primarily in relation to the ways in which *Hotel World* speaks to, absorbs or exploits the potentials of other texts or works of literature and culture referenced within its pages. Smith is a writer who creates text, at least in part, against pre-existing text which she strains against, deforms, milks for alternative meanings, and reforms. At the same time, she is able to take abstract notions (such as death, grief and the afterlife) and moral precepts (advice about how to live) and make stories out of them, using playful yet simple language. She makes language, which can seem dead and clichéd through overuse, fresh and reinvigorated. A tragicomic accident in a dumb waiter – a fall to one's death – becomes a 'flight to the bitter end' (p. 5), as opposed to the normal usage of the expression, 'a *fight* to the bitter end': Sara's end is indeed bitter in that she is now deprived of life, and her family is left to grieve a young life cut short. Yet 'flight' in the context of Sara's diving activities and her desire to shave time off her swimming (butterfly), as well as Clare's timing of the fall by throwing a shoe down the lift shaft and checking the second hand of a borrowed watch, connects speed with success and with effortless competition. From Clare's perspective, the fact that her sister did not intend to die and that she was fast in her descent means that she can retain a positive, rather than a negative, image of her sister. Dust (from which we come and to which we all return, according to the Bible) is rendered as 'the glamorous leavings of breathing creatures' (p. 5), something to be treasured rather than cleaned up or swept away.

In connection with Clare's section and the issue of works which recall, speak to or cite other works (a very loose way of understanding intertextuality), as readers of Thomas Hardy, you may have picked up on the references in *Hotel World* to *Tess of the D'Urbervilles*, a novel which Clare is studying in class. Hardy's novel is referred to in relation to Clare's thoughts on how her sister would have turned 20 years old in a couple of months' time (p. 188). She remembers how:

> there is that bit in it [*Tess of the D'Urbervilles*] where she is looking in the mirror suddenly she thinks that we all know our

> dates of birth but that every year there is another date that we pass over without knowing what it is but it is just as important it is the other date the death date
>
> (p. 188)

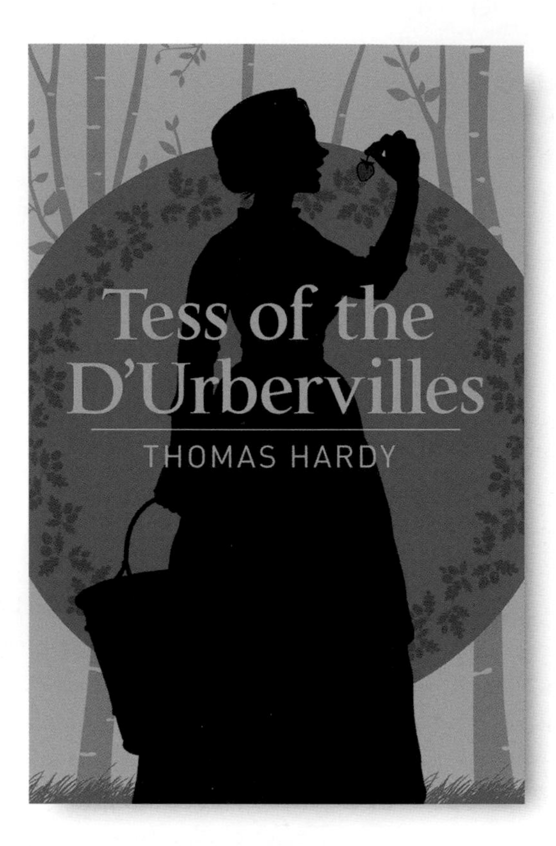

Figure 7.6 Front cover of Thomas Hardy, *Tess of the D'Urbervilles*, 2018, London, Arcturus Publishing, ISBN 9781788881890. Photo: Arcturus Publishing Ltd.

Clare is aware of some of her classmates' eyes on her, as they think about her sister Sara whose death date has already been written. Clare says, 'for once … I had been thinking of something else' (p. 188) but she is forced, by the looks following her – 'sympathetic fucking sad eyes' (p. 188) – to remember her sister's death date. She comments on how if such a thing hadn't happened in her life, she would have found the idea in the book cool, 'even though it's in *such an old long book with all those boring bits about fate*' (p. 189; my italics), and goes on to itemise the bits she can remember: 'the horse getting killed & the baby & the man with the moustache' (p. 189). She comments that 'there was obviously a lot more death in those days' (pp. 189–90) and refers to the film adaptation that they were shown '& the blood on the ceiling'. What Clare refers to as 'the date thing in the book' (p. 190) could have been cool but because of its connection to the reality of Sara's death, she feels it's like reading a book which seems to stop halfway through '& it's all just blank nothing to tell you' (p. 190). Clare's references to Hardy's work embed in *Hotel World* a reference to a different late nineteenth-century novelistic world. In the section narrated by Clare (pp. 185–221), the reader learns that she collects dust from the vacuum and from the top of the bedroom door, hardened syrup from the cough mixture and a crumpled five-pound note – all reminders of her sister. She leaves sweets, rather than flowers, at the graveside, something to give her sister energy and the kind of thing that sisters would trade or share.

Realism and the novel

A work such as Smith's *Hotel World*, which begins with a story told by the ghost of a dead girl, might seem a strange choice for inclusion in a book about realism in the novel and beyond. However, as we have been finding out, it is a work that addresses serious social and familial issues (homelessness; inclusion and exclusion; the aftermath of death; grief). It is also set at a particular historical and political juncture: the late 1990s in Britain when Tony Blair, the Labour Party leader, was Prime Minister. Under Blair, the party became known as 'New Labour', its 'newness' involving a shift away from the party's traditional focus on the interests of the working class and the poorer and more disadvantaged segments of society, towards a friendlier attitude towards **capitalism**, the market and globalisation. To many observers, Labour no longer seemed to represent the interests of the poor and the working classes but were more interested in economics and a new world order.

Writers (and readers) belong to a social world and are, to an extent, products of their own time and place. Therefore, the work that writers produce (or engage with), depending on genre, is likely to reflect on and interact with aspects of the so-called real world. In *Hotel World*, there are a series of characters (Sara and Clare Wilby; Else Freeman; Penny Warner; Lise O'Brien) who temporarily occupy the same space – the space of the Global Hotel, located in a northern town somewhere in Blair's Britain where the division between rich and poor is rife in the approach to the new millennium. Yet as characters in a novel, they also occupy the space(s) of our imaginations for as long as we engage with the fictional world of the book (and perhaps for a while thereafter). The extent to which this fictional world incorporates recognisable aspects of the world beyond the book may imply a critical attitude. So, for example, the question of the extent to which Smith is critiquing capitalism (however we understand that term) would require us to think about what is being represented and how that representation signals a critical evaluation. Put more concretely, we might wish to consider the extent to which journalist Penny is negatively evaluated in the text through use of irony and consider what she might stand for. As a character, we see her perhaps as someone who is fast and loose with the truth (compare the contents of her review with her actual thoughts about the hotel), a cynic who is bored and on the hunt for adventures and someone who fails to notice reality around her (e.g. she thinks that Else is house-hunting). This satiric portrait of the self-serving journalist – for whom words are cheap and who is wrapped up in her own very comfortable, material world where money matters, to the exclusion of all else – may serve as a critique of a particular set of values. Smith is often seen as an ethical writer by critics who read her work as constituting 'a creative, critical response to capitalist modernity by closely engaging with its materials and contexts, carving out an alternative to the marketplace from within it' (Horgan, 2016, p. 155).

In the case of Smith, there is clear engagement in *Hotel World* with aspects of reality, and a certain interplay between narrative discourses and the social world beyond the book in which they are indexed and/or reproduced (e.g. advertising jingles, bureaucratic language). For example, we might consider Lise the receptionist's section, entitled 'Future Conditional' (pp. 81–122), which includes an account of her grappling with bureaucracy following illness. The manner in which the forms she has to fill in are presented suggests a critical stance – the type of information required appears trivial and unsympathetic towards the sick. The forms focus on the collection of facts making visible things which may not have a tangible or physical cause. This box-ticking exercise involving indices and measurement is seen to be at odds with the complexities of psychological illnesses in particular. Presentation of time in this section is also complex and multilayered. The present tense is used to signal Lise's attributes as she considers filling out the form; it is also used to replay the events of the night when Lise gives a free room to Else. While the events of that night are now in the past from the perspective of Lise's current condition, they are recounted in the present: 'Lise, behind Reception, is at work' (p. 101). There is also reference on the part of the narrator to a time in the future when Lise, now cured of her illness and travelling in Canada, will seek refuge from poor weather in a Global Hotel in Ottawa. On entering the hotel foyer, she will remember some aspects of her previous life, memories triggered by the similarities in design, layout, smells and sounds of the hotel. These workings of memory and of time are shown to be part of the substance of human experience, and link Smith's work with a modernist tradition intent on finding new modes of representation capable of treating complexity and multiplicity.

Context in focus: Modernism and post-modernism

These terms can refer to a period as well as a style (of art, architecture and literature). For our purposes, in the context of a module focusing on realism(s) and fantasy/the fantastic in the novel and beyond, perhaps the best starting point is Virginia Woolf's declaration in her essay, 'Character in Fiction' that 'on or about December, 1910, human character changed' (Woolf, 2008, p. 79). She goes on to enquire about the nature of reality and argues that new novelistic tools are required for a new age. So in one sense, modernist techniques and narrative strategies such as 'stream of consciousness' and a focus on a character's perspective, developed as a reaction to the novelistic preferences of a previous generation of novelists. Woolf contrasts the work of Arnold Bennett, H. G. Wells, and John Galsworthy, writing in the latter half of the nineteenth century, with that of writers such as T. S. Eliot, James Joyce, and D. H. Lawrence, whose body of work is firmly rooted in the twentieth century. She berates the former group's lack of attention to the 'real' (inner) life of a character (as opposed to the construction of descriptive detail relating to their external circumstances), while defending the failures of the latter as they search for alternative representational means to explore a more complex sense of reality in fiction.

Post-modernism is also a term that applies not only to literature but also to styles of art and architecture. It can be said to be both a continuation of and reaction against modernism, and dates roughly from the middle of the twentieth century. Where it differs perhaps in the literary domain from modernism is in its preoccupation with chance and contingency, its scepticism in relation to '**grand narratives**', its rejection of universalising tendencies and its promotion of a cultural **relativism**. Post-modernist artists and writers generally like to mix styles and **modes**, construct multi-voiced narratives, and often use irony, satire, and humour to critique prevailing ways of thinking.

While Lise's section is recounted in the third person for the most part, there are moments of first-person narrative as she fills in (or tries to) forms from the Department of Social Security (DSS), asking her to describe herself and the symptoms of her illness: 'Well. I am a nice person' (p. 81), in response to a request to 'Tell us about yourself' (p. 81). There is also a high degree of narratorial intervention in this section, in the sense that the narrator flags up their presence by pointing to the differences between: narrative report and individual, subjective experience; between time as it is measured and viewed from the outside and time as it is felt and experienced by an individual person. The narrator provides a kind of commentary on some of what has already been reported, showing the extent to which even apparently uncontentious sentences and 'innocent' facts are part of a network of sentences and contexts, the meaning of which can change if they are recontextualised or woven into a different complex of sentences. The narrator fills in some of the background that allows the reader to better understand Lise's actions and motivations on the night in question. Lise sees herself, the reader is told, as 'a good but unimportant worker' (p. 112). She has had some money problems – the bank is concerned about her overdraft. Working in a hotel where for most of the guests money is not a problem confronts her with a sense of her own unimportance and flags up the material differences between rich and poor. Tonight, the narrator tells us, given how Lise feels, 'anything is possible' (p. 113). Life is about change but we don't always know, as in Lise's case, what awaits us ('She is ill and she doesn't know it yet' (p. 30)), as Sara informs the reader in her first-person narrative section at the novel's beginning.

Smith's major literary influences are, broadly speaking, modernist writers such as Katherine Mansfield and Virginia Woolf. At the same time, Smith is a product of a different era and a different sensibility: in this sense and in others, she might be considered a post-modernist writer. In *Hotel World*, her treatment of the hotel as a site where people come and go and are serviced by an array of mostly hidden workers (including chambermaids), and in her presentation of multiple voices and partially overlapping stories from different perspectives, she is certainly a writer who draws on post-modernist **tropes** such as **liminality** (standing on the threshold between one thing and another) and fluidity. Her combination of playfulness and critique, of realistic and somewhat fantastic elements – such as the ability of a departed spirit (Sara's ghost) to inhabit the grave where her physical body is laid and converse with that corpse – makes her a writer for whom **binary oppositions** are just further resources in the storytelling toolbox.

Conclusion

This chapter has situated Smith's *Hotel World* as a novel that indexes aspects of a recognisable world beyond the text (Blair's Britain at the end of the twentieth century) using setting (the space of the Global Hotel) and multiple narratives from different perspectives to further extend the possibilities of fiction already set in motion by modernist writers such as Woolf. Smith deals with serious issues (the aftermath of death; grief; loss) in a playful, linguistically exuberant and technically innovative way in a text displaying 'modernist techniques combined with postmodernist strategies' (Latham, 2015, p. 205). It is a work that is concerned with time, modes of consciousness and the subjective nature of experience; it is also 'a text aware of the artifice behind its fictionality and textuality (punning, blank spaces, playing with liminal boundaries between reality and fiction)' (p. 205). In so far as it employs craftsmanship and artifice to create a multidimensional and immersive fictional world, inhabited by a series of characters to whom the reader attends and gives credence, it can be said to be a work that continues a tradition of creating an illusion of reality – albeit one that may be at odds with strict notions of verisimilitude, probability and plausibility. While a ghostly narrator (Sara) may be said to imbue the work with an otherworldly or supernatural element, it is important to recognise that *Hotel World* is a work that creates its own associative textual logic to discuss, at a deeply serious level, what it means to live, to love and to come to terms with loss and mortality. It does this partly through the use of intertexts which open up alternative imaginational and representational spaces, partly through temporal juxtaposition and condensation and partly through the multiplicity of voices that haunt the various narrative sections. A highly original text, it responds to 'a new spectrum of aesthetic, political, cultural and economic demands' (Latham, 2015, p. 207) by creating a liminal space between outside and inside, reality and fiction, the world of the everyday and the extraordinary or fantastic.

References

Set text

Smith, A. (2002) *Hotel world*. London: Penguin Books.

Other references

Davison, C. and Germanà, M. (2017) 'Borderlands of identity and the aesthetics of disjuncture: an introduction to Scottish gothic', in *Scottish gothic: an Edinburgh companion*. Edinburgh: Edinburgh University Press, pp. 1–13. Available online via the OU Library.

Germanà, M. (2010) 'Ghosts: dissolving the boundaries', in *Scottish women's gothic and fantastic writing: fiction since 1978*. Edinburgh: Edinburgh University Press, pp. 134–172. Available online via the OU Library.

Hensel, K. (2017) *Dance by the canal*. Translated by J. Calleja. London: Peirene Press.

Horgan, M. (2016) 'About change: Ali Smith's numismatic modernism', *Contemporary Women's Writing*, 10(2), pp. 155–174. Available online via the OU Library.

Latham, M. (2015) 'The artful ornament of ordinariness', in *A poetics of postmodernism and neomodernism*. London: Palgrave Macmillan, pp. 167–207.

Miller, L. (2014) '*How to be both* by Ali Smith review – playful, tender, unforgettable', *The Guardian*, 13 September. Available at: https://www.theguardian.com/books/2014/sep/13/how-to-be-both-ali-smith-review-novel (Accessed: 11 April 2019).

Ovid (2004) *Metamorphoses*. Translated by D. Raeburn. London: Penguin Classics.

Smith, A. (2007) *Girl meets boy*. Edinburgh: Canongate.

Smith, A. (2013) 'My hero: Lydia Davis', *The Guardian*, 24 May. Available at: https://www.theguardian.com/books/2013/may/24/my-hero-lydia-davis-smith (Accessed: 11 April 2019).

Smith, A. (2014) *How to be both*. London: Hamish Hamilton.

Spark, M. (2014) 'The desegregation of art', in Jardine, P. (ed.) *The golden fleece: essays by Muriel Spark*. Manchester: Carcanet Press, pp. 26–30. Available online via the OU Library.

Woolf, V. (2008) *Virginia Woolf: selected essays*. Edited by David Bradshaw. Oxford: Oxford University Press.

Chapter 8 Edmund Blunden, *Undertones of War*: Telling stories about the First World War

Edmund G. C. King

Contents

Introduction

The events immediately preceding Britain's entry into the First World War took place over a bank holiday weekend. Germany declared war on Russia on Saturday 1 August 1914. On Sunday 2 August 1914 – the day Germany sent an ultimatum to Belgium demanding free passage for its troops across Belgian soil – British socialists organised an anti-war protest in Trafalgar Square. On the bank holiday Monday, 3 August 1914, as parliament convened to assess the situation, thousands of curious onlookers, who had travelled into the city to witness what one newspaper called 'the exciting scenes' assembled near Whitehall (Gregory, 2008, p. 14). When Britain declared war on Germany the following day, few would have predicted the final human cost. Between 4 August 1914 and 11 November 1918, when the Armistice was called, at least 761,000 British service personnel died. Another 1,663,435 British soldiers, sailors and airmen were wounded during the war, many of whom were permanently maimed. Estimates put the total number of troops killed across all combatant nations at over ten million (Prost, 2014, pp. 5, 8). The sheer scale of human loss that the conflict led to came as a profound shock to many observers. Never before in history had a single war killed so many in such a short space of time.

Another unprecedented aspect of the conflict was its social reach. Previous European wars had been largely fought by small professional armies. In Britain, poor pay and working conditions meant that the ranks of the peacetime army usually attracted only the most economically desperate recruits (Beckett, Bowman and Connelly, 2017, p. 33). However, the magnitude of the First World War demanded much larger and more diverse fighting forces. This led to the recruitment of a 'citizens' army', made up of millions of men who would never ordinarily have donned a military uniform. Over 22 per cent of the total male population in Britain served in the Army at some point between 1914 and 1918 (p. 96). This body of fighters was supported by a much larger group of men and women – doctors, nurses and stretcher-bearers; labourers, clerks, munitions and transport workers – who did the work necessary to keep the war machine running.

When war was declared, Edmund Blunden (1896–1974) was in the sixth form at Christ's Hospital, a public school in West Sussex. In 1915, he won a prestigious scholarship to read classics at The Queen's

College, Oxford. Instead of taking up his place, he volunteered for war service. Because of his social class and public school background, he was immediately seen as officer material. In September 1915, only a month after enlisting, he was commissioned as a Second Lieutenant in the 11th Battalion, Royal Sussex Regiment. This was one of many new battalions created to accommodate the masses of 'citizen soldiers' who had joined the army as a result of the war.

In the final words of Blunden's memoir *Undertones of War*, Blunden describes his wartime self as 'a harmless young shepherd in a soldier's coat' (Blunden, 2010, p. 191). This disarmingly modest self-portrait significantly understates the nature of Blunden's war experience. In fact, he saw more continuous frontline service than many other prominent British war writers, including Siegfried Sassoon (1886–1967), Wilfred Owen (1893–1918), and Robert Graves (1895–1985). After going into the trenches for the first time in May 1916, Blunden spent most of the second half of that year in battlefields around the Somme. His battalion fought two major actions in the Somme region, during which they lost hundreds of men killed or missing: at Hamel (3 September 1916) and during the attempt to capture and hold Stuff Trench during the Battle of Ancre Heights (21 October 1916). During this time, Blunden was awarded the Military Cross for bravery in action. In December 1916, his battalion was posted to the Ypres sector, in Belgium, where he took part in the Battle of Passchendaele. In early 1918, Blunden was sent back to Britain on a six-month attachment to a training centre and saw no further fighting. After the Armistice, he was discharged from the army and took up the place at Oxford he had won four years earlier. However, he found it difficult to adjust to student life and left after only one year. After working first as a journalist and then as an English lecturer, he started writing *Undertones of War* in 1924 and saw it finally published in 1928.

In this chapter, you will explore some of the literary techniques Blunden uses to construct his memoir. Truth and factual accuracy were extremely important to him. Those who had served alongside him regarded *Undertones of War* as an 'accurate and judicious chronicle of events' (Blunden, 2010, p. viii). Nevertheless, as Hew Strachan observes in the Introduction to your set text, Blunden did not approach his task as a military historian would (p. viii). He saw himself primarily as a poet and an imaginative writer, and he accordingly chose to describe his wartime experiences in a highly literary fashion. *Undertones of War* uses narrative and descriptive techniques drawn

Figure 8.1 Edmund Blunden: From Edmund Blunden's Minute Book, 1916. Blunden Family Private Collection. Photo: © The Estate of Edmund Blunden, reproduced by permission of David Higham Associates Limited.

from both realist and **genre fiction**. Some of the incidents described in prose in the main text of the book are reimagined in poetic form in the appendix of 'Poetical Interpretations and Variations' at the end of the book. Blunden also approached his war experience as a *reader* of literature. He refers to the books he read while in uniform, as well as the literary works he was reminded of while serving in France and Belgium. This chapter will focus on three aspects of Blunden's literary reimagining of the First World War. You will examine Blunden's use of first person narrative to depict the lived experience of the serving soldier. You will also look at Blunden's use of **literary allusions**. In the final section, you will analyse Blunden's handling of a non-realist literary genre, the ghost story, to portray some of the more **uncanny** aspects of the battlefield. Before you begin, however, we will look at an episode that happened shortly after the publication of *Undertones of War*, one that illustrates in more detail Blunden's attitude to factual accuracy.

War, memoir and truth

On 7 November 1929, Blunden and the poet Siegfried Sassoon sat down together to annotate a pre-publication copy of Robert Graves' First World War memoir, *Good-bye to All That*. Blunden and Sassoon had both been close friends of Graves for years, but on this occasion they were outraged by what they read. By the time they finished, they had scrawled 5631 words into the book's margins, identifying what they saw as its factual errors and Graves' deliberate exaggerations of his war experience (Moorcroft Wilson, 2018, pp. 386–8; p. 437, note 19). Even this marathon effort was not enough for Sassoon. He soon acquired a further copy of the book and filled *its* pages with additional comments, often one-word dismissals such as 'rot', 'fiction' or 'faked' (p. 388). Blunden meanwhile gave an account of his objections to *Good-bye to All That*, and what he and Sassoon hoped to achieve by 'correcting' a copy of it in this way, in a letter to a friend:

> R. Graves has published, for money and to create a sensation, a most ugly and untruthful autobiography. It is the season of gross and silly war books, and he has succeeded in selling his. But he has lost all the respect … of Sassoon and other old friends. I am collecting the comments and corrections of those persons concerned, and hope the British Museum will soon accept a copy in which (nearly) every page will have corrective marginalia.
>
> (Blunden, letter to Takeshi Saito, quoted in Webb, 1990, p. 170)

Writing about the war in the sensationalised way that Graves had done was, Blunden thought, 'equivalent to using the cemeteries that crowd the old battle line from north to south as latrines' (Webb, 1990, p. 171). These attempts to refute Graves ultimately came to nothing: *Good-bye to All That* sold 30,000 copies in its first month (Moorcroft Wilson, 2018, p. 391). Graves himself was thoroughly unrepentant. He freely admitted that he had written the book to make money and he ascribed any mistakes in it to the destabilising effects of the war on the soldier's brain. 'High-explosive barrages will make a temporary liar or visionary of anyone', he wrote (Graves, 1930, p. 42).

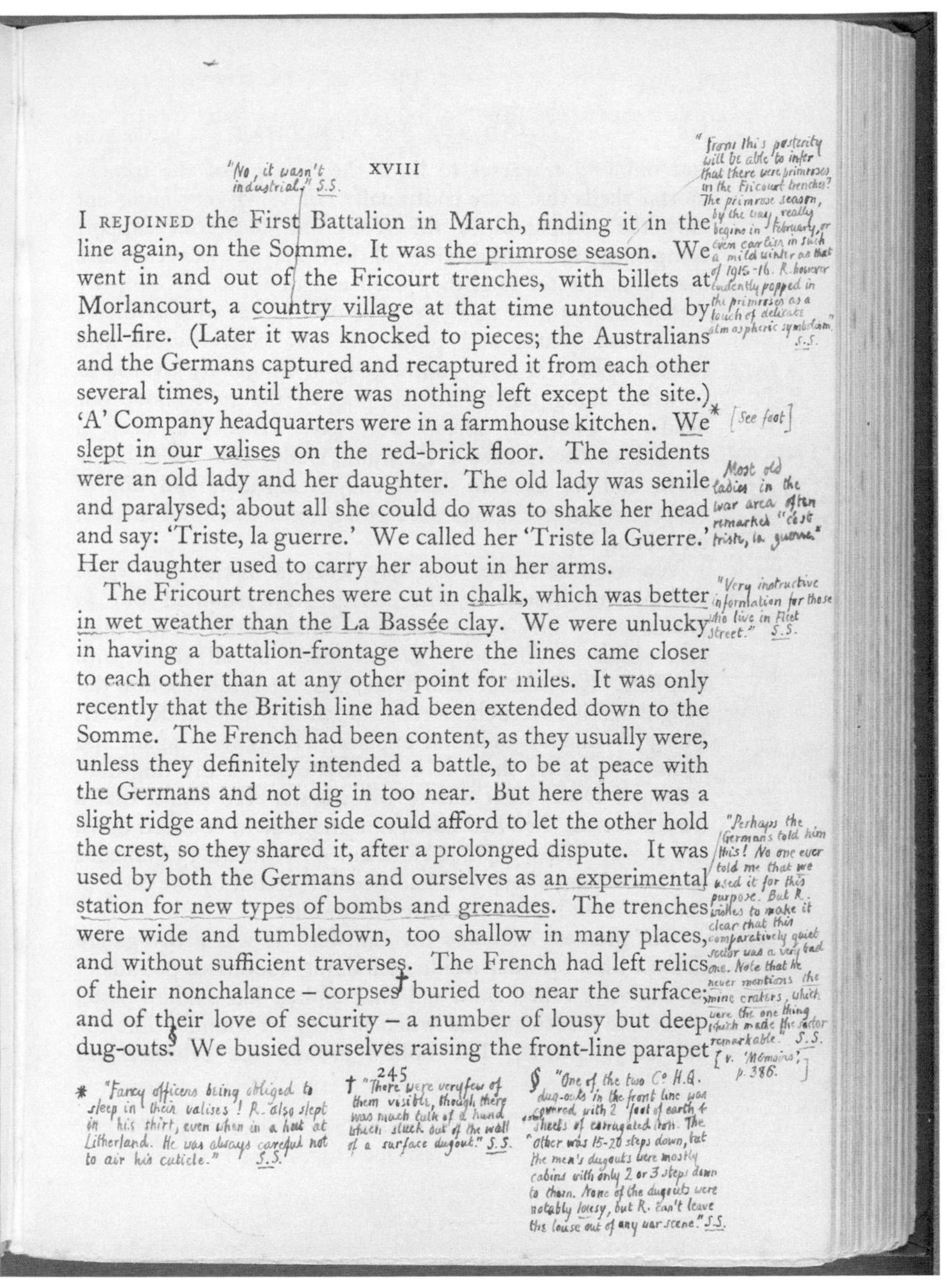

XVIII

"No, it wasn't industrial." S.S.

I REJOINED the First Battalion in March, finding it in the line again, on the Somme. It was the primrose season. We went in and out of the Fricourt trenches, with billets at Morlancourt, a country village at that time untouched by shell-fire. (Later it was knocked to pieces; the Australians and the Germans captured and recaptured it from each other several times, until there was nothing left except the site.) 'A' Company headquarters were in a farmhouse kitchen. We* slept in our valises on the red-brick floor. The residents were an old lady and her daughter. The old lady was senile and paralysed; about all she could do was to shake her head and say: 'Triste, la guerre.' We called her 'Triste la Guerre.' Her daughter used to carry her about in her arms.

The Fricourt trenches were cut in chalk, which was better in wet weather than the La Bassée clay. We were unlucky in having a battalion-frontage where the lines came closer to each other than at any other point for miles. It was only recently that the British line had been extended down to the Somme. The French had been content, as they usually were, unless they definitely intended a battle, to be at peace with the Germans and not dig in too near. But here there was a slight ridge and neither side could afford to let the other hold the crest, so they shared it, after a prolonged dispute. It was used by both the Germans and ourselves as an experimental station for new types of bombs and grenades. The trenches were wide and tumbledown, too shallow in many places, and without sufficient traverses. The French had left relics of their nonchalance – corpses† buried too near the surface; and of their love of security – a number of lousy but deep dug-outs.§ We busied ourselves raising the front-line parapet

"From this posterity will be able to infer that there were primroses in the Fricourt trenches? The primrose season, by the way, really begins in February, or even earlier in such a mild winter as that of 1915–16. R. however evidently popped in the primroses as a touch of delicate atmospheric symbolism." S.S.

[See foot]

Most old ladies in the war area often remarked "c'est triste, la guerre."

"Very instructive information for those who live in Fleet Street." S.S.

"Perhaps the Germans told him this! No one ever told me that we used it for this purpose. But R. wishes to make it clear that this comparatively quiet sector was a very bad one. Note that he never mentions the mine craters, which were the one thing which made the sector remarkable." S.S. [v. 'Memoirs', p. 386.]

245

* "Fancy officers being obliged to sleep in their valises! R. also slept in his shirt, even when in a hut at Litherland. He was always careful not to air his cuticle." S.S.

† "There were very few of them visible, though there was much talk of a hand which stuck out of the wall of a surface dugout." S.S.

§ "One of the two Co. H.Q. dug-outs in the front line was covered with 2 feet of earth & some sheets of corrugated iron. The other was 15–20 steps down, but the men's dugouts were mostly cabins with only 2 or 3 steps down to them. None of the dugouts were notably lousy, but R. can't leave the louse out of any war scene." S.S.

Figure 8.2 Annotated page from Robert Graves, *Good-bye to All That: An Autobiography*, 1929. Annotated by Siegfried Sassoon and Edmund Blunden. Photo: Henry W. and Albert A. Berg Collection of English and American Literature, The New York Public Library. © Carcanet Press/© Siegfried Sassoon by kind permission of the Estate of George Sassoon/© The Estate of Edmund Blunden, reproduced by permission of David Higham Associates Limited.

This episode is an example of the controversies that have sometimes surrounded autobiographical writing. How can we trust that the writers of autobiographies are who they claim to be? How can we be sure that they are telling the truth about what happened to them? Before returning to the questions of truth and reliability, however, perhaps we should deal with some definitions first. The French critic Phillippe Lejeune defines an autobiography as a 'retrospective prose narrative produced by a real person concerning his own existence, focused on his individual life, in particular on the development of his personality' (quoted in Anderson, 2011, p. 2). The autobiographical genre's inward focus – its concern with 'individual life' – has some important consequences for the way autobiographies are written. While a historian might use official documents to reconstruct the past, autobiographers draw on their own personal memory of events as their main source of evidence. Another word traditionally associated with autobiography makes this point explicitly. The English word 'memoir' derives from the French 'mémoire', meaning a written memorandum. However, in French, 'mémoire' has an additional sense: it can also mean 'memory'. On a basic level, of course, the life-story told in an autobiography or a memoir is still a *kind* of history – a sequence of facts about the writer's life. Autobiographical writers, however, usually go far beyond simply cataloguing life events. Instead, they explain how it felt to experience history first-hand. Their life-stories become an occasion for setting down their own thoughts, opinions and personal philosophies on the page. We might say that autobiographers and memoirists aim above all to record emotional and psychological truths. Autobiographical narratives also tend to be highly rhetorical documents. They seek to persuade readers that their version of events is the correct one. This is because, as the critics Sidonie Smith and Julia Watson point out, the details of a story derived from personal memory are not always easy to independently verify. Their status as truth relies ultimately on the autobiographical narrator's own authority – their ability to convince their readers that they are a trustworthy source (Smith and Watson, 2000, p. 6).

Some critics suggest that autobiographers therefore have an ethical responsibility to tell the truth about themselves. Lejeune calls this the 'autobiographical contract'. Any autobiographical writer, he argues, 'implicitly declares that he is the person he says he is and that the author and the protagonist' of the book 'are the same' (Anderson, 2011, p. 3). When applied to retrospective accounts, this is perhaps a slightly more problematic argument than it first appears. *Undertones of*

War, for instance, is a first-person narrative – it frames the story it tells around the thoughts and emotions of its central character, Blunden himself. However, the Blunden whose actions we follow in the book is not necessarily exactly the same as the older Blunden who tells the story. At the beginning of *Undertones of War*, Blunden creates a **persona** – a perhaps slightly idealised version of his younger self as an 'innocent' who is yet to experience the events that unfold over the course of the book (Edwards, 2005, p. 18). The story draws on the young Blunden's memories and impressions, but the decisions about how to order, select and describe that material are those of the older Blunden, in his role as author. It is worth paying attention to these acts of arrangement and inclusion. These are the means by which autobiographical writers derive meaning from the stories they tell.

Writing *Undertones of War*

You can get a clearer sense of the relationship between Blunden as author and the younger version of himself who is the book's protagonist from two of the brief introductions he wrote to *Undertones of War*. These are the 'Preliminary' (printed on pp. xli–xlii of your set text) and the 1929 'Preface to the Second Edition' (p. xliii). One of the most revealing details in the 'Preliminary' lies in the two words – 'Tokyo, 1924' – which appear right at the very end, just above Blunden's initials. He wrote *Undertones of War* in a Japanese hotel room six years after the conflict ended, when he was a Professor of English at what is now the University of Tokyo. This provided him with a sense of distance, in both time and space, from the experience of war. Writing in the mid-1920s rather than during the war itself, he could explore fresh perspectives. He would not be limited by the meanings attached to the war while it was still being fought. In the 'Preface' to the second edition of *Undertones of War*, Blunden makes a further claim about the practical constraints that writing at a geographical distance imposed upon him. The book was written, he claims, 'with no other assistance than the old maps Hazebrouck 5A and Lens 11 and one of the Cemeteries in the Ypres Salient' (Blunden, 2010, p. xliii). This is a remarkable claim, and one that places the comments in the 'Preliminary' that 'memory has her little ways' (p. xli) in true perspective. If Blunden were indeed writing with no other external reference points than the trench maps he was issued with as a young officer, then the book is a remarkable feat of memory as well as literary composition.

In fact, Blunden wrote an earlier attempt at wartime autobiography in 1918, a brief narrative which he called *De Bello Germanico* – literally, 'The German War'. This is a reference to the Roman Emperor Julius Caesar's classic Latin text about his wars in France or 'Gallic Wars', *De Bello Gallico*, a copy of which Blunden had with him during his time in France (Blunden, 2010, p. viii). He also kept notebooks and a personal diary for at least some of the time he was in uniform. Two notebooks and part of a Collins diary covering July and August 1917 still survive. Blunden also served for part of the war as his battalion's Intelligence Officer, collecting information, updating maps and compiling daily reports. As Intelligence Officer, he was tasked with writing up the battalion's official war diary, now held in the National Archives at Kew ('War Diary'). The pages of the diary that are written in his hand are vivid and meticulous records of events. Like other soldiers, Blunden regularly wrote letters home to family and friends and he also jotted down a number of war poems. However, Blunden left these personal records in England when he went to teach in Japan, so he would not have had access to them during the writing process. Likewise, he would not have been authorised to keep a copy of the official battalion war diary. Nevertheless, we could consider these earlier texts as being in some way 'rough drafts' of *Undertones of War*. The fact that he wrote continuously about the war at the same time as he fought in it enabled him to record events and impressions while they were still fresh in his mind. These earlier acts of writing may well have acted as prompts to memory later on.

Figure 8.3 Soldiers from the Auckland Regiment, New Zealand Expeditionary Force, in a switch trench, Battle of Flers (Somme campaign), September 1916. Imperial War Museum, London, Catalogue no. Q194. Photo: © IWM.

There is one other important detail to note. In the 'Preface to the Second Edition', Blunden says that he hadn't attempted to revise the book in order to correct errors in the original text. Why has he left 'uncertainties of time and situation' intact, when he could now potentially fact-check his version of events against more official 'authorities and papers'? Because, he says, 'their character was genuine' (p. xliii). That is, he has retained inaccuracies because to his mind they truthfully reflect the chaotic nature of battle and the limited perspective of the serving soldier. In some ways, this is similar to Graves' point that the very nature of battle – with its 'High-explosive barrages', chaos and unpredictability – made any objectively truthful account of the war difficult if not impossible to assemble (Graves, 1930, p. 42). An incoherent or confused account, according to this argument, is actually a more authentic document than a version that has been retrospectively corrected according to the 'true facts'. We might relate this to the autobiographer's concern with recording emotional and psychological truths, rather than literal ones.

Truth, fiction and realism in *Undertones of War*

Telling truths about war extended beyond documenting events and describing objects. War memoirists also wanted to convey the emotional, physical and psychological aspects of the war experience. These included exhaustion and sleeplessness, the pulverising effects of shell-fire on both body and mind, and the mental trauma generated by witnessing violence and constantly anticipating one's own death (Leese, 2014, pp. 25–7). To write about these parts of the combat experience, war memoirists turned to the storytelling and descriptive techniques of poetry and novelistic fiction. Graves had initially started writing down his war experiences in the form of a novel, only later deciding to recast them as a memoir (Graves, 1929, p. 127). Blunden himself later said that *Undertones of War* could be read as 'a sort of long poem' as well as a memoir (Blunden, 2010, p. viii). Fiction and poetry provided these authors with a storehouse of modes, techniques and genres that they could draw upon to record their memories and impressions.

This melding of fact and fiction might seem at first to be contradictory. How could the tools of the poet and the fiction writer be used to represent fact? War memoirists, however, saw no such contradiction. They readily adopted the techniques developed by realist novelists to depict the thought processes of fictional characters in order to describe their own inner lives (Saunders, 2010, pp. 161–2). Fictional storytelling techniques were familiar, adaptable and easily understood by reader and author alike. The descriptive techniques of poetry and other forms of imaginative writing also provided a way of creating atmosphere and giving readers a sense of place. Let's look in detail now at how Blunden uses literary devices to evoke the emotional and psychological side of the war.

Activity 8.1

Allow around 30 minutes to complete this activity

Read carefully through the second half of Chapter xii, 'Caesar Went into Winter Quarters', in *Undertones of War*, from the paragraph beginning 'Now November's advancing date' to the end of the chapter (pp. 101–5). As you do so, look for literary devices. Pay particular attention to describing words and metaphors – that is, figures of speech in which 'one thing or idea is expressed in terms of another' (Ritchie, 2013, p. i).

1. What atmosphere or effects do you think Blunden is trying to create?
2. Do you feel that these effects give you any sense of Blunden's inner, subjective viewpoint as he experiences events?

Discussion

1. The literary effects in the early paragraphs of this passage emphasise the physical discomforts of trench life during winter. Blunden uses metaphorical descriptions – 'Sluggish … mists'; 'stinging wind' – to convey the hostility of the climate (p. 101). By suggesting that the wind literally 'stings' and that the mist deliberately hangs about in a 'sluggish' manner, Blunden uses personification, attributing a sense of agency to these aspects of the natural environment. They become like living beings, additional enemies in the narrative, consciously inflicting suffering on the soldiers in the line. Further descriptions of the physical landscape add to the sense that the elements here are both alive and hostile. The 'grey chalky mud' of the Somme literally 'crawls' down dugout entrances, as though deliberately trying to occupy them, and the 'fog' seems to be actively fighting against the sunrise. Blunden increases the sense of threat in this passage with his description of the trees in Thiepval Wood. Not only are they denuded 'ghosts' of their former selves, due to the effects of winter and prolonged shell-fire, but Blunden also uses metaphor to depict them as 'gallows-trees' – trees from which the body of a criminal might be hung during execution. The overall atmosphere is one of impending death.
2. Obviously, we cannot know if the impressions recorded here are precisely the same as those the young Blunden actually experienced. They may be sense memories, or they could be ideas retrospectively ascribed to him by the older Blunden in his role as writer. Nevertheless, the effect is to give readers the illusion, at least, of seeing things through the younger Blunden's eyes as he experiences them in real time. We get an insight into the sense-making processes within Blunden's brain. The ideas he uses as reference points for his metaphors, meanwhile, give us clues about his education, background and personality. He hears the noise created by exploding artillery shells, for instance, as a kind of music – 'the double bass of high explosives' vibrating above 'on the dugout exit' (p. 102). To portray the experience of the reconnaissance mission, he again turns to the natural world, metaphorically describing the shell-fire that he and Johnson experienced as a 'waterfall' that they must plunge through to reach safety on the other side (p. 104).

Figure 8.4 A wiring party advancing over shell-swept ground, *c.*1914–1918. National Library of Scotland, Shelf. Acc. 3155. Photo: Reproduced by permission of the National Library of Scotland.

Figure 8.5 Christopher Richard Wynne Nevinson, *After a Push*, 1917, oil on canvas, 57 × 80 cm. Imperial War Museum, London, Catalogue no. Art.IWM ART 519. Photo: © IWM.

No matter how many poetic and novelistic devices Blunden uses, *Undertones of War* is still ultimately an autobiography. The book's first-person narrative provides us with a strictly limited point of view. Unlike a novelist, Blunden cannot directly incorporate the private, unspoken thoughts of other people into the narrative because he has no access to them. We as readers perceive other characters only as Blunden does, from the outside. He (and we) can only know what they are thinking if they tell him outright (or if he overhears them talking), or by making inferences based on their expressions and behaviour. In Chapter xii, for instance, our introduction to Private Johnson, the message runner, is Blunden's scanty impression of a 'red-cheeked silent youth' (p. 103). The only insight we gain into what *Johnson* might be thinking is Blunden's subsequent observation that he 'turned very white' when safely back at battalion headquarters, which we can infer was probably a symptom of shock (p. 105). Because Blunden does not record anything that Johnson might have said during the reconnaissance mission, we are never allowed to get under his skin.

Despite these limitations, this chapter is a good example of how Blunden attends to both documentary and psychological truth through his use of realist storytelling techniques. We are given a sense of Blunden's shock and exhaustion after surviving the artillery barrage from descriptive hints in his first-person narrative of events. He tells us, for instance, that he and Johnson needed to lie down in a shell hole after returning to the British lines in order to 'recover … our senses' (p. 105). Most of the information we are given about Blunden's psychological state after returning from the reconnaissance mission, however, is conveyed from the outside, through reported speech. Lieutenant-Colonel Harrison's telephone call to Brigade Headquarters tells us that, from Harrison's perspective, Blunden and Johnson look like 'men who have been through terrific shelling' (p. 105). Harrison's evident care when addressing Blunden at the end of the chapter – 'take it easy, Rabbit, we'll go and see the General when you feel a bit better' (p. 105) – gives us additional hints about how traumatic the experience had been. The effect of these two strands of narrative working together is to provide readers with two distinct perspectives on events, one of which we could think of as being in 'close-up' and the other in 'long shot'. Through his first-person narrative, Blunden gives us his own immediate impressions of events as they unfold. By incorporating the reported speech of other officers – Lieutenant-Colonel Harrison and Captain Lupton – discussing battle strategy, he is able to place these within a broader military context. Like a camera pulling back from a central figure into a long shot that positions it in a wider landscape, this effect reveals Blunden to be one small cog operating in a much larger military machine.

We can get a further sense of how carefully Blunden has shaped this material in his role as author by looking at another description of the same event, this one written much closer in time to the original experience. As you saw earlier, one of Blunden's tasks as Intelligence Officer was to keep the battalion's official war diary. The page for 13 November 1916 contains an entry describing the reconnaissance mission, which Blunden probably wrote within a day or so of its taking place. The existence of these two written versions gives us a chance to place the two Blundens – the young officer experiencing events and the older memoirist recalling his experiences in order to write *Undertones of War* – side by side.

WAR DIARY
or
INTELLIGENCE SUMMARY
(*Erase heading not required.*)

Army Form C. 2118

Instructions regarding War Diaries and Intelligence Summaries are contained in F. S. Regs., Part II. and the Staff Manual respectively. Title Pages will be prepared in manuscript.

Place	Date	Hour	Summary of Events and Information	Remarks and references to Appendices
SENLIS	Nov. 8		Troops rested. Church service in afternoon. 7 Casualties rejoined Bn. Weather bad.	EB.
	9		Weather better. Brigadier-General HORNBY inspected boots, and the C.O. inspected Billets.	EB.
			Orders received to take over SCHWABEN REDOUBT next day.	
	10		Battalion relieved the 1/1st CAMBS. in SCHWABEN REDOUBT, and were fortunate in having no	
SCHWABEN REDOUBT			casualties on the relief. B & C Companies were in the front line, D being in Support and	
			A in Reserve in THIEPVAL. Sergeant ASHFORD contrived to put Bn H.Q. in communication not only	
			with the Reserve and Support Coys but also with both front line Coys. The Battalion worked very	
			hard at clearing out dugouts. A Coy. carried Rations etc. to the front line. 1 O.R. was killed	
			while carrying SAA and 3 wounded. B Coy continued work on three T-saps in front of SPLUTTER	EB.
			WAY. A number of dead were buried by parties detailed only for this work.	
	11		Dull and heavy. Organised bombardment of enemy line in the early morning drew only moderate	
			retaliation. Work carried on: in the evening a Bombing Raid under Sergeant Stickland attempted	
			to rush the German Block R 19 a 91 but found it very thickly wired and could not force an	
			entry. They bombed it and managed to catch two prisoners: and waited outside the wire for	
			further orders. These were that they were to withdraw. Prisoners were of the 95th Regt.	EB.
	12		Dull but no rain. Another morning bombardment was carried out by our gunners and the enemy	
			retaliated with 20 minutes' shrapnel and whizzbang fire followed by methodical 'heavies' on our	
			front and support lines. During the day four fresh dugouts were cleared in THIEPVAL. The front	
			line companies were relieved after midnight by the assembling troops due to attack on the 13th,	
			but the sentry posts in RIDDELL TRENCH were retained until the attack had been made when	EB.
			they too withdrew to THIEPVAL (1 O.R. killed) ~~At 4 p.m.~~	
	13		Battalion in THIEPVAL. At 4 p.m. orders came through for 300 men and a proportion of officers under	
			CAPT. COOLING to carry coils of wire and wire pickets to point R 19 c 01, and a patrol of 1	
			officer and runner were immediately sent up to find out the best way. They had a lively	

1875 Wt. W593/826 1,000,000 4/15 J.B.C. & A. A.D.S.S./Forms/C. 2118.

Figure 8.6 11th Battalion Royal Sussex Regiment 'War Diary', *c.*1916–1918. The National Archives, Kew, ref: WO 95/2582/1. Photo: © Crown Copyright.

Activity 8.2

Allow around 30 minutes to complete this activity

Read the following extract taken from the 11th Battalion Royal Sussex Regiment official war diary and written by Blunden on or about 13 November 1916:

> 13 [November]. Battalion in THIEPVAL. At 4 p.m. orders came through for 300 men and a proportion of officers under Capt. COOLING to carry coils of wire and wire pickets to point R19 c 01, and a patrol of 1 officer and runner were immediately sent up to find out the best way. They had a lively journey and overshot their mark, almost reaching GRANDCOURT. Eventually returning via HANSA LINE, SERB WAY, ST PIERRE DIVION, MILL ROAD & THIEPVAL WOOD, they reported a heavy barrage behind SCHWABEN and a worse on the HANSA LINE. The orders were then modified and the party carried the wire up to the SCHWABEN REDOUBT, point 86. The Battalion went back to huts in PIONEER ROAD. [signed] EB.
>
> ('War Diary')

1 Note down any differences you can find between this account and the later one in *Undertones of War*, which you read in Activity 8.1 (pp. 101–5). If you do detect any differences, what *kinds* of differences are they? Are they factual differences? Descriptive differences? Differences of focus or emphasis?

2 Thinking about how an official document like a battalion war diary and a published memoir differ in terms of purpose and readership, what do you think might be the reason for the differences you found between the two accounts?

Discussion

1 The first thing I noticed is just how accurate the passage in *Undertones of War* is when comparing it with an official source. Blunden has remembered the size of the wiring party (300 men), the exact time the order came through (around 4 p.m.), and his recall of places and waypoints on his journey (St Pierre Divion, Thiepval Wood) is strikingly accurate. One possible discrepancy is that Blunden remembers the wiring party being cancelled, whereas

the war diary says that the orders were only 'modified' and the wiring party sent to a different place. However, this would effectively have amounted to the same thing.

The differences I noted are mainly in the language that the younger and older Blundens have used to describe the events of 13 November 1916. Writing for his superior officers, the young Blunden was unlikely to use highly imaginative language in his narrative report – although something of his literary personality and dark sense of humour can be glimpsed in the understated phrase, 'lively journey', used to describe what had in fact been a thoroughly harrowing patrol. The emphasis in an official document like this was on recording events and places as accurately and clearly as possible, rather than evoking subjective experience. We might remember how, earlier in the book, Blunden recalls his officer colleague, Second Lieutenant Kapp, being criticised by the General in command of their brigade for using language that was 'Too flowery for a military report' (Blunden, 2010, p. 16).

2 What we might conclude from comparing these two pieces of writing is that there is more than one way to write about events. This part of *Undertones of War* uses the same basic framework of facts and places as the war diary does, but its author makes very different choices of language and description in order to convey meaning. We could certainly relate this to the audience and purpose of the two documents. The war diary entry was written for senior officers and the official record and aimed to set forth established facts of place and action. *Undertones of War*, however, is an attempt by its author to convey to a general readership what it felt like to experience these events first-hand.

Blunden's literary allusions

One feature of *Undertones of War* that you may have noticed while reading it is how full of quotations and allusions to other literary works it is. A literary allusion can be defined as a deliberate reference by an author to another work of art or literature (Wetzsteon, 2012). Allusions encourage readers to draw upon their own stocks of literary knowledge and apply to them to the text at hand. In Chapter v, to select just one example, Blunden recounts what it was like to enter the trenches near the village of Richebourg Saint-Vaast, where the British defences had been constructed amidst ruined fragments of medieval church architecture: 'It was a district of shrines and keeps. St Vaast had resplendent examples of both; a white marble shrine, if I remember, looked eastward there, its saints gleaming like Byron's Assyrians' (Blunden, 2010, p. 36). In this passage, Blunden is alluding to Lord Byron's 1815 poem, 'The Destruction of Sennacherib', which was taught in schools and widely anthologised in the late nineteenth and early twentieth centuries. The poem begins:

> The Assyrian came down like the wolf on the fold,
> And his cohorts were gleaming in purple and gold;
> And the sheen of their spears was like stars on the sea,
> When the blue wave rolls nightly on deep Galilee.
>
> (Byron, 1992, lines 1–4)

By alluding to this poem, Blunden hopes that his readers might remember Byron's description of the light reflecting off the Assyrian army's spears and armour, filling in the gaps in the text's brief description of 'gleaming' marble saints with their own literary memories. This allusion to Byron gives readers a glimpse of Blunden's mind at work in the trenches at Richebourg in 1916, where he had made the same literary connection while watching the play of light on the marble statues at Saint-Vaast.

Throughout *Undertones of War*, Blunden gives us glimpses of how other soldiers used popular culture as a form of temporary mental escape from war. Kapp delights in traditional folk songs and tries to get his fellow officers to sing them with him (Blunden, 2010, p. 18). In Chapter xviii, Blunden describes how he would file past exhausted soldiers dozing alongside 'a fragment of some rural newspaper' posted to them from home, or perhaps 'Mr Bottomley's oracle', the popular patriotic magazine, *John Bull* (p. 141). The sheer density of literary allusions in *Undertones of War*, however, suggests that it was above all books that Blunden turned to for emotional and intellectual relief. Soldiers during the First World War could be prodigious readers (King, 2014), but Blunden's wartime appetite for books was unusually voracious. 'All are amused and amazed by my book habits', Blunden wrote from the trenches in a letter to his mother (quoted in Webb, 1990, p. 55). Blunden read eighteenth- and nineteenth-century poetry when he was at the front, as well as more contemporary authors, such as Thomas Hardy and H. G. Wells. He also souvenired books from ruined houses behind the lines before they could be destroyed by rain or artillery fire (see, for example, Blunden, 2010, p. 100). It was in one of these houses that he found the edition of Julius Caesar's *De Bello Gallico* that he carried with him from then on, and which inspired the title of his first attempt at a war memoir, *De Bello Germanico* (Blunden, 2015, p. 317). Allusions to these and other works in *Undertones of War* show how Blunden was able to draw connections between the books he read and what he was experiencing at the front. It is by no means necessary, however, to identify allusions in order to appreciate their effects. What they show us is a bookish young man drawing upon his memories of reading in order to make sense of the war. Allusions give us access to a mind responding to and processing events in real time, deriving a sense of structure and meaning from prior experiences of reading. They also provide us, as readers, with a set of ready-made guidelines for understanding events.

A supernatural war? Blunden and the uncanny battlefield

As you have already seen, a limited first-person narrative – such as the one Blunden uses in *Undertones of War* – poses some particular challenges for an author. Conveying the thoughts, emotions and subjective experiences of other characters, besides the storyteller, can be a difficult narrative problem for any writer using such a limited point of view. In the last section in this chapter, you will look at one final example of Blunden using techniques developed by fiction writers to give emotional and psychological depth to his narrative. We have already examined Blunden's use of literary realism to evoke a sense of the subjective experience of war. Here, we will explore Blunden's use of a non-realistic storytelling genre – that of the ghost story and the supernatural tale. Starting from the early chapters set in Festubert, we will look at how Blunden's use of these story elements enables him to convey a sense of the 'inner lives' of the soldiers serving alongside him, as well as his own psychology. Examining Blunden's deployment of supernatural elements in the passages leading up to the disaster at Hamel on 3 September 1916, when the battalion lost almost 300 men, we will explore how these supernatural motifs shape our expectations as readers and contribute to the book's atmosphere.

Rereading the early chapters of *Undertones of War*, it is striking how many supernatural references Blunden incorporates into the text. In Chapter ii, Blunden describes how the early morning mists rising off the landscape could create uncanny effects. Inspecting the British lines early one morning in Festubert, Blunden sees what he thinks is 'a rising' spectral 'shroud over a wooden cross in the clustering mist'. Blunden's immediate response is to imagine he has seen a ghost – 'Horror!' – but this 'apparition' turns out to be a false alarm. Someone has draped a gas helmet over the old seventeenth-century shrine in the woods at Festubert, creating the illusion of a ghostly human form (Blunden, 2010, p. 19). Other men in the battalion see portents and warnings in the mists over Festubert. A working party witnesses a 'luminous' white mist moving across the sky one evening, which some interpret as a cross, while others see a sword. Blunden's servant, Private Shearing, confides in him that 'he read coming disaster in this sword' (p. 20). A similar environment exists at Richebourg Saint-Vaast. Describing the spooky night-time effects produced by gas alarms and heavy mists, Blunden calls it 'all a ghost story' (p. 36). Nearby, the church graveyard has been uprooted by artillery fire, and soldiers walk over to gaze with morbid curiosity at the 'vaults' that 'gaped unroofed', the 'greenish water', and the 'bones and skulls and decayed cerements' (burial shrouds) emerging from within (p. 37).

Figure 8.7 Shell-stricken church, *c*.1914–1918. Photographed by John Warwick Brooke. National Library of Scotland, Shelf. Acc. 3155. Photo: Reproduced by permission of the National Library of Scotland.

Blunden's descriptions draw upon the literary techniques of the English ghost story – a very popular genre in the years leading up to 1914, and one that influenced other British war writers, including Graves, Sassoon and Owen (Davies, 2018, p. 74). However, these descriptions also represent an underlying psychological reality. As the historian Jay Winter writes, many First World War soldiers 'believed in the supernatural' (1995, p. 64). Supernatural stories and superstitions circulated freely among troops on all sides of the conflict. Some also kept amulets to which they attributed magical powers of personal preservation. Faith in the existence of an afterlife, along with a belief that future events could be foretold from signs, provided soldiers with a means of coping with the always-present threat of death (Winter, 1995, pp. 65–7). Blunden uses these tropes in *Undertones of War* to represent soldiers' psychological responses to the uncanny aspects of the First World War battlefield. In the fighting areas that Blunden describes, this sense of strangeness stems from the upheavals of war. The landscapes of battle exist in a state of confusion, in which things that would normally be kept well separated – the modern and the ancient; the living and the dead – are mingled together in chaotic and unpredictable ways. At Festubert, living soldiers occupy the lines alongside the skeletons of those killed in the battles of 1914, which already seem uncannily ancient due to decay and exposure to the weather (Blunden, 2010, pp. 12–3). At Richebourg Saint-Vaast, the war has opened up the tombs in the graveyard, a scene recalling the biblical prophecy that 'the earth shall cast out the dead' on the day of judgement (Isaiah 26:19). In each case, the environment is saturated with reminders and manifestations of death.

Writing about the English ghost story, the critic David Punter observes that 'ghosts have virtually always to do with fear' (Punter, 2017, p. 182). 'In the realm of the ghost', he writes, 'nothing is true, nothing is verifiable' (p. 181). The ability of ghosts to resist rational explanation simply adds to the fear associated with them. A ghostly apparition therefore creates an 'apprehension as to what *might* happen', what 'messages' the ghost might bring (p. 182), and what misfortunes its appearance might foreshadow.

Activity 8.3

Allow around 30 minutes to complete this activity

Bearing Punter's definitions in mind, reread Chapter ix of *Undertones of War*, 'The Storm' (pp. 61–74).

1 Which incidents in this chapter could we perhaps identify as 'ghostly'?
2 Can you find any commonalities between these incidents?
3 Can you see any parallels between these incidents and what happens in the last section of the chapter, the attack on German trenches at the 'Boar's Head'?

Discussion

1 I found three incidents that seem 'ghostly' in the chapter. The first occurs at Monchy-Breton. Examining a map in preparation for the coming attack at battalion headquarters, Blunden and his fellow officers suddenly feel as though 'something was wrong' and one of them notices a 'face at a window', looking in. Rushing out to catch the presumed spy, they find no one there (Blunden, 2010, p. 62). Blunden experiences another incident on the day of the attack.

Waiting in the trenches, he is approached by a 'stranger' in non-standard-issue clothing, 'white-faced as a ghost', who asks directions to the German lines. Blunden assumes he too is a spy and directs him down a communication trench instead (pp. 70–1). The third and most overtly supernatural of these incidents happens to the battalion's orderly room clerk, Corporal Candler. Sitting alone in his tent, Candler looks up to see 'a man wearing a black cloak appear in the doorway' (p. 68). He follows the figure outside, into the trees of Mailly Wood, but is unable to locate it.

2 Regarding commonalities among these incidents, each ends inconclusively, without explanation. In the first, the officers rush out 'to catch a spy', but 'miss' him (p. 62). Describing his encounter with the 'white-faced' man in the trenches, Blunden writes that 'I have never explained to myself' who the figure was (p. 71). Of Corporal Candler's spooky encounter with the man in the black cloak, Blunden writes similarly that 'no explanation could be got' (p. 68). Blunden's emphasis on the unexplained nature of each sighting certainly accords with Punter's observation that 'nothing is verifiable' in the 'realm of the ghost' (Punter, 2017, p. 181). Another parallel linking the three sightings is that each figure is out of place and unknown to its witnesses. The first and third are called 'strangers', and the clothing of the man in the black cloak and the man in the trench makes each stand out as not belonging to the time and place in which each was seen; for example, a 'black cloak' is something a medieval monk might wear – he therefore seems out of place in time. Similarly, no soldier about to take part in the attack would do so wearing a mackintosh and a soft cap. Blunden has already told us that 'steel helmets' had become the rule in the Somme sector, 'dethroning' the 'soft cap' the men had previously worn for head protection (Blunden, 2010, p. 53).

3 I spotted several parallels between these incidents and the outcome of the attack. As Blunden and the other men behind the British lines wait for news, they find that they 'could make very little sense of ourselves or the battle' (p. 71). Harrison asks Blunden for an update on progress. In the absence of information, Blunden 'could not say'. Everything, he writes, 'was in ominous discommunication' (p. 72). The one piece of definite-seeming news – that the Germans were counterattacking and about to take the British front trench – turns out to be a false alarm. Later, as stragglers from the attacking companies start to return to the British lines, Blunden and his colleagues discover that 'not even these ... could say what had happened, or what was happening ... the general effect was the disappearance of the attack into mystery' (p. 73). Just as the

three 'ghost' sightings earlier in the chapter were left unexplained, so too is the fate of the men in the attacking companies. The men had been so completely overwhelmed by the German defences that few survived to bring back any information.

Now that you have read the chapter, as well as Punter's observations about ghost stories, we can draw some more general conclusions about Blunden's use of the ghost story motif. Perhaps the first thing to note is the care with which Blunden situates the sightings firmly within the reality of the Somme in 1916. Reading the anecdote about Candler in his tent, we can see how Blunden brings it to life with small, mundane details. Candler adjusts his glasses and addresses the ghost, assuming that it might be another soldier playing a trick. Although Blunden is drawing here upon the motifs of a fictional genre, the ghost story, realistic details make this anecdote seem as grounded and reliably sourced as anything else in the book. It has a named witness and enough description provided for us, as readers, to be able to 'see and hear [Candler] exactly' (p. 68). A later piece of memoir called 'Infantryman Passes By' (1968) suggests that Blunden genuinely thought that Mailly Wood, where Candler had his encounter, was haunted. 'Our position in a dusky wood', he writes, 'was not only gas-scented but ghost-ridden – the sense of some intolerable presences had nothing to do with us, presumably, but that wood was deadly in gunfire fact and in some other way' (Blunden, 2014, p. 126).

Figure 8.8 Panoramic view of the battlefield at Guillemont during the Somme campaign, 1916. Photographed by Lieutenant Ernest Brooks. Imperial War Museum, London, Catalogue no. Q1281. Photo: © IWM.

By deploying these ghostly encounters in the earlier parts of the chapter, Blunden is able to foreshadow the disaster that overcomes the battalion in the attack on the Boar's Head. One meaning attributed to ghosts in western culture has been as omens of pending misfortune or harbingers of death (Davies, 2018, p. 72). Blunden hints at a similar mystical cause-and-effect relationship here. These passages are positioned where they are in the narrative to give us, as readers, our own 'premonition' of the disaster about to overcome the battalion. They also add to the uncanny atmosphere that Blunden has created through his descriptions of disrupted and skeleton-strewn French landscapes. Here, as at Festubert and Richebourg Saint-Vaast, the dead seem to lie in layers underneath and alongside the living, reminding them of their own impending mortality in a wartime environment. The ghosts that Blunden and his colleagues evidently believed inhabited Mailly Wood are a supernatural counterpart to the 'deadliness' of the 'gunfire' that soldiers occupying it endure (Blunden, 2014, p. 126).

Conclusion

In this chapter, we have explored some of the ways in which *Undertones of War* approaches the lived experience of soldiers on the Western Front through the descriptive lenses of literature. Through an examination of Blunden and Sassoon's hostile responses to Graves' *Good-bye to All That*, we have gauged the importance of truth and accuracy to First World War memoirists. Looking at three specific episodes in the first half of *Undertones of War*, we have seen how Blunden draws upon the techniques of the poet and the fiction writer to describe his emotional and psychological responses to war. We have analysed in detail one of the many instances of literary allusion in *Undertones of War*. Finally, in our reading of Chapter ix, we have looked at Blunden's deployment of a non-realist storytelling genre, the ghost story, to foreshadow future events and create an uncanny atmosphere. In the next chapter, we will continue our explorations of *Undertones of War*, examining how Blunden writes about wartime landscapes and the problems posed for the memoirist by the quirks and idiosyncrasies of personal memory.

References

Set text

Blunden, E. (2010) *Undertones of war*. Edited by Hew Strachan. London: Penguin.

Other references

Anderson, L. (2011) *Autobiography*. 2nd edn. Abingdon: Routledge. Available online via the OU Library.

Beckett, I., Bowman, T. and Connelly, M. (2017) *The British Army and the First World War*. Cambridge: Cambridge University Press.

Blunden, E. (2014) *Fall in, ghosts: selected war prose*. Edited by Robyn Marsack. Manchester: Carcanet Press. Available online via the OU Library.

Blunden, E. (2015) *Undertones of war*. Edited by John Greening. Oxford: Oxford University Press. Available online via the OU Library.

Byron, G.G. (1992) 'The Destruction of Sennacherib', *Literature Online*. Cambridge: Chadwyck-Healey. Available at: http://gateway.proquest.com.libezproxy.open.ac.uk/openurl?ctx_ver=Z39.88-2003&xri:pqil:res_ver=0.2&res_id=xr i:lion&rft_id=xri:lion:ft:po:Z300294270:3 (Accessed: 11 April 2019).

Davies, O. (2018) *A supernatural war: magic, divination, and faith during the First World War*. Oxford: Oxford University Press. Available online via the OU Library.

Edwards, P. (2005) 'British War Memoirs', in Sherry, V. (ed.) *The Cambridge companion to the literature of the First World War*. Cambridge: Cambridge University Press, pp. 15–33. Available online via the OU Library.

Graves, R. (1930) *But it still goes on: an accumulation*. London: Jonathan Cape.

Graves, R. (1929) *Good-bye to all that*. London: Jonathan Cape.

Gregory, A. (2008) *The last Great War: British society and the First World War*. Cambridge: Cambridge University Press. Available online via the OU Library.

King, E.G.C. (2014) '"A Priceless Book to Have Out Here": Soldiers Reading Shakespeare in the First World War', *Shakespeare*, 10(3), pp. 230–44. Available online via the OU Library.

Leese, P. (2014) *Shell shock: traumatic neurosis and the British soldiers of the First World War*. 2nd edn. Basingstoke: Palgrave Macmillan.

Moorcroft Wilson, J. (2018) *Robert Graves: from Great War poet to* Good-bye to all that. London: Bloomsbury Continuum.

Prost, A. (2014) 'War losses', in Daniel, U., Gatrell, P., Janz, O., Jones, H., Keene, J., Kramer, A. and Nasson, B. (eds) *1914–1918-online: international encyclopedia of the First World War*. Berlin: Freie Universität Berlin, pp. 1–14. Available at: https://encyclopedia.1914-1918-online.net/article/war_losses (Accessed: 11 April 2019).

Punter, D. (2017) 'The English ghost story', in Brewster, S. and Thurston, L. (eds) *The Routledge handbook to the ghost story*. Abingdon: Routledge, pp. 179–87. Available online via the OU Library.

Ritchie, L.D. (2013) *Metaphor*. Cambridge: Cambridge University Press.

Saunders, M. (2010) *Self-impression: life-writing, autobiografiction, and the forms of modern literature*. Oxford: Oxford University Press.

Smith, S. and Watson, J. (2000) *Reading autobiography: a guide for interpreting life narratives*. Minneapolis, Minn.: University of Minnesota Press. Available online via the OU Library.

'War Diary', 11 Battalion, Royal Sussex Regiment, March 1916–June 1918, The National Archives, Kew, WO 95/2582/1.

Webb, B. (1990) *Edmund Blunden: a biography*. New Haven, Conn.: Yale University Press.

Wetzsteon, R. (2012) 'Allusion', in Green, R., Cushman, S. and Cavanagh, C. (eds) *The Princeton encyclopedia of poetry and poetics*. 4th edn. Princeton, N.J.: Princeton University Press. Available online via the OU Library.

Winter, J. (1995) *Site of memory, sites of mourning: the Great War in European cultural history*. Cambridge: Cambridge University Press. Available online via the OU Library.

Chapter 9 Edmund Blunden, *Undertones of War*: Memory, trauma and landscape

Edmund G. C. King

Contents

Introduction

The previous chapter looked at some of the literary storytelling techniques in *Undertones of War*, focusing on episodes from the first half of the book, corresponding to Blunden's service in France and on the Somme battlefields in 1916. This chapter will explore new territory, examining the relationship between writing, memory and trauma in Blunden. You will have already encountered the topic of memory in our earlier discussions, when we looked at Blunden's claims that he wrote *Undertones of War* based on nothing more than a pair of trench maps and his own recollections. This chapter will examine the theme of memory in more detail. You will look at the methods that Blunden uses to convey what it feels like to both remember war and to try and reconstruct it in writing afterwards. You will examine the relationship between the prose section of *Undertones of War* and the poems in the appendix, seeing how Blunden uses the poems to reflect on or develop events depicted in the main narrative. In the second part of this chapter, you will examine the ways in which the book's emphasis on memory enables Blunden to structure his material. Focusing on Blunden's use of pastoral imagery to represent the destructive impact of war on the landscapes of the Western Front, you will discover how the pastoral enabled Blunden to impose order on to his memories of wartime service and derive meaning from them.

First World War memory and trauma

In the early morning hours of 1 January 1931, Blunden was woken from his sleep by what he called 'the most dreadful dreams of War' (Rothkopf, 2012, p. 311). In a letter to Siegfried Sassoon that he wrote the following day, Blunden described how he was 'in those dreams an utter coward and the battalion including me is about to raid'. Another recent dream that he related to Sassoon in the same letter, in which he was about to be sent into enemy lines to look for a new German gun, had been triggered by the sounds of the family dog barking downstairs (Rothkopf, 2012, p. 311). Sassoon described his own experience of having 'ugly thoughts' about the war that 'you've gagged all day come back to scare you' in a poem written in 1917, when he was recuperating from war trauma at his mother's house (Sassoon, 1918, p. 51). Trying to adjust to university life at Oxford in 1919, Robert Graves would suddenly find himself overwhelmed by vivid memories of the war while sitting in the lecture hall. 'These daydreams', he wrote, 'persisted like an alternate life' (Graves, 1929, p. 361).

Blunden, Sassoon and Graves would go on to publish their war memoirs within a short space of time of one another. *Undertones of War*, Graves' *Good-bye to All That* (1929), and Sassoon's *Memoirs of a Fox-Hunting Man* (1928) and *Memoirs of an Infantry Officer* (1930) were all commercially successful books. They quickly established themselves as the most prominent titles within what historians now refer to as the 'war books boom': the wave of war memoirs that appeared in print in the late 1920s and early 1930s (Wilson, 2012, pp. 19–21). We saw in the previous chapter how outraged Blunden and Sassoon were about what they saw as Graves' careless attitude to the truth. However, in *Good-bye to All That*, Graves raises larger questions about the relationship between memory, trauma, and the act of writing that could be applied to *all* war memoirs of the period. Outlining his rationale for producing the book, Graves wrote that 'once all this has been … written down and published it need never be thought about again' (Graves, 1929, p. 13). Later, in his account of meeting Blunden when they were both studying at Oxford in 1919, he expanded on this point. 'Edmund', he wrote, 'had war-shock as badly as myself, and we would talk each other into an almost hysterical state about the trenches. We agreed that we would not be right until we got all that talk on to paper' (pp. 358–9).

What Graves is describing here is less an act of remembering than one of deliberate forgetting. Putting traumatic memories into print, he suggests, effectively cleanses them from an author's mind. Life-writing for Graves therefore becomes a kind of therapy, where getting 'right' involves putting things out of one's mind by writing them down. The title of the book is a literal expression of this idea. Graves sees it as his chance to bid 'good-bye to you and to you and to you and to me and to all that' through the act of putting pen to paper (Graves, 1929, p. 13). How does Blunden's approach to memory and trauma compare with this? There is no doubt that Blunden retained unpleasant memories of his wartime service. In Chapter xii of *Undertones of War*, for instance, he describes what he calls his own 'unwelcome but persistent retrospect', a disturbing image of 'two flattened German bodies', 'tallow-faced and dirty-stubbled', lying at the bottom of the shell-hole near Thiepval Wood that Blunden's unit used as a latrine (Blunden, 2010, p. 96). This unwanted visual memory apparently stayed with Blunden after the war much as Graves's persistent wartime 'daydreams' did.

Undertones of War also contains occasional flashes of straightforward horror. In Chapter vi, Blunden provides a detailed sketch of what shellfire was capable of doing to the human body. After passing a 'young and cheerful lance-corporal' brewing tea in the trenches and assuming that a nearby German shell has exploded harmlessly, Blunden is called back to the scene by a 'cry'. Coming down the trench he discovers that:

> the shell had burst all wrong. Its butting impression [i.e. the mark the explosion had left] was black and stinking in the parados [the raised lip on top of the trench wall facing away from the firing line] where three minutes ago the lance-corporal's mess-tin was bubbling over a little flame. For him, how could the gobbets of blackening flesh, the earth-wall sotted with blood, with flesh, the eye under the duckboard, the pulpy bone be the only answer? At this moment … the lance-corporal's brother came round the traverse.
>
> (p. 46)

Reading this passage over, you can see how carefully Blunden has structured it to derive maximum emotional effect. He establishes the scene with positive adjectives that convey a sense of calm. The lance-corporal is 'young' and 'cheerful', the afternoon 'warm', the fall of the shell apparently 'lucky'. All of this changes abruptly once the shell bursts, and the language alters in turn to become a catalogue of escalating horrors. Each new phrase introduces an additional disturbing element – the 'gobbets of blackening flesh', the 'blood' on the earth-wall, the 'eye under the duckboard' at the bottom of the trench, the 'pulpy bone' – culminating in the tragic entry of the dead man's brother from around the side of the trench (p. 46). This sense of increasing horror continues as Blunden and one of his sergeants are then faced with the task of 'shovelling' the young soldier's dismembered remains into a sandbag.

Figure 9.1 Captain A. C. Morris, Commander of No. 3 Section, 3rd Australian Tunnelling Company, standing near an intermediate entrance to Hythe Tunnel, 1918. The Australian War Memorial, Acc no. E01712. Photo: Australian War Memorial.

These descriptions of traumatic scenes suggest that Blunden's approach to memory in *Undertones of War* is quite different from the one Graves sets out in *Good-bye to All That*. Blunden does not seem to think that traumatic memories can be simply expunged and forgotten through the act of writing. Instead, the care and clarity with which each detail is described suggests that what is at stake here for Blunden is not forgetting, but *remembering*. As Blunden describes the horrific consequences of the shell-burst at Cambrin, it seems as though he is recollecting the scene for us in real time. We are given a sense of both what it feels like to have witnessed such a scene, and what it feels like to then recover it, piece by piece, from the depths of personal memory.

Blunden expands upon some of these ideas later in the memoir. In Chapter xviii, Blunden describes a similar event that occurred near Ypres in 1917. 'Towards Hooge one … morning', he writes:

> Kenward the corporal and I saw a sentry crouching and peering one way and another … He spoke, grinned and shivered; we passed; and duly the sentry was hit by a shell. So that in this vicinity a peculiar difficulty would exist for the artist to select the sights, faces, words, incidents, which characterized the time. The art is rather to collect them, in their original form of incoherence.
>
> (p. 141)

This is undoubtedly a difficult passage, and in order to grasp its full meaning, it needs to be unpacked carefully. What Blunden means is that he simply has too many memories of events around Ypres to know which were the most significant. Writing a memoir involves selecting which events and memories from the past work best to tell the story. The problem with wartime, however, is that a soldier's experience is so overloaded with events and impressions, 'faces' and 'sights', that it is hard to know what is representative and what is merely incidental to the story. When viewed up close, war is, as the critic Allyson Booth writes, 'as disordered, incomprehensible, and illogical an experience as it is possible to imagine' (Booth, 1996, p. 118). Any war writer therefore faces two choices: either to exclude the 'incoherence' – and risk telling a less truthful account – or to try and incorporate it somehow into the narrative.

The death of the young sentry near Hooge becomes an example of this artistic problem. He clearly lodged in Blunden's memory, but Blunden suggests that it would be difficult to include such a seemingly incidental death within a conventionally structured narrative. The alternative, Blunden says, is to 'collect' rather than 'select'. By 'collecting' so many small incidents and fleeting impressions, Blunden is trying to give readers a sense of the actual experience of war, in all its 'incoherence' and confusion. His expectation is that larger truths about what war was actually like will emerge from the pattern made by the various memorial fragments. There is, as the critic Paul Edwards points out, no way in which a lone death like that of the sentry at Hooge had any significance in the wider context of the war. However, by including it in the book, Blunden is able to give it a meaning that it would otherwise lack. It becomes, like the lance-corporal's death at Cambrin, a representative symbol of the seemingly endless stream of background casualties that took place during the war – each one 'unique', but also ultimately meaningless when measured against the war's larger objectives (Edwards, 2005, p. 20). Blunden's 'collecting' strategy shows how memory works: it produces connections between unrelated events, putting them into an artificial sequence that exists only in the mind of the witness.

When we place Blunden's accounts of these two deaths side by side, we can start to detect other patterning effects at work. Although these two events are completely unrelated, the death of the sentry at Hooge seems almost like a repeat version of the lance-corporal's death at Cambrin. We could compare this with Blunden's 'persistent retrospect' of the dead Germans at Thiepval Wood, 'tallow-faced and dirty-stubbled, one spectacled, with fingers hooking the handle of a bomb' (Blunden, 2010, p. 96), and a later episode in which Blunden encounters German dead. As he describes it in Chapter xvi, a small group of German soldiers conducted a successful trench raid on the battalion's positions near Railway Wood on 25 January 1917. It was one of Blunden's jobs as battalion Intelligence Officer to look out for any potential weaknesses in the defensive line. When he revisits the scene the next morning, he finds that the culvert the raiding party had hidden in 'appeared painfully prominent', and it is clear that Blunden blames himself for failing to spot it. Surveying the scene, he finds, among other German casualties of the raid, the 'corpse … of a youth, perhaps eighteen years old, fair-haired, rough-chinned … and his right hand clutched the wooden handle of a bomb' (p. 127).

The echoes between the descriptive elements that Blunden chooses to pick out from the two scenes – the dead men's stubble and the fact that both are holding unexploded bombs – are striking. They make the latter scene, at Railway Wood, seem like a repetition of the shell-hole at Thiepval and its human contents. The linkages that Blunden creates between these two scenes suggest something about how the mind processes trauma. The corpses in the latrine at Thiepval Wood were incidental to Blunden's war, so there is no reason why the memory of them should 'persist' so strongly after the war. Blunden's use of repetition here provides a possible explanation. In her account of trauma in British First World War narratives, the critic Deborah Parsons describes how painful events can detach 'shards of memory' from their original contexts. Once created, these memorial fragments reappear in nightmares and flashbacks, and can become associated with subsequent traumatic experiences (Parsons, 2005, p. 186). We could speculate that something similar happened to Blunden. His memory has created an unconscious association between the two traumatic scenes. The 'persistent retrospect' of the corpses at Thiepval therefore becomes his mind's way of processing the guilt he feels over failing to predict the trench raid at Railway Wood. You will find out more about trauma in your study of Arundhati Roy, *The God of Small Things*, later on in Part One.

Figure 9.2 Ernest Brooks, 'A flourishing village once stood on yonder hill', *c.*1916–1918. National Library of Scotland, Shelf Acc. 3155. Photo: Reproduced by permission of the National Library of Scotland.

Poetry, prose and memory

Undertones of War is not solely a prose memoir. As you can see when you look at the contents page of your set text edition, the book is rounded out by what Blunden calls 'A Supplement of Poetical Interpretations and Variations' – 32 war poems printed after the main text as an appendix. A number of these poems were prompted by events also described in the prose part of the book. Let's turn now to two incidents that Blunden was involved in while serving near Ypres, during the Battle of Passchendaele, to see how the two parts of the book – prose and poetry – work together. In Chapter xxi, Blunden describes the events of 31 July 1917, when his battalion was ordered to participate in the British advance that marked the beginning of the battle. After taking the first line of German trenches, the 11th Battalion Royal Sussex are then pinned down by German shellfire in the defensive positions they had just captured. While sheltering in a captured German pillbox – a concrete fortification – Blunden and the rest of the battalion headquarters experience a sustained artillery barrage. One shell hits the pillbox entrance, just above Blunden's head. This explosion could have easily killed everyone inside, but the concrete absorbs the shock, no one is killed, and Blunden pulls the injured battalion doctor, Captain Gatchell, to safety (pp. 158–9). Soldiers in a neighbouring pillbox are not so lucky – a direct hit kills or wounds 30 men from another battalion.

In Chapter xxiii, there occurs what seems almost like a repetition of these events, but this time with a tragic twist for Blunden's battalion. Ordered to advance down the Menin Road, south of Ypres, on 25 September 1917, the battalion is once again pinned down by German shellfire and Blunden once more finds himself sheltering in a captured German pillbox. Shells strike the concrete walls and one of Blunden's men dies of shock after being hit by a shell fragment. Feeling fortunate to have survived, Blunden is then horrified to discover that there has again been a hit on a neighbouring pillbox, but this time it is men from Blunden's own battalion who have been killed, including Captain Gatchell, whose life he had saved less than two months earlier (pp. 169–70).

Figure 9.3 Massive concrete dugout for German battery, *c.*1916–1918. Photographed by John Warwick Brooke. National Library of Scotland, Shelf Acc. 3155. Photo: Reproduced by permission of the National Library of Scotland.

The prose section of *Undertones of War* is not, however, the only place where Blunden describes the events of 25 September 1917. There are two poems in the appendix, 'Pillbox' and 'The Welcome', which provide their own accounts of what happened to the battalion that day.

Activity 9.1

Allow around 45 minutes to complete this activity

Read the whole of Chapter xxiii, 'The Cataract' (pp. 167–72), and then read the poems 'Pillbox' and 'The Welcome', printed on pp. 212–4 at the back of the set text. Once you have done this, answer the following questions for each of the two poems:

1 Which parts of Chapter xxiii does each poem correspond to?

2 Can you find any differences between the two accounts?

3 Thinking about our earlier discussion on Blunden's technique of 'collecting' memories 'in their original form of incoherence', why do you think Blunden has chosen to include both prose and poetry versions of this incident? How do the different versions (prose and poem) work together to tell a story?

Note, in Greek mythology Charon, referred to in the poem 'Pillbox', was the ferryman who carried the souls of the dead to their final resting place in Hades, the Greek underworld.

Discussion

'Pillbox'

1. This poem elaborates on a single sentence in the main prose narrative: 'One man in my headquarters died of shock from a heavy shell striking just outside' (p. 169).
2. The sentence, as it appears in the prose part of *Undertones of War*, is written in the official language of war – it would not be out of place in an officer's report or the battalion's official war diary. In 'Pillbox', however, Blunden is able to tell a more expansive story. Reading the two versions side by side, we are given an insight into the anxiety and stress that those within the pillbox experienced during the shelling, culminating in the death of the man Blunden calls 'Sergeant Hoad' (effectively from fright). This is an aspect of the experience that is almost entirely repressed in the prose narrative, which simply relates a sequence of events. It is this variation in tone – between the restraint and near emotionlessness of the prose narrative and the panic and terror in the poem – that is most strikingly different about the two accounts.
3. Perhaps Blunden felt that there was simply no space to include his memories of 'Sergeant Hoad's' mental breakdown and eventual death in the main narrative. The poem gives him the opportunity to revisit the scene, process it, and through the act of writing, come to terms with what must have been a traumatic event to witness. We might also think of it as a kind of memorial to 'Sergeant Hoad' – 'a good man ... for weeks' – as well as to Sergeant Worley, who desperately tries to keep the dying man focused on his family to stop him succumbing to shock.

'The Welcome'

1. This poem takes place in the other pillbox. It begins with a character whom we can assume to be 'Colonel Millward', whose return from leave is referred to in a single sentence on pp. 169–70.
2. 'The Welcome' deviates much less from the prose version of the narrative than 'Pillbox' does, describing once again how the adjutant, Captain Lewis, invites Blunden to dinner, and how Blunden's servant, Private Shearing, went over to see what had happened and came back warning Blunden not to go and see it for himself. In both versions, Blunden declines to describe in any

detail the carnage in the other pillbox. In both cases, the horror of the sight is implied in Shearing's shocked reactions to it – 'Don't go over, sir; it's awful' (p. 170) and 'Don't go there!' (p. 214).

3 'The Welcome' functions as a kind of counterpart to, or mirror image of, the prose narrative, focusing on survival, rather than death. By a kind of twist, the poem ends with the fact that the officer who has just returned from leave miraculously survives (and was not driven mad by the experience). While 'Pillbox' describes a death that really should not have happened, 'The Welcome' ends with an act of survival that seems equally inexplicable.

Context in focus: Note on historical accuracy

You may have noticed that, in my discussion, I have placed the name of the soldier whose death is described in 'Pillbox' in quotation marks. Blunden did indeed serve with a Sergeant F. A. Hoad, although the next of kin details on his grave registration report indicate that he was from Lewes rather than Eastbourne, as suggested in the poem.

However, this man died more than a year before the events described in the poem, during the attack on Hamel on 3 September 1916. (No one named Hoad died on 25 September 1917.) It may be, as John Greening observes in his edition of *Undertones of War*, that the poem merges two separate incidents (Blunden, 2015, p. 464). Details like this should make us bear in mind that, while *Undertones of War* is based on real events, they are filtered through Blunden's organising powers as an author and he does occasionally take liberties with names and the sequence of events he records.

Landscape, memory and the pastoral

In his 'Preliminary' note to the 1928 edition, Blunden notes that, even as he was producing poetry that dealt with the 'image' and 'horror' of his war experience, he felt that there was more to say. Justifying the existence of his memoir, and hinting at the kind of book it is, he writes, 'I must go over the ground again' (p. xlii). We might assume that 'ground' is simply another word for 'subject matter', but in the context of the First World War it also has a literal meaning – the war on the Western Front was fought for control of particular areas of French and Belgian soil. The experience of war was, as the critic Kate McLoughlin points out, inextricably bound up with the 'geographical space' in which the war was fought (2011, p. 102). As we have seen, Blunden claims to have written the book with no other reference materials than a pair of trench maps showing the areas he had served in. We could think of the geography of war as a kind of memory aid for Blunden. In Chapter xvii, for instance, he writes that, even though the exact 'chronology' of his experiences has 'withered away', he still retains 'topographical' impressions (Blunden, 2010, p. 133). These enable him to provide us, as readers, with a geographically highly accurate account of his daily routine as Brigade Intelligence Officer in February 1917, visiting observation posts from Zillebeke Lake to Observatory Ridge, south of Ypres (pp. 133–6).

However, there is also another way in which 'ground' is significant in *Undertones of War*. Throughout his life, Blunden was obsessed with both the landscape itself and with writing about landscape. In *Undertones of War*, he uses a literary mode – the pastoral – to place the events and impressions he describes within a wider interpretive framework. Documenting the effects of modern warfare on landscapes – and the living things that populated them – enabled him to represent something of the emotional experience of war and gesture towards what it had all meant. In the final section of this chapter, we will return to some of the earlier sections of *Undertones of War* to explore Blunden's use of pastoral imagery. In doing so, we will bring together the various themes we have examined so far: Blunden's use of literary modes and genres to describe his wartime experiences; the importance of memory as a theme in *Undertones of War*; and Blunden's concern with portraying emotional and psychological truths, as well as literal ones.

By the time he entered the army, Blunden had already written a series of poems on rural themes. These were published in the Christ's Hospital school magazine and then reissued in a slim volume entitled *Pastorals* in June 1916. When he was posted to France, he took with him a volume written by the Northamptonshire landscape poet John Clare (1793–1864) (Blunden, 2010, p. 23). In the previous chapter, we looked at Blunden's reading habits while on active service, seeing how he scavenged for books left behind by other soldiers or abandoned in the ruined houses behind the fighting areas (see, e.g., p. 100). It is important to note, however, that some of the books he prized most had pastoral themes. In late 1918 in Arras, for instance, he picked up a copy of the soldier-writer Edward Thomas's 1916 study of the pastoral poet John Keats, imagining that it might once have belonged to Thomas himself (Webb, 1990, pp. 55–6). (Thomas was killed in action at Arras in 1917.) Soon after returning from the war, Blunden started work on a new edition of John Clare's poems (Blunden, 2015, p. 343) and he later wrote a book on Thomas Hardy. In his post-war writing, he returned repeatedly to childhood memories of the Kent and Sussex countryside and lamented that rural traditions were not being passed on to coming generations (Blunden, 1932, p. 111). Blunden's background as an avid reader and writer of landscape poetry is clearly an important context for understanding *Undertones of War*. It gave him a specifically literary set of resources for making sense of his experiences and organising them into a larger framework of meaning.

We can see Blunden's pastoral imagination at work in Chapter ii, 'Trench Education' (Blunden, 2010, pp. 7–20), where he describes his first spell of trench duty in the line at Festubert in May 1916. The Royal Sussex were occupying a part of the line that had seen fierce fighting in 1914 and 1915, and there had been little chance to clear the battlefields of earlier casualties. Skeletal human remains were still lying in the former German line and just below the surface in the reserve trenches. Such grotesque details seem a long way from the idylls of the pastoral, but Blunden mixes the two modes until they intertwine. Live bullet rounds sound, to Blunden's untrained ear, like insects flying by. The rounded curves of skulls emerging from the sides of the trenches 'appeared … like mushrooms' (p. 11). This blurring of the boundaries between the natural world and the world of battle – the living and the dead – continues as Blunden surveys the landscape with his poet's eye. Eroded and overgrown since the Battle of Aubers Ridge 13 months before, the old German line has come to resemble a sunken 'lane' dug into a country landscape (p. 13). The anti-gas machines remind

Figure 9.4 An old German trench overgrown with flowers, captioned 'How nature prevails – flowers overgrowing an old front line German Trench', *c.*1916–1918. Photographed by John Warwick Brooke. National Library of Scotland, Shelf Acc. 3155. Photo: Reproduced by permission of the National Library of Scotland.

Blunden of the devices used to spray insecticide in Sussex cherry orchards. Later, he recalls how the sounds of rural tranquillity and modern warfare would blur together and form one unique sound environment: 'the frogs in their fens were uttering their long-drawn *co-aash, co-aash*; and from the line the popping of rifles grew more and more threatening' (p. 19). Blunden's extended description of his company headquarters, situated in a ruined French farmhouse, is perhaps the most vivid example in the chapter of Blunden's wartime pastoral, with its thorough intermingling of the picturesque and the deadly:

> our garden was lovely, with flowering shrubs, streaked and painted blooms, gooseberry bushes, convenient new gaps and paths, and walks between evergreen hedges — 'unsafe by day', as the notice-boards said. Not far down the road was a wooden bathhouse, where one splashed in cold water agreeably, yet with a listening

> ear. Not far, again, was a red brick wall, to which fruit-trees reached their covert; this red wall was an instance of man's duplicity, for part of it, being but painted wood, presently swung open, and a field battery glaring brutally out would 'poop off'.
>
> (pp. 17–18)

The elements of traditional pastoral description in this passage – flowers, trees and bushes, the rustic architecture of the bathhouse – are juxtaposed against pieces of the war machine with which they now share a landscape. The result is a disconcerting jumble of conflicting information, one that subverts traditional pastoral expectations (Fussell, 2000, p. 261). The country walks between the hedges are 'unsafe' for rambling due to being in the German line of fire. The red-brick wall, which at first sight forms part of an idyllic country landscape, is merely a means for concealing a large field gun. Any activity performed within this formerly pastoral space is accompanied not with pleasure but instead by a constant shadowing anxiety – the need to keep 'a listening ear' out for incoming artillery shells.

Many soldiers wrote about the odd moments of natural beauty they encountered on the Western Front. A snatch of birdsong, the blue flash of a moth's wings, or the green shoots of a young plant would stand out markedly against the monotonous sound and colour palettes of the trenches. While such small details might pass unnoticed in peacetime, they could gain a heightened sense of emotional significance to a serving soldier (Heyde, 2015, pp. 186–7). We might regard Blunden's attention to these details as part of his wider quest to document the emotional and psychological truths of war. These fragments of pastoral represent the military experience at the level of individual perception – momentary thoughts and impressions pieced together by the sense-making powers of the mind.

There is one further way in which this chapter functions as a kind of pastoral. Traditionally, pastoral writing has looked back to a lost 'golden age' of relative innocence located in the distant past (Gifford, 1999, pp. 17, 21). Blunden subtly suggests that the 'quiet life' (2010, p. 19) in the trenches around Festubert represents (despite its dangers) its own kind of 'golden age', both for his battalion and for himself as an inexperienced young officer, before the trials and casualties to come.

As Chapters ii and iii indicate, soldiers on the Western Front did not spend all their time in the frontline trenches. By the time Blunden arrived in France in May 1916, the British army had developed a regular troop rotation system designed to limit casualties and ensure units got at least some rest. Soldiers would typically spend between four and eight days in the frontline trenches, followed by a similar period in the slightly safer reserve trenches behind them. After rotating between these lines of defence, they would then be rested in billet accommodation well away from the fighting (Holmes, 2005, pp. 275–81). All soldiers were entitled to leave and officers were sometimes sent away on training courses. In Chapter iii, 'The Cherry Orchard' (pp. 20–4), Blunden tells his readers what it felt like to experience these periods of respite.

Figure 9.5 Swans and soldier in the back areas, captioned 'Two swans well known to the Tommies in a certain area in France: midst pretty surroundings', *c.*1914–1918. Photographed by Tom Aitken. National Library of Scotland, Shelf Acc. 3155. Photo: Reproduced by permission of the National Library of Scotland.

Activity 9.2

Allow around 45 minutes to complete this activity

Read Chapter iii, 'The Cherry Orchard' (pp. 20–4), carefully and answer the following questions:

1 What elements of the natural world and the pastoral can you find in this chapter?
2 What are the literary effects created by these descriptions?
3 How do they contribute to the book's overall atmosphere?

Discussion

1 Passages of descriptive nature writing feature prominently in this chapter. Blunden narrates his journey away from the lines to the village of Hinges – where the battalion would be rested – largely by describing features in the rural landscape he sees as he walks. There are abandoned farmhouses and farm equipment and fields of 'self-sown wheat' (Blunden, 2010, p. 21). At several points in the chapter, Blunden lets his potted descriptions develop into something that seems like full-blown pastoral: 'Life, life abundant sang here and smiled; the lizard ran warless in the warm dust; and the ditches were trembling quick with odd tiny fish, in world[s] as remote as Saturn' (p. 21). Hinges is also described in terms that deliberately evoke Romantic-period pastoral poetry. Blunden imagines that the farmhouse that would serve as company headquarters was just the sort that the poet Percy Bysshe Shelley (1792–1822) might once have sat and written in. Later, as Blunden leaves Hinges for Essars – where he is assigned to a three-day gas course – the focus on precise, detailed nature writing becomes increasingly prominent. The canal is filled with 'glittering roach', while Blunden, 'swinging' his 'stick' like a countryside rambler, notices 'the yellow-hammer and the wagtail' flying around him (p. 23). At the gas course itself, he meets like-minded young officers, talks about poetry, and luxuriates in the idyllic country setting:

> so long as the war allowed a country-rectory quietude and lawny coolness three kilometres from the line, and summer had even greater liberty than usual to multiply his convolvulus, his linnets and butterflies … an inestimable sweetness of

> feeling beyond Corot or Marvell made itself felt through all routine and enforcement; an unexampled simplicity of desire awoke in the imagination and rejoiced like Ariel in a cowslip-bell.
>
> (p. 24)

2 There are multiple layers of meaning operating in this chapter. On the most basic level, these heightened descriptions of the natural world serve to illustrate how beautiful and richly populated the French countryside could still be, only three kilometres from the fighting front. At the same time, these descriptions also draw attention to the organising powers of Blunden's imagination. Allusions to the poet Andrew Marvell (1621–1678), the French landscape painter Camille Corot (1796–1875), and Ariel in Shakespeare's *Tempest* suggest some of the aesthetic frames through which Blunden viewed and constructed this scene.

3 Blunden's purpose in marshalling all of these pastoral images is, I would suggest, to evoke a sense of loss and looming danger. The abandoned farmhouses would have inevitably become 'effigies of agony' and 'mounds of punished … materials' (p. 21) when the war moved into the area during the battles of 1918. Blunden says that his memory of his two officer friends from the Gloucestershire Regiment remains fixed in the setting of the fields outside Essars. He does not say what ultimately happened to them. The sense of threat that Blunden manages to derive from his use of the pastoral in this scene is perhaps most obvious in the image of the 'ponderous and ugly carp' that startles him as he looks into the dyke. This 'lurking … monster' (p. 24), which momentarily awakens Blunden's childhood terrors, punctures the idyllic tone and foreshadows the dangers that lie ahead in the narrative. Blunden's suggestion that the natural world around him conveyed a sense of foreboding is an example of pathetic fallacy, which you learned about in Chapter 2. This is a literary technique in which a writer suggests that nature is capable of experiencing human emotions (Siddall, 2009, p. 123). In this instance, the carp in the dyke seems to register Blunden's unease and reflect it back at him. You may be able to identify other examples of this technique at work in Blunden's descriptions of French and Belgian landscapes.

Pastoral as critique: the ruined landscape

We have already touched on the idea that the pastoral can be used as a form of critique. Oliver Goldsmith's poem 'The Deserted Village' (1770) depicts the 'desolation' wrought on the landscapes surrounding a formerly idyllic English village by the actions of a wealthy landowner. Closer in time to Blunden, Edwardian novelists such as E. M. Forster (1879–1970) and D. H. Lawrence (1885–1930) also used this form of pastoral to represent the changes brought about by urban development (Hynes, 2018, p. 123). The historian Jay Winter has described the First World War as a 'counterrevolutionary moment' in the arts; many war writers went back to traditional literary modes to make sense of their wartime experiences and find ways of mourning their losses (Winter and Wohl, 2009, p. 170). We can certainly regard Blunden's return to the pastoral both as a means of bearing moral witness to the consequences of war and as its own act of mourning. His minutely detailed depictions of the effect of war's destructive potential on landscapes, villages and animals symbolise the costs of war, both human and environmental.

In traditional pastoral, a spectator usually derives either straightforward pleasure or an intense aesthetic experience from contemplating nature. In *Undertones of War*, Blunden consciously subverts this norm. Many of his descriptive passages work by untethering pastoral beauty from the aesthetic or emotional responses they would usually evoke. Contemplating the picturesque sight of a 'German kite balloon … hanging in the blue like a boat swinging idly at a mooring' (Blunden, 2010, p. 59) would be fatal. Its observer was scouting targets for German artillery. The beauty of an evening sky in autumn goes unappreciated due to the 'succession of typewritten decrees' Blunden has to attend to as Field Works Officer (p. 78). Indeed, war as Blunden depicts it seems to target for destruction the most conventionally beautiful elements in the landscape, perpetually frustrating the pastoral imagination. At Hamel, he writes, 'peace and innocence' still clung to some of the landscape, such that a 'cow with a crumpled horn' and

Figure 9.6 Entrance to a captured French village, *c.*1916–1918. Photographed by John Warwick Brooke. National Library of Scotland, Shelf Acc. 3155. Photo: Reproduced by permission of the National Library of Scotland.

Figure 9.7 A shell-wrecked farmhouse near Hannebeek, in the Ypres sector, where severe fighting took place on 20 September 1917. The Australian War Memorial, Acc no. E00894. Photo: Australian War Memorial.

'a harvest cart should have been visible here and there' (p. 64). In the trench lines, however, conditions were 'not so pastoral':

> Ruined houses with rafters sticking out, with half-sloughed plaster and dangling window-frames, perched on a hillside, bleak and piteous that cloudy morning; half-filled trenches crept along below them by upheaved gardens, telling the story of wild bombardment... South of the Ancre was broad-backed high ground, and on that a black vapour of smoke and naked tree trunks or charcoal, an apparition which I found was called Thiepval Wood.
>
> (pp. 64–5)

Shellfire has systematically destroyed every aspect of what would before the war have been material for a conventionally pastoral scene, completely overturning its aesthetic potential. The once picturesque farmhouses have been turned literally inside out, their gardens uprooted, while Thiepval Wood is now simply a collection of blackened and denuded tree trunks. The emotions evoked by this scene are now 'bleakness', 'pity', and the horror suggested by Blunden's choice of the word 'apparition' to describe Thiepval Wood.

In the passage you will read in the following activity, Blunden describes the events of 30 October 1916, as the 11th Battalion Royal Sussex return to the lines to occupy the Schwaben Redoubt. This was a heavily fortified strongpoint that formed part of the Somme trench system. It had been captured by the Ulster Division on the first morning of the Somme Offensive on 1 July 1916, only to be retaken by German forces in a counterattack. It was then continuously bombarded by British artillery before being finally taken from the Germans on 14 October 1916, after a complex battle that lasted over two weeks (Prior and Wilson, 2016, pp. 85–6, 256–8).

Activity 9.3

Allow around 30 minutes to complete this activity

Turn to Chapter xii, 'Caesar Went into Winter Quarters', and read Blunden's description of his battalion's journey through the Thiepval area to take over the Schwaben Redoubt at the end of October 1916, from the paragraph starting 'Soon enough ...' to the paragraph ending '... an uncertain sentence of days' (pp. 97–8).

Figure 9.8 Christopher Richard Wynne Nevinson, *That Cursed Wood*, 1918, drypoint, 24 × 35 cm. Private collection. Photo: © The Fine Art Society/Bridgeman Images. While this evocative print does not depict Thiepval Wood, it uses (albeit in a different artistic medium) some of the same effects as *Undertones of War* does to show the effects of shellfire on forest landscapes.

1. What are the features to be found in the landscape described in this passage?
2. How do Blunden's descriptions contribute to the book's overall meaning?

Discussion

1. Blunden's detailed prose descriptions suggest just how much devastation this period of concentrated fighting had caused and what the cost had been in human terms. As Blunden narrates the journey his battalion took from their billets into the line, he describes the landscape in a way that reflects his 'melancholy'. (As

we discussed earlier, this is a literary technique termed the pathetic fallacy.) They pass over 'Black Horse Bridge', through 'the scanty skeleton houses' of the ruined village of Authuille, and finally up a 'dirty little road' until they reach what Blunden evocatively terms 'the land of despair' (Blunden, 2010, p. 97). All of these landscape features have names or descriptions associated with darkness, dirt or death. The emphasis on death continues as Blunden develops his verbal sketch of the landscape around the former village of Thiepval. The area is covered in human corpses in various states of decay, including one Scottish soldier whose uncanny kneeling posture in death is described in detail. Thiepval itself is merely a 'whitish tumulus of ruin' (p. 97), again linked with death by colour (whitishness: the colour of bones) and Blunden's choice of the word 'tumulus' (an ancient burial mound). What would have been the features of its pre-war landscape have been almost completely blotted out by shellfire, leaving only fragments ('some spikes that had been pine trees, a bricked cellar or two'). In this altered landscape, Blunden finds his map almost tragically misleading. The village pond ('so blue on the map') has gone altogether. In its place, British artillery has left shell holes containing 'small lakes' full of dirty water that looks and smells uncannily like blood.

2 According to Blunden's descriptions, war has systematically transformed every aspect of the French countryside that had existed here prior to 1914, leaving almost no living remains of its former self visible. The pastoral has disappeared. What exists here instead is something that seems more like its opposite – an 'anti-pastoral', or even an 'anti-landscape' – imposed on what was formerly an 'idyllic' countryside space by the forces of industrial warfare. We could compare this with other passages in *Undertones of War* in which features in the former landscape have been replaced by elements of the war machine. We could think, perhaps, of what Blunden calls the 'ritual of the sunrise' – the fusillade of 'indiscriminate rifle fire' each morning in the trenches which functions as a kind of wartime version of the dawn chorus (p. 86).

Conclusion

In this chapter, we have continued to explore how Blunden uses literary techniques to describe his experiences on the Western Front. We have examined Blunden's use of an unconventional structuring device, which he calls the 'collection' of 'incoherent' fragments of experience. As we have seen, this enables him to convey to readers something of the chaos and confusion of war experience itself, as well as a sense of what it is like to carry traumatic memories of combat into the post-war world. We have also seen how the prose section of the book works alongside the poetry printed in the book's appendix. Finally, we have returned to the earlier sections of the book and analysed in detail Blunden's use of a literary mode, the pastoral, seeing how Blunden uses it as a literary framework for organising his memories of war and deriving meaning from them. Blunden's extended descriptions of abandoned rooms, houses and fields, where the normal rhythms of life have been suspended, is part of his wider moral critique of war. It implies the absence of the rural population whose land it had been before the war, and who have been forcibly moved off it by the battles Blunden takes part in.

Blunden was in many ways an idiosyncratic and unique witness to war. Very few soldiers in the British Army would have been as well equipped with literary references as he was, and as we have seen, the men in his battalion regarded his dedicated and voracious reading habits as rather unusual. Nevertheless, Blunden found a way of using his immersion in the poetic tradition of nature writing to recast the war as a pastoral tragedy. The pastoral enabled Blunden to find a way of expressing the emotional and psychological truths of war, both as he saw them while fighting the war, and when writing about it from the vantage point of a hotel room in Tokyo in 1924.

References

Set text

Blunden, E. (2010) *Undertones of war*. Edited by Hew Strachan. London: Penguin.

Other references

Blunden, E. (1932) *The face of England: in a series of occasional sketches*. London: Longmans, Green and Co.

Blunden, E. (2015) *Undertones of war*. Edited by John Greening. Oxford: Oxford University Press. Available online via the OU Library.

Booth, A. (1996) *Postcards from the trenches: negotiating the space between modernism and the First World War*. Oxford: Oxford University Press. Available online via the OU Library.

Edwards, P. (2005) 'British war memoirs', in Sherry, V. (ed.) *The Cambridge companion to the literature of the First World War*. Cambridge: Cambridge University Press, pp. 15–33. Available online via the OU Library.

Fussell, P. (2000) *The Great War and modern memory*. 25th anniversary edn. Oxford: Oxford University Press. Available online via the OU Library.

Gifford, T. (1999) *Pastoral*. Abingdon: Routledge. Available online via the OU Library.

Graves, R. (1929) *Good-bye to all that*. London: Jonathan Cape.

Heyde, S. (2015) 'History as a source for innovation in landscape architecture: the First World War landscapes in Flanders', *Studies in the History of Gardens and Designed Landscapes*, 35(3), pp. 183–97. Available online via the OU Library.

Holmes, R. (2005) *Tommy: the British soldier on the Western Front, 1914–1918*. London: Harper Perennial.

Hynes, S. (2018) *On war and writing*. Chicago, Ill.: University of Chicago Press.

McLoughlin, K. (2011) *Authoring war: the literary representation of war from the Iliad to Iraq*. Cambridge: Cambridge University Press. Available online via the OU Library.

Parsons, D. (2005) 'Trauma and war memory', in Marcus, L. and Nicholls, P. (eds) *The Cambridge history of twentieth-century English literature*. Cambridge: Cambridge University Press, pp. 173–96. Available online via the OU Library.

Prior, R. and Wilson, T. (2016) *The Somme*. New Haven, Conn.: Yale University Press. Available online via the OU Library.

Rothkopf, C.Z. (2012) *Selected letters of Siegfried Sassoon and Edmund Blunden, Volume I: Letters 1919–1931*. London: Pickering & Chatto.

Sassoon, S. (1918) 'Repression of war experience', in *Counter-attack and other poems*. London: William Heinemann, pp. 51–3.

Siddall, S. (2009) *Landscape and literature*. Cambridge: Cambridge University Press.

Webb, B. (1990) *Edmund Blunden: a biography*. New Haven, Conn.: Yale University Press.

Wilson, R.J. (2012) *Landscapes of the Western Front: materiality during the Great War*. Abingdon: Routledge. Available online via the OU Library.

Winter, J. and Wohl, R. (2009) 'The Great War: midwife to modern memory?', in Winter, J. (ed.) *The legacy of the Great War: ninety years on*. Columbia, Mo.: University of Missouri Press, pp. 159–84. Available online via the OU Library.

Chapter 10 Arundhati Roy, *The God of Small Things*: Context and story structure

Alex Tickell

Contents

Introduction

Arundhati Roy (1961–) famously started her novel *The God of Small Things* with a single generative image in mind, an image which became the central scene in Chapter 2, 'Pappachi's Moth': a railway level-crossing in the southern Indian state of Kerala, a sky-blue Plymouth car with tailfins, containing twin children and their family, and a political procession. Out of her initial image Roy builds a complex, meticulously structured story – a kind of mosaic – that conceals its own pattern in its inexorable movement towards tragedy. On its publication in 1997, Roy's debut novel was recognised as a new departure for Indian writing in English, and its experimental style and haunting story gained fulsome praise but also some significant criticism. Over 20 years later, it has become a canonical work of **postcolonial** literature, having sold an estimated six million copies globally and been translated into 42 languages. Because its release coincided with India's fiftieth year of independence, the publication of *The God of Small Things* made its author the reluctant representative of the energies of a 'new' emergent India, but Roy's subsequent outspoken criticism of a number of Indian government policies – ranging from dam-building to nuclear testing – has since turned her into a campaigning voice of political dissent.

Reduced to its simplest terms, *The God of Small Things* is the story of two deaths and a love affair. Set in Kerala's ancient Syrian Christian community, the plot revolves around the Ipe family, and centres on their disgraced daughter, Ammu. Having divorced her alcoholic husband, Ammu has returned, with her two children, to live unhappily as a single mother in the family home, in the small backwater town of Ayemenem. The love affair is an illicit cross-caste liaison between Ammu and a lower-caste 'Untouchable' carpenter, Velutha, who is employed by the Ipe family as a servant – a liaison that is forbidden and unthinkable for the older members of the family. To avoid spoiling the plot, the rest of the narrative will not be outlined in detail here, other than to note the pivotal, life-changing nature of the events that occur in the novel.

These events are largely focalised through the perspective of the novel's twin protagonists, Estha and Rahel. However, this perspective is not constant, and the story stretches across two time schemes: the first covering a few days in December 1969, when the twins are seven years old, and the second after they have returned to their family home in Kerala as adults, 23 years later, in 1992/93 (approximately at the same time as Roy started writing her novel). The intricate narrative structure of *The God of Small Things* will be discussed further in this chapter, and it is enough to note here that the distinctive shape of the story mediates, and changes the way we experience, the traumatic events at its centre. As its title suggests, Roy's novel also involves shifts in emphasis and focus, so that 'small things' often take centre stage and the hidden connections between 'big' and 'small' things are exposed. This technique has a highly political aim and, as Roy has stated, a central theme of much of her writing is 'the relationship between power and powerlessness and the endless, circular conflict they're engaged in' (Roy, 2004, p. 13).

In the beginning

The story of *The God of Small Things* is inextricably bound up with the history and social and cultural worlds of its setting: the south Indian state of Kerala. Indeed, as indicated by Roy in her novel, History (with a capital H) is much more than just a knowledge of the past or an account of change across time; it is also one of the big forces in the novel, a thing that can be manipulated through tradition or forms of institutional power, and is essentially a plot device and an active presence in the book. Another expression of History in Roy's novel is as an inquiry into narrative starting points, and an investigation into where a story might begin:

> In a purely practical sense it would probably be correct to say that it all began when Sophie Mol came to Ayemenem. Perhaps it's true that things can change in a day. That a few dozen hours can affect the outcome of whole lifetimes. …
>
> Still, to say that it all began when Sophie Mol came to Ayemenem is only one way of looking at it.
>
> Equally, it could be argued that it actually began thousands of years ago. Long before the Marxists came. Before the British took Malabar, before the Dutch Ascendency, before Vasco da Gama arrived, before the Zamorin's conquest of Calicut … It could be argued that it began long before Christianity arrived in a boat and seeped into Kerala like tea from a teabag.
>
> That it really began in the days when the Love Laws were made. The laws that lay down who should be loved, and how.
>
> And how much.
>
> (Roy, 2017, pp. 32–3)

This is an original way of looking at what might be termed narrative patterning, and at the shape of a story, but it is also a way of thinking about the power of beginnings to shape subsequent events and beliefs. Remember that an explanation of beginnings is key to many religions as creation myths – we'll discuss myth further in the next chapter – and that both Christianity and Hinduism present influential versions of how the world began and explain the place of people in this created world. Curiosity about beginnings is also perhaps a common human characteristic and has long been the basis of scientific and philosophical inquiry about origins.

If we look carefully at the passage quoted above, we can see that, before starting the 1969 sections of the story, Roy effectively second-guesses us, as readers, by asking rhetorically where the story we are reading begins. Its 'practical' beginning occurs when we meet the main protagonists, but the earlier, projected beginning makes us think of the story as a 'small' result of 'big' historical forces, and a narrative connected with and shaped by other things/times. This way of starting *The God of Small Things* reminds us, too, that this is a story with children at its centre. Children are notoriously interested in personal beginnings, and where we come from, and parents have often been inventive in their responses to such questions. As a way of commencing narration, a reflection on ancient beginnings – 'long long ago', 'once upon a time' – is deeply reminiscent of stories we listen to as children. Accounts of personal beginnings in childhood are also a feature of certain kinds of realist novel, which we'll look at shortly. Later in this chapter, we'll also reflect on connections between psychology and narrative – we'll find that in its early influential forms, **Freudian psychoanalysis** used personal stories, often stories about childhood and adolescent development, as a way of understanding a patient's repressed fears and subconscious conflicts.

Lastly, reflecting on beginnings is also a strategy that allows us to think about how History and society narrate *us*, and make us part of a pre-existing story. In Roy's novel these social forces are specific to south India, and include the postcolonial history of Kerala as a communist state, the cultural legacies of British rule, and the central theme of the Hindu caste system and the practice of 'untouchability'.

Because *The God of Small Things* is the first work you have encountered on A233 that is not written from a European or an American perspective, it is important to familiarise yourself with its historical and cultural contexts. One of the criticisms sometimes levelled at Indian fiction written in English, in contrast to literary works published in India's many state languages, is that it exoticises and misrepresents India for an international audience (Tickell, 2003). We will return to discuss this process of reading postcolonial fiction as 'exotic' later. In the next section you will look at some of the contexts of the novel and think in more detail about the 'Love Laws' that Roy identifies as the presiding, punishing force in her story.

Theme and context: caste, classification and colonialism

A key theme of *The God of Small Things* is signalled in Chapter 1, 'Paradise Pickles & Preserves', when Rahel reflects on her family's long-standing problem with classification and rules, a problem that even extends to the products they make in their factory:

> Paradise Pickles & Preserves …
>
> They used to make pickles, squashes, jams, curry powders and canned pineapples. And banana jam (illegally) after the FPO (Food Products Organization) banned it because according to their specifications it was neither jam nor jelly. Too thin for jelly and too thick for jam. An ambiguous, unclassifiable consistency, they said …
>
> Looking back now, to Rahel it seemed as though this difficulty that their family had with classification ran much deeper than the jam-jelly question.
>
> Perhaps, Ammu, Estha and she were the worst transgressors. But it wasn't just them. It was the others too. They all broke the rules. They all crossed into forbidden territory. They all tampered with the laws that lay down who should be loved and how. And how much. The laws that make grandmothers grandmothers, uncles uncles, mothers mothers, cousins cousins, jam jam, and jelly jelly.
>
> (pp. 30–1)

In the novel, then, classification is associated with the power of History to make laws, enforce rules and maintain power structures (sometimes quite arbitrarily). As Ammu's children, and therefore as children of a divorcee, Estha and Rahel are representative of broken rules; and at a more fundamental level their biological existence, as two-egg twins, represents a 'tampering' with the usual rules of unified individual selfhood. What Roy wants us to notice in particular here is the way classification and social rules operate to privilege certain groups and preserve long-standing injustices. An obvious example is Ammu's lack of what her children call 'Locust stand-I' – this is a mispronunciation of the legal term *locus standi*, which means the right to be heard in a law court – and which indicates her disempowerment

Figure 10.1 Green Label Indian Mango Chutney *c.*1925. Photo: Shawshots/Alamy.

as a divorced woman. Ammu's brother Chacko jokes about her exclusion from any legal claim on property, saying 'What's yours is mine and what's mine is also mine' (p. 57); in response, Ammu's anger and frustration at her lack of opportunities and her marginalisation as a divorced single mother in the male-orientated world of rural Kerala gives her an 'Unsafe Edge' and fills her with 'An unmixable mix. The infinite tenderness of motherhood and the reckless rage of a suicide bomber' (p. 44). Chacko has in fact also broken convention by marrying outside the community, and he even conducts illicit affairs with women workers at the pickle factory, but as the son of the family his sexual conduct is excused and condoned as 'Man's Needs' (p. 168).

Caste and the 'Love Laws'

The most visible and damaging forms of social hierarchy in the novel are the 'Love Laws' mentioned earlier in the section titled 'In the beginning', that refer to the division of society in ancient Indian religious texts into four main social groups. Known as the caste system, this socio-cosmic ordering is still a significant, pervasive social force in India today. The concept of caste appears in some of the creation myths of Hinduism: in the *Rig Veda* – a sacred hymn composed between 1200 and 1000 BCE (which is the earliest text of the Vedic religion, and a foundation of modern Hinduism) – caste is associated with the creation myth of Purusa, the primeval cosmic man out of whom the universe is formed. In this myth, humankind comes into being through the dispersal of Purusa's limbs after he has been sacrificed by the gods:

> When [the gods] divided the Man, into how many parts did they disperse him? What became of his mouth, what of his arms, what were his two thighs and his two feet called? His mouth was the brahmin [the priest class], his arms were made into the nobles ['Ksatriyas'], his two thighs were the populace ['Vaisyas'], and from his feet the servants ['Sudras'] were born. The moon was born from his mind; the sun was born from his eye.
>
> (O'Flaherty, 1975, p. 28)

The boundaries of caste as a social hierarchy solidified in the last centuries BCE, as numerous occupational subdivisions or *jati* were established, and the laws that defined caste were codified and set down in one of the founding works of the Hindu legal system, titled the *Manava Dharmashastra*, and attributed to the thinker Manu.

The law code of Manu, also known as the *Manusmriti* (Figure 10.2), emphasises the purity and superiority of the 'Brahmin' priest caste, and lists the punishments to be inflicted upon those who break caste rules. This ancient legal work first differentiated the lowest Sudra caste between servants and 'Untouchables', the latter being considered symbolically 'impure'. In it we also find the nearest textual equivalent to the 'Love Laws' that are broken in Roy's novel. The *Manusmriti* was burned as a symbol of caste oppression during some of the first political demonstrations against untouchability in the 1920s.

The long history of the caste system in Kerala is registered in *The God of Small Things* in the crushing sense of inferiority felt by older 'Untouchable' characters. One example is Velutha's father, Vellya Paapen, who is a product of the 'Crawling Backwards Days' (p. 76) of

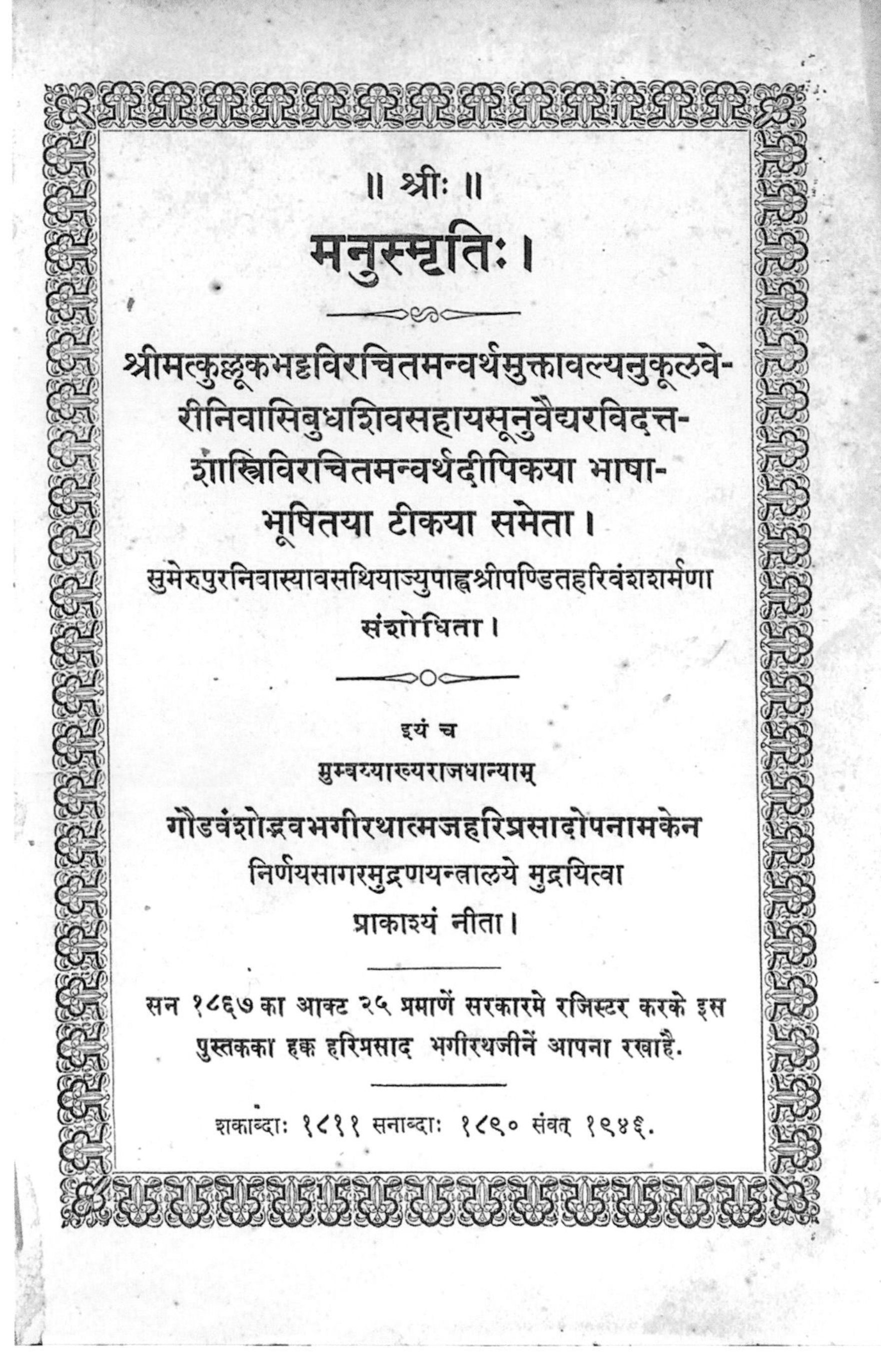

॥ श्रीः ॥

मनुस्मृतिः ।

श्रीमत्कुल्लूकभट्टविरचितमन्वर्थमुक्तावल्यनुकूलवे-
रीनिवासिबुधशिवसहायसूनुवैद्यरविदत्त-
शास्त्रिविरचितमन्वर्थदीपिकया भाषा-
भूषितया टीकया समेता ।

सुमेरुपुरनिवास्यावसथियाज्युपाह्वश्रीपण्डितहरिवंशशर्मणा
संशोधिता ।

इयं च
मुम्बय्याख्यराजधान्याम्
गौडवंशोद्भवभगीरथात्मजहरिप्रसादोपनामकेन
निर्णयसागरमुद्रणयन्त्रालये मुद्रयित्वा
प्राकाश्यं नीता ।

सन १८६७का आक्ट २५ प्रमाणें सरकारमे रजिस्टर करके इस
पुस्तकका हक्क हरिप्रसाद भगीरथजीनें आपना रखाहै.

शकाब्दाः १८११ सनाब्दाः १८९० संवत् १९४६.

Figure 10.2 *Manusmriti* manuscript, 1890, Nirnaya Sagar Press. Photo: Ishwar Ashram Trust/Internet Archive.

Figure 10.3 Procession of Untouchables on their way to the Kalaram temple in Nashik, 1931. Photo: Granger Historical Picture Archive/Alamy.

the pre-independence period, when 'Paravans' (a subdivision of the lowest caste group) 'were not allowed to walk on public roads, not allowed to cover their upper bodies, not allowed to carry umbrellas' (p. 74).

Activity 10.1

Allow around 30 minutes to complete this activity

Review your reading of *The God of Small Things* so far and note down some other instances of caste discrimination in Roy's novel. You may want to reflect on Roy's presentation of the history of caste or find some examples of the effects of the caste system elsewhere in the novel. This might be an attitude or opinion voiced by one of Roy's characters, or it may be an account of the physical effects or experiences of caste discrimination.

Discussion

The description of Velutha's childhood and early adulthood (pp. 73–8) is a good example, as it includes a summary of the proscriptions against Untouchables enforced by the Ipe family (Untouchables are not allowed in the compound of the Ayemenem House; they are not allowed to touch anything that 'Touchables' touch). This section also details the historical taboos associated with untouchability. You may have also thought about the response of the Ipe family to Velutha's personal confidence and assurance, which is a 'perfectly acceptable, perhaps even desirable' quality in Touchables, but which is construed as 'insolence' in a Paravan (p. 76). Velutha is also a gifted mechanic and carpenter, and you may have considered how his technical skills are greeted by his employers – they benefit from them but also lament, with 'Touchable logic', that had he not been a Paravan he might have been an engineer. Another example of how caste inequality is 'embodied' is in the figure of Velutha's disabled brother Kuttapen (pp. 206–7), who exists on the edge of insanity because, as a lower-caste man and a paraplegic, he has no rehabilitative support or occupation. Ammu's affair with Velutha is another instance in which the severe taboos against cross-caste involvement and intimacy become horrifyingly apparent.

At the beginning of the twentieth century, Kerala had one of the most restrictive systems of caste regulation in the subcontinent; this was exacerbated by an imbalance in the main caste groups, with Naboodiri Brahmins settling in the region from the eighth century, and becoming landowners, temple administrators and priests, and most agricultural work being conducted by the Nayars, a comparatively high-status Sudra group. You may have noticed that in *The God of Small Things*, members of the Ipe family, who are Syrian Christians – a religious minority group in Kerala that traces its roots back to the mythical arrival in India of the apostle St Thomas – still observe rules of caste segregation even though they are not Hindu. Historically, the Syrian Christians, who integrated themselves into the local economy, fulfilled some of the region's intermediate caste occupations such as business and banking, and saw themselves as upper caste.

The communist movements which gained power in Kerala in the 1960s were complacent about the history of caste oppression, and the CPI (M) (Communist Party of India (Marxist)) tended to work tactically from *within* caste divides rather than challenging them. Roy registers this complacency in her characterisation of the manipulative party worker Comrade K. N. M. Pillai, whose house, once a hotbed of revolutionary fervour, is now decorated by a limp, faded party flag from which, ironically, 'the red [has] bled away' (p. 13).

Figure 10.4 Communist symbols on the streets of Varkala, Kerala, India. Photo: Oleksandr Rupeta/Alamy.

Classification and colonialism

Rules and forms of classification are also apparent in the legacy of colonialism in India. Between 1757 and 1947, much of India was ruled by the British, first under the authority of a trading concern – the East India Company – and then, after 1858, as a colony of the British crown. While British influence varied throughout directly and indirectly controlled regions of the subcontinent (Cochin was governed indirectly as a nominally independent princely state), and relied on the threat of military force, the so-called British Raj also promoted itself through cultural means, primarily through English language and literature. From the latter half of the nineteenth century, British colonial rule in India also justified itself through assumptions about the racial dominance of Europeans, and the innately civilising superiority of British culture. In their dealings with Indians, British colonial officials, military personnel and plantation managers developed a system of racial segregation and exclusion that rivalled the caste system (while also emphasising existing caste divisions). They were also similarly fearful of obvious evidence of intermixing. For Indian nationalists like Mohandas K. Gandhi and Jawaharlal Nehru – who led the Indian independence movement against British rule in the 1920s, 30s and early 40s – one of the greatest challenges was to reverse the ingrained assumption that the British had an innate ability to govern and a mandate to rule.

Reflecting on this legacy in her early prose essays, Roy states: 'Fifty years after independence, India is still struggling with the legacy of colonialism, still flinching from the "cultural insult" [and …] we're still caught up in the business of "disproving" the white world's definition of us' (Roy, 2001, p. 13). For the Ipe family, with its history of educating its sons in Europe (Pappachi trains to be an Imperial entomologist in Vienna, and the children's uncle Chacko is an undergraduate at Oxford), this history has particular implications. Chacko admits their cultural alienation in a self-deprecating way early in the text:

> Chacko said that the correct word for people like Pappachi was *Anglophile*. He made Rahel and Estha look up *Anglophile* …
>
> Chacko told the twins that though he hated to admit it, they were all Anglophiles. They were a *family of* Anglophiles. Pointed in the wrong direction, trapped outside their own history, and unable to retrace their steps because their footprints had been swept away.
>
> (p. 52)

The effects of this self-damaging Anglophilia – or what we might call a general equation of European-ness with a racial and cultural superiority – is apparent in Pappachi's predilection for wearing three-piece woollen suits even in the hottest weather, and in the family's identification and familiarity with English culture, especially **canonical** English literature.

The toxic rules and classifications of colonial racism come back to haunt Estha and Rahel in their sense of themselves as 'Other' (their sense that as Indians they are not equivalent to a normalised European identity). This realisation literally comes home to them in the perceptions of non-Indian characters such as Sophie Mol, who – as their cousin and 'the harbinger of harsh reality' – confidently informs them: '*You're both whole wogs and I'm a half one*' (p. 16). It could also be argued that Estha's perception of the Von Trapp family in the 1965

Robert Wise musical *The Sound of Music*, although bound up with his own feelings of self-loathing after he is sexually abused by the Orangedrink Lemondrink Man, is also shaped by his perception that he is not like the children in the film: 'And there was Captain von Clapp-Trapp … A captain with seven children. Clean children, like a packet of peppermints … They all loved each other. They were clean, white children, and their beds were soft with Ei. Der. Downs' (p. 105).

Figure 10.5 *The Sound of Music*, advertising poster, 1965. Photo: Pictorial Press Ltd/Alamy.

As a way of clarifying your thoughts about the theme of classification and how it bears on the institutional and political contexts of *The God of Small Things*, ask yourself who enforces rules and how they are policed. As one critic of Roy's novel notes: 'Rather than present[ing] us with a definite separation between the world of power that makes the laws, and the world of the transgressors, the narrative uncovers a multiplicity of intersecting, sometimes contradictory, sets of rules, and

[…] ways they are tampered with' (Baneth-Nouailhetas, quoted in Tickell, 2007, p. 9). These contradictions are apparent in Ammu's concerns with her children's cleanliness, which echo a fear of caste-pollution, even though her actions later transgress caste laws much more irrevocably. We might also remember that while Baby Kochamma is unmarried as well, she has little sympathy for Ammu: 'Baby Kochamma resented Ammu, because she saw her quarrelling with a fate that she, Baby Kochamma herself, felt she had graciously accepted. The fate of the wretched Man-less woman' (p. 45). Like Velutha's father, who reports the news of his son's scandalous caste-breaking affair to Mammachi, Roy's novel suggests that it is not only those in power who have a stake in enforcing rules: sometimes the powerless also eagerly collude in the preservation of the very structures that rob them of agency.

Looking backwards and forwards: story structure in *The God of Small Things*

By this point you should have a better sense of *The God of Small Things* as an *Indian*-English fiction, as well as an understanding of some of the novel's thematic concerns and key contexts, such as caste and colonialism. It is now worth thinking about how Roy constructs her narrative (the arrangement of events into a story). You may recall from your reading of other literary works that authors sometimes start stories not at their actual beginnings, but at some, often more exciting, point in the middle of the action (termed ***in medias res***, a Latin phrase meaning 'in the middle of things'). Authors may then use flashback (analepsis), or other devices of non-linear storytelling, to fill in the story until it catches up with itself. As we shall see, Roy employs a variation on the device of *in medias res* but, highly originally, she ends her story in this way. As Roy herself states, describing her novel's structure:

> the novel ends in the middle of the story, and it ends with Ammu and Velutha making love and it ends on the word 'tomorrow'. And though you know that what tomorrow brings is terrible, the fact that the book ends there is to say that even though it's terrible it's wonderful that it happened at all.
>
> (Simmons, quoted in Alexandru, 2007, p. 181)

Don't worry if this sounds complicated: we'll think about what this non-linear mode of storytelling means for our understanding of Roy's novel and look at the structure of *The God of Small Things* in more detail in the next section.

Writing across time

At the start of this chapter we noted that the narrative of *The God of Small Things* works across two time schemes, which might be said to operate backwards and forwards simultaneously. Put simply: the story moves *forwards* in the sections set in 1969, towards the two deaths mentioned earlier, and often anticipates them by intimating that something is *going to happen*; and at the same time it moves *backwards* in the sections set in 1992/93, retrospectively, long after the main plot events have happened, to show us their delayed effects on the now grown-up protagonists.

It is helpful to think of this alternation or narrative '**anachrony**' by looking at the contents page of Roy's novel and quickly mapping her time scheme around the chapter structure. Table 10.1 does this and includes page spans, to show the relative size of each chapter. Roy's first chapter, 'Paradise Pickles & Preserves', is one of the most complex: it switches across a number of narrative perspectives and time schemes, starting in the present but moving into the past and providing backstories for characters like Baby Kochamma. However, from Chapter 2, 'Pappachi's Moth', onwards the alternation between past and present is clearer, with even-numbered chapters set in the past, and odd-numbered chapters taking place largely in the present, but involving complex recollection and inset flashbacks, which have been marked in square brackets in Table 10.1. However, after Chapter 10, and what we might call the structural centre of the novel, this balanced, alternating chapter pattern changes tempo, and the narrative moves increasingly into the past, with sections set in the present only in Chapters 12, 'Kochu Thomban', 17, 'Cochin Harbour Terminus', and 20, 'The Madras Mail' (with even these latter sections dominated by the past).

By looking at their relative page lengths, we can see that the chapters set in the present are often much shorter than those set in the past. Only about a fifth of the entire novel is actually set in the present, and the impression we have of chronological balance given by the alternating chapter pattern is actually an emphasis on the past. It is the narrative of the past that has precedence. Another way of thinking about this narrative structure is to understand that it occupies two positions with which we are all familiar: the curious split between our perceptions during childhood, with all their immediacy and rawness, and our more or less failing attempts in adulthood to make sense of our earlier selves. This kind of splitting is clearly evidenced in Chapter 7, 'Wisdom Exercise Notebooks', in which the now adult twins retrieve some exercise books written by the seven-year-old Estha, who has fallen into silence in response to the earlier events of the story.

Table 10.1 Mapping past and present in *The God of Small Things*

Chapter	'Past' 1969	'Present' 1992/93
1. Paradise Pickles & Preserves	pp. 3–9, pp. 23–26	pp. 1–3, pp. 10–22, pp. 26–34
2. Pappachi's Moth	pp. 35–87	
3. Big Man, the Laltain, Small Man the Mombatti		pp. 88–93
4. Abhilash Talkies	pp. 94–123	
5. God's Own Country		pp. 124–131 [pp. 132–134], p. 135
6. Cochin Kangaroos	pp. 136–154	
7. Wisdom Exercise Notebooks		pp. 155–159 [pp. 159–164], p. 164
8. Welcome Home, Our Sophie Mol	pp. 165–186	
9. Mrs Pillai, Mrs Eapen, Mrs Rajagopalan		pp. 187–188 [pp. 189–190], pp. 191–192
10. The River in the Boat	pp. 193–214	
11. The God of Small Things	pp. 215–227	
12. Kochu Thomban		pp. 228–237
13. The Pessimist and the Optimist	pp. 238–251, pp. 252–267	
14. Work is Struggle	pp. 268–282, pp. 283–288	
15. The Crossing	pp. 289–290	
16. A Few Hours Later	pp. 291–294	
17. Cochin Harbour Terminus		pp. 295–299 [pp. 300–303]
18. The History House	pp. 304–312	
19. Saving Ammu	pp. 313–322	
20. The Madras Mail	pp. 323–331	pp. 327–328 [pp. 328–330]
21. The Cost of Living	pp. 331–340	

Estha's notebooks have all the strangeness of such writings because they allow the adult self, in this case Rahel, a glimpse of an earlier self. They also have the effect of emphasising the 'childishness' and vulnerability of Estha, but because Ammu has corrected the mistakes in the notebook and is referred to as 'little Ammu' in one of the pieces of writing, her predicament come into focus too, and at a distance of over 20 years she seems diminished and tragic.

The seamlessness of this narrative construction – with its interlocking or intertwining double time scheme – is one of the most impressive aspects of Roy's writing in *The God of Small Things*, and has often been cited as evidence of her deep interest in structure. Roy trained as an architect before becoming a writer and in her first novel, her authorial voice states that the 'Great Stories', performed in Kerala's Kathakali dramas, are those that can be 'enter[ed] anywhere' (p. 229). In the foreword to a screenplay she wrote based on her experiences at college, she likens her writing process to an architectural plan: 'studying architecture taught me to apply my understanding of structure, of design and of minute observation of detail to things other than buildings. To novels, to screenplays, to essays. It was an invaluable training' (Roy, 2003, p. xii). Roy asks us to think about her story as a constructed thing here, as having something like a three-dimensional design, in which the narrative gives the impression that a clear beginning and ending is not as important as a cumulative effect. Roy's writing style reminds us that the process of storytelling in the novel can be highly varied and does not always follow a conventional progressive pattern. More accurately, we could say that the modern novel is a form that allows for immense flexibility and inventiveness in how a story can be arranged.

Activity 10.2

Allow around 45 minutes to complete this activity

In Table 10.1 some of the chapters set in the present – such as Chapters 5, 7 and 9 – have page spans marked in square brackets within the larger page span of the chapter. As you already know, these indicate points or 'flashbacks' when the narrative digresses from the present to recall an isolated scene or moment set in the past. Look again at these sections in turn and, for each one, think about how Roy presents the process of remembering, using the following questions as prompts: how is the memory triggered in each case? Is there a mnemonic trigger or cue that causes the act of recall? Are particular objects or words implicated in the process of remembering?

Discussion

In Chapter 5, 'God's Own Country', the act of digressive recall is triggered for Rahel when Comrade Pillai shows her some photos of his son Lenin, who is almost the same age as Rahel and Estha. Comrade Pillai tells Rahel that Lenin is now working for a foreign embassy in Delhi. In contrast to Rahel's inability to imagine the manipulative Comrade Pillai as anything but an adult ('He looked as though he had been *born* middle-aged' (p. 130)), her response to the pictures of the grown-up Lenin (who is now unfamiliar, with 'his wife, his child, his new Bajaj scooter' (p. 131)) is to recall him as a 'Real Person', aged three or four years old, when they had both visited the creepy Dr Verghese Verghese – who is described as 'Kottayam's leading Paediatrician and Feeler-up of Mothers' – because, coincidentally, they both had small objects lodged up their noses. Roy is perceptive here in connecting childhood recall to a traumatic event and elaborating on its coincidental associative link between the two children. She even makes the respective lodged objects symbolic of the class differences between Rahel and Lenin: 'she a glass bead, and he a green gram' (p. 132).

In Chapter 7, 'Wisdom Exercise Notebooks', as we have seen, the digression is triggered by a kind of jointly authored text: the spelling corrections and comments which Ammu writes on the 'Wisdom Exercise Notebooks'. Finding and reading the notebooks, the adult Rahel is transported back in time to the very end of Ammu's life. Rahel recalls the occasional visits her seriously ill mother made to the Ayemenem house, visits that betrayed Ammu's misery at not being part of her children's lives in the presents she brings for Rahel, which are too young for her:

> They were presents for a seven-year-old; Rahel was nearly eleven. It was as though Ammu believed that if she refused to acknowledge the passage of time, if she willed it to stand still in the lives of her twins, it would. As though sheer willpower was enough to suspend her children's childhoods until she could afford to have them living with her.
>
> (p. 159)

In Chapter 9, 'Mrs Pillai, Mrs Eapen, Mrs Rajagopalan', the triggering of memory is caused by the adult Rahel looking at toads in the garden pond (we will discuss this scene in more detail in the next chapter). Here we encounter one of Roy's idiosyncratic linguistic riffs: looking at the toad blinking with its specialised amphibious eyelid, Rahel remembers that she and Estha and Sophie Mol once spent the whole day saying 'Nictitating Membrane' while dressed up as 'Hindu ladies' in half-saris and clumsily applied makeup. It is notable that all these flights into childhood memory are prompted by specific things – pictures, notebooks, a toad's eye – which are effectively bridges to the past.

Narrating memory and trauma

We have spent some time considering the two distinctive chronological threads of the story of *The God of Small Things*, and we can now focus on how these narrative strands connect in the novel. If we think again about the way *The God of Small Things* is organised around 'returns' – in this case the return of both Estha and Rahel to the ancient Ipe family house in Ayemenem – we can see that, like all such experiences of revisiting a familiar place, the narrative not only moves over the setting of the past (the family home), but also uses the physical act of return as a way of returning through time to the personal past. Memory, in other words, provides the unstable bridge or link between the two parts of the narrative. Keeping the previous activity in mind, we will now review some of the ways in which memory operates in Roy's novel.

Authors of literary fiction, especially in the longer form of the novel, frequently use memory to structure their narratives, most often in works that read like memoirs or autobiographies. The *Bildungsroman* – a kind of novel that follows the life of a single individual from childhood to maturity – was part of the development of the realist novel in the eighteenth and nineteenth centuries, and canonical works such as Charlotte Brontë's *Jane Eyre* (1847) and Charles Dickens' *Great Expectations* (1861) are examples of the *Bildungsroman*: both employ forms of recollection and remembered childhoods as part of their narrative structure. The form of the *Bildungsroman* has also been used by writers from South Asia, Africa and the Caribbean to dramatise the difficulties of a postcolonial claiming of identity in the twentieth century. In many cases in these novels, the non-European protagonist's growth to maturity mirrors or comments on the political development of a new nation. Yet, as you may already suspect, *The God of Small Things* is not really a *Bildungsroman* in the conventional sense: it presents a much bleaker, more broken or disjointed passage from childhood to adulthood than we would usually expect from this 'progressive' form. Estha and Rahel, who, as twins, share aspects of their identity (and therefore modify the conventional individualism of the form), do not appear to have developed through time, but rather seem to have almost been prevented from emerging into a resilient or confident sense of selfhood by the events they have experienced.

Memory is central to Roy's book. Indeed, critics who are interested in **narratology** (a literary-critical approach that analyses the structure and effects of narratives and story forms) have suggested that memory is not only key to the way the story is constructed, in two overlapping or interlocking parts, but also integral to the style of writing in *The God of Small Things*:

> The importance of memory, recollection and their corollaries (the sense of foreboding or of 'déjà-vu', of expectation or of familiarity) is somehow hammered into the reader through the stylistic characteristics of this text: mainly, the unabashed, sometimes disconcerting use of repetition, semantic and structural, in a spiralling narration that brings the past to bear on the future, and the present to reconstruct the past … the meaning of the present comes together through the action of remembering the past.
>
> (Baneth-Nouailhetas, 2007, p. 144)

Baneth-Nouailhetas uses some terms – '**semantic**', 'structural' – that you may find unfamiliar, but her point is relatively easy to grasp. Not only does memory operate as a way for Roy's characters to gain access to the earlier time period from the novel's 'present', but the distinctive style of Roy's writing – with its repetitions, repeated phrasing and 'returning' structure – is organised in such a way that it is *like* memory. Most of us tend not to remember the past in a continuous unbroken narrative but recall it through vivid images or situations, which are often (as we saw in the previous activity) 'triggered' by associations such as a familiar smell or taste, or a piece of music. In *The God of Small Things*, it could be said that Roy is interested in recreating, in fiction, what it feels like to remember, or to be defined by memory.

However, as we noted in relation to the conventions of the *Bildungsroman*, it is a particular kind of memory that takes hold of the grown-up child protagonists of Roy's novel, not a happy or an enabling recollection of the past but a haunting memory of terrible events: instances of violence and death in which they are, or feel themselves to be, implicated. In relation to the distinctive repeating or 'spiralling' structure of the novel just discussed, we can think of the effect of memory in the following way: if you have ever listened to a piece of music on a vinyl record, you'll know that these analogue recordings scratch easily, and that the scratch can be heard as a repeated noise on the recording. (Sometimes, if badly scratched, the recording simply repeats a phrase or the same few notes over and over again.) Memory seems to work in this way in relation to the 'spiralling' narrative in *The God of Small Things*: as though running over a physical scratch in the material of the novel's time, the things that have happened to Estha and Rahel continually return to them, often unbidden, through memory.

You have already encountered traumatic memory as a literary subtext in the module materials on Edmund Blunden's *Undertones of War*. In fact, some of the writing we most strongly associate with the irrepressible return of disturbing images and negative memories of past events is war writing, and the delayed psychological effects of conflict in war veterans, termed 'Post Traumatic Stress Disorder' (or 'PTSD'), are now well known. In *The God of Small Things*, the kinds of recall that take place and the way that Estha and Rahel are helplessly shackled to their own memories conform to a 'post-traumatic' pattern, and some further reflection on trauma and its literary expression is therefore necessary.

Defining trauma

The word 'trauma' comes from Greek and has an original meaning of a 'wound'. In clinical medicine, a physical injury is called a 'trauma', but the more usual definition is that of a 'deeply distressing or disturbing experience', or of 'emotional shock following a stressful event' (Stevenson, 2015). The memory of a distressing experience is therefore something like a psychological 'wounding', but as the founder of psychoanalysis, Sigmund Freud, noted in his work, the characteristic experience of trauma is a return of the event to the sufferer: as nightmares in which they relive the trauma, as 'fateful' behavioural repetitions in their lives, or forms of flashback in which the trauma is vividly present again in the mind of the sufferer (in Part 3 of Freud's essay, 'Beyond the Pleasure Principle', first published as 'Jenseits des Lustprinzips' [1920], Freud, 2003, p. 60). To illustrate this process, Freud refers to a detail of a narrative poem, *Gerusalemme Liberata* (1581), by the sixteenth-century Italian poet Torquato Tasso. In the poem Tancred, a Christian knight involved in the first crusade, falls in love with a Muslim warrior, Clorinda. Then, when Clorinda disguises herself in another knight's armour, Tancred inadvertently kills her in a duel. After her burial, Tancred and his crusader knights find themselves in a magical forest, where Tancred slashes at a tree with his sword and is horrified when the wound gushes with blood and a voice, which sounds like Clorinda's, complains that he has wounded her again.

For critics interested in how literature can illuminate trauma, the Freudian example of Tasso's lovers is instructive because it presents trauma as a kind of double wound. Freud suggests that because trauma is so unexpected, so shocking, it cannot be assimilated (or 'processed') mentally and therefore returns to us: what returns to haunt the victim, these stories tell us, is not only the reality of the violent event but also the reality of the way its violence has yet to be fully known. As the critic Cathy Caruth argues:

> The returning traumatic dream perplexes Freud because it cannot be understood in terms of any wish or unconscious meaning, but is, purely and inexplicably, the literal return of the event against the will of the one it inhabits. Unlike the symptoms of a normal neurosis, whose painful manifestations can be understood

Figure 10.6 Louis Jean Lagrenee, *Tancred and Clorinda*, 1761, oil on canvas, 195 × 261 cm. Tretyakov Gallery, Moscow. Photo: Tretyakov Gallery/Bridgeman Images.

> ultimately in terms of the attempted avoidance of unpleasurable conflict, the painful repetition of the flashback can only be understood as the absolute inability of the mind to avoid an unpleasurable event that has not been given psychic meaning in any way.
>
> (Caruth, 1996, p. 59)

These insights into the structure of traumatic recall give us a way of thinking about the numerous repetitions of Roy's narrative in *The God of Small Things*. As something resistant to meaning, the shock of the traumatic event seems to inhibit later explanation or working out in language. (Recalling Blunden's writing, you might reflect here on the tendency of a whole generation of veterans of the First World War *not* to talk about their experiences.)

In Estha's case, two traumatic events in the novel have a silencing effect: the first is the incident in the lobby of the Abhilash Talkies cinema, when he is sexually abused by the Orangedrink Lemondrink Man. In the sudden unexpectedness of this event we, as readers, feel something of Estha's shock at finding himself not holding a '*moonbeam in [his] hand*' (p. 101) like the nuns at Maria's convent but, in an abusive, exploited situation, holding something else entirely. Like the other traumas of the novel, this one will be recalled throughout the novel by Estha, triggered by the sickly flavour of the fizzy 'Lemondrink'.

Figure 10.7 The exterior of the Raj Mandir Cinema in Jaipur, Rajasthan, India. Photo: 1Apix/Alamy.

The other traumatic experience that haunts and silences Estha is his betrayal of Velutha, which Baby Kochamma presents to both children as a necessary step in 'Saving Ammu', when actually it is to save their aunt from being charged for lodging a false report with the police:

> In the years to come they would replay this scene in their heads. As children. As teenagers. As adults …
>
> The inspector asked his question. Estha's mouth said Yes.

Childhood tiptoed out.
Silence slid in like a bolt.
Someone switched off the light and Velutha disappeared.

(pp. 318, 320)

The Judas-like betrayal that Estha is forced into by his aunt is directly connected here to the 'wounding' experience of seeing Velutha's grotesquely mutilated body in the police station. In both instances, the trauma that causes a kind of narrative recurrence is not directly physical, but is highly damaging in other ways. The critical theorist Judith Butler explains the effects of violence in the following way: 'Violence is surely a touch of the worst order, a way in which the human vulnerability to other humans is exposed in its most terrifying way, a way in which we are given over, without control, to the will of another' (Butler, 2006, pp. 28–9). Estha is not the actual victim of this violence, but witnessing its terror in this way, he becomes ethically and psychologically implicated in it, to such an unbearable extent that he must convince himself and Rahel that he really saw the body of Velutha's brother Urumban, and that Velutha has 'Escaped to Africa' (p. 320). As readers we realise that this desperate switching strategy will not work, and that later, the scene will return to both twins in the psychological replaying described above. Indeed, the traumatic moment of betrayal marks the exact moment at which innocence and 'childhood' depart from Estha and Rahel's lives.

Conclusion

The pattern of repetitions and 'returns' that cuts through and across *The God of Small Things* is a storytelling technique that reflects the workings of post-traumatic memory in the way it scrambles a linear arrangement of events and fragments the main narrative. In some instances, this means that Roy's writing is highly attuned to objects as linguistic 'signifiers', and we will be discussing language in *The God of Small Things* in further detail in the following chapter. Like the resonance of the scattered objects 'found' after an accident or a disaster, the objects (especially 'small' childhood objects) and phrases scattered through the novel have an associative force that enhances the narrative. We should note that in some cases, however, repetition is connected to trauma in opposite ways. Explaining her use of rhymes and repetitions, Roy states that they were included, in part, to insulate us against the horror of what has happened: 'Repetition [was] used because it made me feel safe. Repeated words and phrases have a rocking feeling, like a lullaby. They help take away the shock of the plot' (Jana, 1997). Far from contradicting our earlier discussion of memory and trauma, however, this insight deepens our understanding of how the novel recreates a narrative response to a highly traumatic event: as return, as recurrence and in forms of silence and inventive linguistic evasion.

References

Set text

Roy, A. (2017) *The god of small things.* London: 4th Estate.

Other references

Alexandru, M-S. (2007) 'Towards a politics of the small things: Arundhati Roy and the decentralization of authorship', in Hadjiafxendi, K. and Mackay, P. (eds) *Authorship in context: from the theoretical to the material.* Houndmills: Palgrave Macmillan.

Baneth-Nouailhetas, E. (2007) 'The structures of memory', in Tickell, A. *Arundhati Roy's the god of small things: a reader's guide.* Abingdon: Routledge. Available online via the OU Library.

Butler, J. (2004) *Precarious life: the powers of mourning and violence.* London: Verso.

Caruth, C. (1996) *Unclaimed experience: trauma, narrative and history.* Baltimore, Md: Johns Hopkins. Available online via the OU Library.

Freud, S. (2003) *Beyond the pleasure principle and other writings.* Translated by J. Reddick. London: Penguin.

Jana, R. (1997) 'Arundhati Roy', *Salon*, 30 September. Available at: https://www.salon.com/1997/09/30/00roy/ (Accessed: 11 April 2019).

O'Flaherty, W. (ed.) (1975) *Hindu myths.* Translated by W. O'Flaherty. Harmondsworth: Penguin.

Roy, A. (2001) *Power politics.* 2nd edn. Cambridge, Mass.: South End Press.

Roy, A. (2003) *In which Annie gives it those ones: the original screenplay.* New Delhi: Penguin.

Roy, A. (2004) *The ordinary person's guide to empire.* London: HarperCollins Flamingo.

Stevenson, A. (ed.) (2015) 'Trauma' in *Oxford dictionary of English* (2010). Available at https://www-oxfordreference-com.libezproxy.open.ac.uk/view/10.1093/acref/9780199571123.001.0001/m_en_gb0878840 (Accessed 18 June 2019).

Tickell, A. (2003) '*The god of small things*: Arundhati Roy's postcolonial cosmopolitanism', *Journal of Commonwealth Literature*, 38(1), pp. 73–89. Available online via the OU Library.

Tickell, A. (2007) *Arundhati Roy's the god of small things: a reader's guide*. Abingdon: Routledge. Available online via the OU Library.

Chapter 11 Arundhati Roy, *The God of Small Things*: Questioning realism

Alex Tickell

Contents

Introduction

In the final chapter in the 'Realism' book of the module we will be continuing our discussion of Arundhati Roy's novel *The God of Small Things*, and asking how it challenges and modifies our understanding of realism in contemporary global or postcolonial fiction. Additionally, we will be thinking about Roy's use of child perspectives and her manipulation of language in the novel. We'll also consider how she incorporates non-realist elements from other genres into her work. At this point, you may want to return to the Introduction to Book 1 and reread the summary of realism there. Remember that while realism is often associated with the rise of the novel in the eighteenth and nineteenth centuries, it has never really stopped being a widespread literary mode; instead, through the twentieth and into the twenty-first century, literary realism has proliferated and transformed into different hyphenated forms. In this sense, it is incredibly fluid and adaptable. As one critic points out, it is unlike other kinds of writing: 'it cannot be a genre; instead, it makes other forms of fiction seem like genres … it teaches everyone else; it schools its own truants: it is what allows magical realism, hysterical realism, fantasy, science fiction, even thrillers to exist' (Wood, 2008, p. 186).

Cultural difference and realism

With these insights in mind, there are two things to be noted about realism in relation to Roy's *The God of Small Things*. The first of these is what we might call the concealed 'artificiality' of realism: the way it seems to present itself as a transparent window on the world and almost convinces us that it is not a style at all. To take one dismissive critical comment about realism: '[it is a] mind-set that allows us to think that pictures [representations] of the world are not pictures but the world itself' (Natoli, quoted in Beaumont, 2010, p. 9). You may have realised that it is not really possible to dismiss realism in this way, and that when we look closely at realist novels, we find that they do sometimes incorporate self-conscious formal and stylistic effects. However, what we must remember here is that, as readers, we have become so accustomed to realism's conventions – its focus on ordinary lives, its detailing and its *apparent* lack of linguistic 'artifice' – that we no longer notice them, even though they were once startling, innovative developments. In contrast, Roy's writing draws our attention to the constructedness of fiction through language and is indebted to exactly the creative energies (often associated with forms of experimental writing related to literary modernism) that challenged realism. As a novel by a multilingual Indian writer, Roy's fiction also has a special, self-consciously postcolonial relationship to language that we will discuss in more detail later.

The second point to be made about realism in *The God of Small Things* is the issue of the novel's cultural and geographical location. In the previous chapter, we noted that the majority of the works you will cover on this module are by European or North American authors, and that Roy's novel is the first work you have encountered here by an Indian writer. Roy's novel could, moreover, be said to present the real in ways that might seem 'unreal' to a non-Indian audience. For instance, as the Ipe family return from meeting their British visitors at Cochin airport in Chapter 6, 'Cochin Kangaroos', they see a dead elephant at the side of the road, which had been accidentally electrocuted by a high-tension cable. The scene gives Roy's authorial voice the chance to comment on the family's reaction (they wonder if it is Kochu Thomban, their local temple elephant), and then to reflect that compassion is delicately calibrated around familiarity (they are relieved it is *not* Kochu Thomban). In a novel by Edith Wharton or Thomas Hardy, the appearance of a dead elephant on the roadside would give us pause and make us wonder if the plot involved a circus or a zoo; it would certainly make the narrative seem strange and slightly 'unreal'. Reading Roy's novel we know, or assume from its context, that the scene is quite plausible, but if we are unfamiliar with the south Indian setting, this detail is still significant. Like Sophie Mol, who has just arrived in Kerala, we may well register the dead elephant as something exciting and remarkable.

When we consider the long tradition in English writing of presenting India as a land of enchantment and mystery, and also take into account trends in the formal developments of the Indian novel in English *before* Roy's *The God of Small Things,* the question of how we define and categorise realism in so-called postcolonial or global fiction becomes more complex. Before Roy, the best-known Indian writer internationally was Salman Rushdie (1947–), an author who is now credited with revolutionising the Indian novel in English with his *Midnight's Children* (1981), and starting a boom in South Asian fiction in English (Rajan, 2019, p. 3). One of Rushdie's achievements was to write about the history of modern India in a style called **magical realism**: a mode of writing in which everyday events and more or less conventional characters coexist with the supernatural and with fantastical figures or occurrences.

Beginning as a term used to describe certain kinds of German pictorial art of the 1920s, the 'magically real' in fiction is associated with some European writers of the post-war period such as Günter Grass (1927–2015) and, more often, with Latin American authors of the 1960s and 70s such as Isabel Allende (1942–) and Gabriel García Márquez (1927–2014) (Bowers, 2004). Rushdie successfully adapted the techniques of magical realism to his subcontinental, largely Indian, context, and in his novels children acquire exceptional powers, metaphors are literalised, history is mythologised, and enchantments have actual effects. Magical realism is, it has been argued, a kind of writing well suited to 'complex and traumatic historical themes' (Mullan, 2006, p. 188); notably, when we remember how *The God of Small Things* challenges classification and ordering, magical realism has also been defined as a mode of writing 'suited to exploring – and transgressing – boundaries, whether the boundaries are ontological, political, geographical, or generic' (Zamora and Faris, 1995, p. 5). In this sense we might say that magical realism challenges the stability of accepted views of the world, especially views that depend on ideas of purity and separation (Bowers, 2004, p. 4).

Figure 11.1 Diego Rivera, *Dream of a Sunday Afternoon in the Alameda Central*, 1947, mural, oil on board, 470 × 1560 cm. Museo Mural Diego Rivera, Mexico City. Photo: bimages/Alamy. © Banco de México Diego Rivera Frida Kahlo Museums Trust, Mexico, D.F./DACS 2019.

Activity 11.1

Allow around 10 minutes to complete this activity

On this module you have already encountered a set text that manipulates what we think of as the 'real': Ali Smith's *Hotel World*, with its 'posthumous' narrative perspective. Now think about Roy's *The God of Small Things* and list instances in which Roy seems to introduce magical or supernatural elements into her work.

Discussion

You'll soon realise that there are comparatively few instances of magical or miraculous occurrences in *The God of Small Things*. However, a key scene is in Chapter 1, 'Paradise Pickles & Preserves', when the dead Sophie Mol appears to come alive at her own funeral: '[Rahel] heard the dullthudding through the polished coffin wood, through the satin coffin lining … Inside the earth Sophie Mol screamed, and shredded satin with her teeth. But you can't hear screams through earth and stone' (p. 7).

Also, in the high dome of the church, which is painted to look like the sky, a baby bat turns into 'a jet plane without a crisscrossed trail' (p. 6).

You may recall that, as twins, Estha and Rahel share a form of telepathic connection. Rahel tastes the sandwiches that *Estha* eats on the Madras Mail to Madras (p. 3), and at the Hotel Sea Queen she opens a door for her brother without knowing of his arrival – an extrasensory skill that no longer disconcerts their uncle: 'Chacko didn't bother to wonder how she could possibly have known that Estha was at the door. He was used to their sometimes strangeness' (p. 119).

However, if we read closely, then the details discussed here can also be seen as projections of Estha's and Rahel's highly imaginative child perspectives. For instance, the scene at Sophie Mol's funeral in the church is coloured by Rahel's vivid imagination and its effects: Sophie Mol's 'secret cartwheel' inside her coffin can be attributed to Rahel's *perception* of events. Moreover, the well-known 'telepathic' connection that some twins report, which the Ipe children betray in opening the hotel door, is just convincing enough to remain on the non-magical side of the 'real'.

Figure 11.2 Holy Cross Church, Cavelossim, South Goa, India. Photo: Dinodia Photos/Alamy.

While literary critics usually avoid relying too much on an author's views about their own work, Roy's unequivocal comments about the 'magical realist' label (and what she thinks of her critics) are useful here:

> we are used to thinking that critics judge books but I sometimes think the creatures and characters in the book will judge the critic. The fact is that yes [my writing] is not a realism that people, say, in the West, are used to, but there is nothing magical about [it] … There are ways in which power *absolves* itself, in very sophisticated ways, and … calling [my writing] magical realism is one of those ways.
>
> (Waterstones, 2017)

The self-'absolving' power that Roy talks about in the interview quoted above is the power of institutions, experts and dominant social groups to arrange and categorise our view of the world, and you know from the material you have read so far that this is a theme of *The God of Small Things*. Naming something is an expression of power; postcolonial theorists have pointed out that this extends to calling something 'magical' or 'strange' because we don't understand it, or preserving a 'sanctioned ignorance' about cultural difference (Spivak, 1999, p. 164). Ultimately, the point we should draw from these insights is that we need to use labels like 'realism' and 'magical realism' judiciously, because they can be more reflective of our own assumptions than of the fictional work itself. In the next section, we will look at Roy's use of child viewpoints and her interest in linguistic manipulation as areas of her work that prompt us to question our ideas about literary realism further.

Childhood, language, perspective

An outstanding feature of *The God of Small Things* is Roy's presentation of children's perspectives in the novel, especially her attention to the ways in which children manipulate and play with language. Roy describes language as 'the skin of my thought' (Tickell, 2007, p. 7) and – although this is a slightly enigmatic statement – we might understand it as Roy's way of registering her sensitivity to the 'feel' of words, and to the versatility and expressiveness of language. As I have noted elsewhere (Tickell, 2007), *The God of Small Things* is a novel that could be said to 'hoard' words and play with them in the same way that children sometimes make collections of toys and found objects (p. 7). Roy's novel 'finds' and collects puzzling phrases, neologisms, road signs, rhymes and quotations from other literary works, and rearranges them, scattering them through its chapters.

If we concentrate on a single passage in Chapter 6, 'Cochin Kangaroos', in which the Ipe family meet Margaret Kochamma and Sophie Mol at Cochin airport, it is possible to analyse some of the finer details of Roy's distinctive use of language. Here, both Estha and Rahel – who have been dressed up for the occasion to become what Roy's authorial voice tells us are 'Two-Egg Twin Ambassadors' – disappoint their mother by misbehaving and failing to play their parts in the welcoming performance:

> 'Go on,' Ammu said to Estha. 'How do YOU do?'
>
> Estha's sleepy eyes were stubborn.
>
> In Malayalam Ammu said, 'Did you hear what I said?'
>
> Ambassador Estha felt bluegreyblue eyes on him … He didn't have a How do YOU do? in him.
>
> 'Esthappen!' Ammu said. And an angry feeling rose in her and stopped around her heart. A Far More Angry Than Necessary feeling … She had wanted a smooth performance. A prize for her children in the Indo-British Behaviour Competition.
>
> Chacko said to Ammu in Malayalam, 'Please. Later. Not now'
>
> And Ammu's angry eyes on Estha said, *All right. Later.*
>
> And Later became a horrible, menacing, goose-bumpy word.
>
> Lay. Ter.

> Like a deep-sounding bell in a mossy well. Shivery, and furred. Like moth's feet.
>
> (pp. 145–6)

This exchange demonstrates many of Roy's techniques, including: her use of capitalisation ('Far More Angry Than Necessary'); her tendency to break up words for emphasis ('Lay. Ter.'); as well as her manipulation or running together of adjectives ('bluegreyblue'). Notice, too, that many of the coinages are childlike ('goose-bumpy') in their simple but striking addition of a 'y' to a noun or verb. Roy uses a similar construction when we witness Chacko's humiliation a little later from Estha's perspective: 'Ambassador Estha saw (with stubborn eyes) that Chacko's suit was suddenly looser, less bursty' (p. 147). 'Bursty' is especially telling here, because even though it is a completely unfamiliar word in isolation, the idiomatic association of 'bursting' with 'pride' makes us realise that Estha's uncle is suddenly less proud, and is embarrassed and deflated. Returning to the passage, the threat of the word 'later' is also almost palpable and reminds us that the process of language learning, especially in childhood, can involve a form of synaesthesia (a sense association of one thing with another: for some people this can mean that colours have a particular taste, or letters of the alphabet 'feel' a certain way). From the perspective of Roy's child characters, 'Lay. Ter.' takes on this associative force when Estha likens it, poetically, to a 'deep sounding bell in a mossy well'. Roy adds further symbolic weight with the simile 'moth's feet', which reminds us of the story of 'Pappachi's moth' and recalls the Ipe family's long-standing 'problem with classification', conveying a general all-encompassing feeling of wrongness.

As we can begin to tell from the passage quoted above, Roy's writing is attuned to how our subjectivity (our sense of self) and our perception of the 'real' world is filtered and shaped by our language use. Debates about exactly these issues had a profound influence on **literary theory** in the 1980s and 90s, and we will review these ideas briefly here, and then come back to think about their relevance to *The God of Small Things*.

From the mid-1950s onwards, literary and cultural critics became increasingly interested in how language worked as a system of grammatical rules and a set of words standing for things (termed 'signs'). They asked if similar cultural 'systems', such as fashion or advertising (Barthes, 2009), could also be seen to work like a language, and this approach became known as '**semiotics**'. (You don't need to know about semiotics in detail for this module, but if you are interested in learning more, you can look up 'semiotics' and 'structuralism' using one of the reference works available online through the Open University Library).

Semiotics was developed on a basic understanding of language as: (a) arbitrary; (b) relational; and (c) constitutive. You will know that language is *arbitrary* if you have ever learned a second language, because in doing so, you immediately realise that there is nothing that fixes the word 'tree' to a thing with a trunk, branches and leaves, except our collective agreement, as English speakers, that we will use this word. (In other language communities, everyone has agreed on a different word for 'tree'.) Words in a language are also *relational*, in that they take their meaning from other, similar words: if you look up the word 'tree' in a dictionary, you'll be given synonyms such as 'woody plant' within the definition. Lastly, language is *constitutive* because its rules and vocabulary shape the way we see the world: we might imagine that some languages 'understand' trees differently from the English meaning of 'tree'. These insights about language were used by a later generation of post-structuralist critics to think about the way language makes truth provisional.

Remember in the previous chapter, in connection with the theme of classification, we noted how the banana jam made in Mammachi's factory is considered illegal by the Food Products Organization (FPO) because it is unclassifiable: 'too thin for jelly and too thick for jam' (p. 30). Roy's immediate point here is that the whole Ipe family 'breaks rules', but her underlying insight is that power operates through labelling, categorising and rule enforcement through language. As we all know, or once knew but have forgotten, children are particularly sensitive to how language defines rules in certain ways: as they meet Sophie Mol and Margaret Kochamma in the airport arrivals lounge, Estha and Rahel are expected to say certain things ('How do you do?') and act in a certain way – definitely not remaining silent or ravelling themselves in dirty airport curtains. As adults, we have more or less internalised these rules, but for children, they still appear arbitrary and imposed. (Ammu's concern that her children behave well and follow rules of politeness is, as we realise here, partly a reflection of her own frustration that Estha and Rahel, as the children of a divorcee, can never live up to local standards of respectability.)

There are two sets of rules to be considered here, then: the rules of vocabulary, grammar and syntax, which make language intelligible; and the 'social' rules that are carried *in* language, which shape our world and compel us to act and behave in particular ways. Psychoanalysts such as Jacques Lacan (1901–1981) – who built on Freud's work and was influenced by some of the ideas about language summarised earlier – suggested that it is when we acquire language as children that we start to see ourselves as 'selves', and as subject to social rules. On these terms, language is an ambiguous gift: like some well-known forms of social media, it enables us to communicate for free but once we accept it, it 'colonises' us and prompts us to act in certain 'symbolic' ways (Žižek, 2006, p. 12). Because children are still effectively learning and acquiring language when at Estha and Rahel's age, it could be argued that they occupy a different, potentially freer position in relation to both the grammatical rules of language and the social rules carried in language.

In fact, one of the most gleeful discoveries children make as they acquire language is the ability to manipulate language in rhymes or puns; introducing tabooed or 'naughty' words into speech also brings the realisation that the mere act of saying something has an effect, an impact, in the real world. Deliberately saying the wrong thing, or saying the right thing in the wrong way, is also traditionally one of the few weapons available to the weak: to those who are disenfranchised or marginalised in society. In *The God of Small Things*, it is exactly this power over language that gets the Ipe children into trouble, when they read backwards to Miss Mitten – Baby Kochamma's Australian missionary friend – who interprets the act as ungodly and blasphemous: 'Miss Mitten complained to Baby Kochamma about Estha's rudeness, and about their reading backwards. She told Baby Kochamma that she had seen Satan in their eyes. *nataS in their seye*' (p. 60). Roy's writing involves a subtle irony here, because the phrase that Miss Mitten uses to demonise the twins' backwards reading is partly reversed in the italicised clause, so that we also read it backwards, just as Estha and Rahel have done.

Throughout *The God of Small Things*, then, the twins' playful response to language is also a way of undermining authority and rebelling against certain kinds of received thought. Going further, we can also note how the numerous perspectives and voices in the novel counteract the certainties of any one point of view, such as Miss Mitten's categorical statement, or the wider social and religious 'laws' that operate through a process of imposing a single, fixed world view. The Russian critic Mikhail M. Bakhtin saw this '**dialogic**' multiplicity of voices as one of the most radical features of the novel form (Bakhtin, 1981). It is worth reflecting on how religious works such as the *Manusmriti*, which defines the love laws, admit nothing but a single authoritative voice. At the start of *The God of Small Things*, Roy's epigraph quotes the art critic John Berger – 'Never again will a single story be told as though it's the only one' – and this sentiment is apt when we recall both the narrative complexity of Roy's novel, as discussed previously, and the different voices and points of view that make up the story.

Linguistic complexity and the condition of being many-voiced are also common features of postcolonial writing. As you saw in the previous chapter, British colonialism involved the imposition of the English language as an elite *lingua franca*, and in postcolonial countries once governed by the British, English is now often spoken alongside other state and regional languages. This multilingual experience is apparent in Roy's novel: think again about the scene at Cochin airport we examined earlier. You might have noticed that, during the meeting, the Ipe family speak to their British relatives in English, as part of the welcome 'performance'. However, they speak to each other in Malayalam – the state language of Kerala – when they are angry and don't want their visitors to understand them. This bilingualism gives us some sense of the higher status of English in this situation, and in several scenes in *The God of Small Things*, the cultural worth of English is affirmed through references to, and recitals of, canonical literary works. At the airport, it is Baby Kochamma who recites Ariel's soliloquy from Shakespeare's most 'colonial' play, *The Tempest* – a work you will be studying later on this module – to 'announce her credentials to Margaret Kochamma' and 'set herself apart from the Sweeper Class' (p. 144). Elsewhere, K. N. M. Pillai's niece, Latha, gives a startling recitation of 'Lochinvar' from Walter Scott's *Marmion*: '*O, young Lochin varhas scum out of the vest, / Through wall the vide Border his teed was the bes'* (p. 271). These instances may seem like slightly comical 'Anglophile' attempts at mimicry, but recalling the covert power involved in such repetitions or reiterations of language, we might also see a writing or speaking back to the former authority of the coloniser in these recitals and performances.

Incorporating the fantastic (1): fairy tales and ghost stories

The playful appropriation of language in Roy's novel, outlined in the previous section, brings us back to our initial questions about realism. Many of Roy's experiments and formal innovations are reminiscent of the work of modernist writers such as James Joyce (1882–1941) and William Faulkner (1897–1962), who challenged the conventional 'objectivity' of realism. Given these influences, and taking into account our earlier reflections on magical realism, it may be necessary to find a more accurate label for Roy's style: perhaps we could think of *The God of Small Things* as an example of 'heightened' or 'enhanced' realism. What we must remember, however, is that this enhancement is gained primarily through Roy's attention to the different kinds of awareness that children have of the world.

The enhanced realism of *The God of Small Things* is also an effect of what critics call 'free indirect style' in fiction. This is a technique you have already learned about in your earlier reading of Edith Wharton's *The Custom of the Country* and Ali Smith's *Hotel World*. It is sufficient here to remind ourselves that free indirect style allows a third-person narrative to take on aspects of a first-person point of view. Free indirect style was a development in realist fiction but is now so widely used by writers that it cannot be closely associated with any one mode of fiction. The reason for its prevalence is because it allows authors to expand the views and perceptions of a single character so that they shape the wider narrative texture of the story. In *The God of Small Things*, the point of view is so often that of a child that even when we read the odd-numbered chapters – which feature the adult Ipe children – the overarching effect of free indirect style is one of a child's view of the world. Additionally, in Roy's novel, free indirect style incorporates the fantastic as a matter of course because, for children, ghosts and monsters *might* be possible and are half-believed in.

We can see how this technique works if we look at the start of Chapter 9, 'Mrs Pillai, Mrs Eapen, Mrs Rajagopalan'. Here, the adult Rahel contemplates Baby Kochamma's abandoned garden:

> The green-for-the-day had seeped from the trees …
>
> A squadron of fruit bats sped across the gloom.

> In the abandoned ornamental garden, Rahel, watched by lolling dwarves and a forsaken cherub, squatted by the stagnant pond and watched toads hop from stone to scummy stone. Beautiful Ugly Toads.
>
> Slimy. Warty. Croaking.
>
> Yearning, unkissed princes trapped inside them. Food for snakes that lurked in the long June grass. Rustle. Lunge. No more toad to hop from stone to scummy stone. No more prince to kiss.
>
> (p. 187)

It is evident here that while the third-person narration shares the point of view of the *adult* Rahel in this chapter, it also employs techniques that we associate with the childlike point of view in the sections of the novel focalised on the Ipe *children*. A colour called 'green-for-the-day' is something we might expect a child to notice – that trees only remain green in daylight – and the extraordinary effect is enhanced when we read that Rahel is being 'watched' by 'lolling dwarves' and a 'forsaken cherub'. Before we recall that Baby Kochamma's garden contains ornamental gnomes, this line unsettles, and presents us with a fantastic tableau in which Rahel coexists, for a moment, with dwarves and cherubs. Moreover, when she watches the 'Beautiful Ugly Toads', Rahel thinks of them as a child would: with 'unkissed princes trapped inside them', which is a reference to the fairy tale of the Frog Prince (one of the first stories collected by the Brothers Grimm as 'Der Froschkönig oder der eiserne Heinrich', literally 'The Frog King, or Iron Henry').

Here, the traditionally happy outcome of the fairy tale is curtailed abruptly by the unalterable fact that toads are food for snakes. The scene therefore works as a kind of critique of the naïvety of the fairy tale, reminding us once again that it is the disillusioned, adult Rahel who watches the toads, and who knows that the biological will triumph over the fictional. Yet even here, as Roy breaks the imaginary spell of the fairy tale, the reality of the toads' deaths is conveyed in a childlike way, with an emphatic note on their sudden disappearance: 'No more toad … No more prince' (p. 187). More generally, this scene reminds us that in *The God of Small Things*, there will be no miraculous transfiguration, and that here unexpected romances rarely end happily ever after. You will be studying fairy tales in more detail in Part Two of the module, so we will only look at the genre briefly here in relation to *The God of Small Things*. Reflecting on the origins of fairy tale, the

Figure 11.3 Derelict colonial house, Mumbai, India. Photo: Alex Tickell.

critic Jack Zipes shows how they dramatise the stark realities of power politics, the 'violence and brutality of everyday life' (1979, p. 29), and other critics have identified formulaic structures in the fairy tale. As we have seen, Roy's novel is alive to everyday violence, and her characterisation can be mapped on to the fairy tale 'format' so that Baby Kochamma becomes the wicked fairy or evil stepmother, Ammu is the confined princess, Velutha is the servant turned hero, and Estha and Rahel are lost children. These connections are incidental, but they show us how other genres exist almost subliminally in Roy's novel.

While the fairy tale of the Frog King is invoked in the main narrative of *The God of Small Things*, another self-consciously 'unreal' genre – the ghost story – is incorporated as a story-within-a-story in Roy's novel. This ghostly narrative concerns the abandoned rubber plantation house across the river, and the paedophile British planter who once lived there: Kari Saipu, a cigar-smoking Englishman 'who had "gone native'" (p. 52) and eventually committed suicide after having an affair with a local boy. Vellya Paapen – Velutha's partly blind, superstitious father – tells Estha and Rahel how he swam across the river to gather nutmegs at the old plantation house and encountered Kari Saipu's ghost, and how he pinned the ghost to a rubber tree by throwing his sickle at it: 'Vellya Paapen … had the satisfaction of knowing that his lightning-quick reflexes … had put an end to the bloodthirsty wanderings of a paedophile ghost. As long as no one succumbed to its artifice and unsickled it with a cigar' (p. 199). (Note the plot detail here about not 'freeing' the ghost by giving him a cigar – an injunction that is reminiscent of fairy tale plots in which such warnings are always unheeded.) Because the Kari Saipu ghost story is an embedded narrative told by Vellya Paapen we, as readers, can choose to believe it (as its internal audience, the Ipe children, probably do), or disbelieve it as the made-up bragging of a marginalised character.

However, here again – as with the passing, indirect reference to the fairy tale of the Frog King – the boundaries between the **frame story** and the story within the novel are blurry. The supernatural elements of *The God of Small Things* challenge narrative containment, seeping into and overgrowing the world of the main story like the irrepressible creepers and snaking pepper vines described in the novel's opening page. In thinking about the ghostly aspects of the novel, it is important to remember that many postcolonial writers have conveyed the damaging experience of living in the aftermath of colonialism as a kind of haunting or a general feeling of uncertainty or un-homeliness. *The God of Small Things* is no exception, and you will remember that Estha and Rahel connect the creepy figurative image of the 'History House' that Chacko uses to explain postcolonial history to them with the actual 'haunted' plantation house across the river that once belonged to Kari Saipu. You may also recognise another unsettling colonial story in the naming of the house as the 'Heart of Darkness', the title of Joseph Conrad's 1899 novella of colonising obsession and madness in the Belgian Congo – a connection which is reinforced by Roy's description of Kari Saipu as 'Ayemenem's own Kurtz' (p. 52), a reference to Conrad's character.

Reflecting on the ghost story elements of Roy's novel more generally, however, we can see that the frightening effects of the embedded ghostly narrative are used to foreshadow the terror of later actual events, using the technique of prolepsis or 'flash forward'. Roy's point here is that the truly terrifying story Vellya Paapen narrates is not the one about Kari Saipu's ghost that he tells to the Ipe children, but the true 'story' he confesses to Mammachi about his son's forbidden affair with her daughter Ammu, also conducted in the derelict plantation house, which leads to Velutha's fatal beating by the police in the back verandah of the same building. As we have already established, this event sets up a kind of traumatic 'haunting' of the main characters and is itself a sort of ghost story. In other figures too, elements of the ghostly creep into Roy's novel: in the image of Baby Kochamma's abandoned garden (like the arrested overgrown world of Miss Havisham's Satis House in Charles Dickens' *Great Expectations*); and in the persistence of an ancestral past and the close coexistence of death with the strangely arrested lives of the Ipe children.

Figure 11.4 Illustration from the story of the Rabbit and the Elephant King, from the Arabic text *Kalila and Dimna, or The Fables of Bidpai*. Photo: Niday Picture Library/Alamy.

Incorporating the fantastic (2): fable and myth

It is not only European pre-novelistic traditions and non-realist genres that inform *The God of Small Things*: elements of the fantastic are also apparent in the novel's debt to Indian narratives, especially forms of fable and myth. You may already have noticed how animals inhabit the imagined world of Roy's rural Kerala. Similarly, we find animals incorporated into ancient South Asian story cycles such as the *Panchatantra*, which could have been conceived as early as 100 BCE, allegedly to teach statecraft to Indian princes. The *Panchatantra* is technically a set of beast fables (you may be familiar with the form in *Aesop's Fables*): a type of short story in which the main characters are anthropomorphised animals whose actions convey a moral truth. In *The God of Small Things*, Estha and Rahel listen to Ammu reciting another famous beast fable, set in India: Rudyard Kipling's *The Jungle Book* (1894), in which the abandoned child Mowgli is raised by animals and learns the law of the Jungle. There is some correspondence between Kipling's *The Jungle Book* and Roy's novel (for instance, both works show a concern over various kinds of laws and what happens when they are broken), but their broader equivalence is in the dramatic power of a world filled with animals, and the interaction of children with that world.

Activity 11.2

Allow around 20 minutes to complete this activity

Roy's novel is unusual among contemporary South Asian fictions in its detailed account of the natural world and the animals that populate its rural Kerala setting. Review your reading of the novel and think about how animals appear in the narrative. How are they presented and what figurative or symbolic meanings, if any, do they convey?

Discussion

You may have noticed that in the final chapter, detailing Ammu and Velutha's secret meetings, a tiny spider fascinates them: 'They checked on him every night … to see if he had survived the day. They fretted over his frailty. His smallness … His seemingly self-destructive pride' (p. 339). In some form then, the tiny spider becomes a token for the lovers: a thing in which they invest their own hopes, and a representation of the fragility and danger of their relationship. As a development of the title motif of 'small things', the spider may also be Roy's way of emphasising the relative importance of things that are normally overlooked or neglected. Elsewhere in the novel, such as when Estha and Rahel overturn the old wooden vallom – the boat in which they will try to cross the river with Sophie Mol – the exposed insects underneath become, momentarily, the characters in an anthropomorphic children's story: 'White termites on their way to work. White ladybirds on their way home ... White grasshoppers with whitewood violins' (p. 202).

While Roy makes reference to fables such as *The Jungle Book*, and anthropomorphises animals in certain situations, it is also possible to make a case that her writing often simply tries to capture, with great concision, the texture and detailing of nature. When Rahel is lying awake during her 'Afternoon Gnap', she senses the natural world as a series of sounds and images:

> The yellow wasp wasping against the windowpane in a dangerous dzzzz.
> A disbelieving lizard's blink.
> High-stepping chickens in the yard
> ...
> Red ants on yellow stones.
> A hot cow feeling hot. *Amhoo*. In the distance.
>
> (p. 201)

Anthropomorphised animals and hybrid creatures are also present in Hindu mythology: another point of connection and crossover between nominally realist aspects of Roy's fiction, its setting and the much older narrative traditions of the subcontinent. In probably the most famous early statement on the challenges of writing an Indian novel in English, published in 1937, the author Raja Rao (1908–2006) tells us that the Indian countryside is steeped in Hindu myth: 'There is no village in India, however mean, that has not a rich *sthala-purana*, or legendary history, of its own. Some god or godlike hero has passed by the village – Rama might have rested under this pipal-tree, Sita might have dried her clothes, after her bath, on this yellow stone' (Rao, 1993, Foreword). Rao goes on to note how the 'presence' of myth has a transhistorical aspect: 'In this way the past mingles with the present, and the gods mingle with men [sic] to make the repertory of your grand-mother

Figure 11.5 Mural on temple wall of the Hindu elephant god, Ganesh. Photo: Louise Batalla Duran/Alamy.

always bright' (Rao, 1993, Foreword). Facing the problem identified by Rao of how to convey the spirit of an Indian narrative in English, many twentieth-century Indian authors have used Hindu religious mythology – derived from the great Sanskrit epic poems, the *Mahabharata* and *Ramayana* – to ground their novels in an Indian context.

Previously, in discussing narrative structure and storytelling techniques in *The God of Small Things*, we saw how representations of the 'Great [mythical] Stories' of the Kathakali drama reflect Roy's interest in non-linear forms of storytelling, and in writing a novel that 'feels' like a myth: a novel that resembles 'the [stories] you can enter anywhere and inhabit comfortably' (Roy, 2017, p. 229). Of equal importance is the shaping or warping of our sense of the real by these mythical dramatic inter-texts. Like the story of Kari Saipu, the mythical narrative based on episodes from the *Mahabharata* (Tickell, 2007, p. 44) is bracketed from the main story in the actual night-long Kathakali performance the children watch, described in Chapter 12, 'Kochu Thomban'. A set of correspondences develops in this chapter between the figures of the Kathakali actors as storytellers – whose bodies '[have] been planed and polished, pared down, harnessed wholly to the task of story-telling' (Roy, 2017, p. 230) – and Roy as a different kind of storyteller (Tickell, 2003). (Roy's predicament, as an Indian novelist writing in English, is arguably reflected in the two performances the Kathakali men put on: one a humiliating 'truncated' poolside performance for foreign tourists; and the other a night-long play performed in the temple to 'ask pardon of their gods' (p. 229).) We will not explore these internal reflections in detail here, except to note that through them, Roy's novel betrays an awareness of the comparative distance between so-called 'traditional', ritualised modes of storytelling – like mythical Kathakali drama – and the different situation of the contemporary postcolonial author.

As we might expect, however, as soon as any distinctions are made between the 'real' and the 'mythical', Roy challenges them, in a subtle mythologising of the everyday world of Kerala. Roy's title is instructive here, as it points to her technique of weighting 'small things' and marginal characters with a transcendent quasi-religious significance. The 'God of Small Things' appears as a one-armed man in Ammu's dreams, and is associated with Velutha, who can be read both as a Christ figure and as reminiscent of the 'little gods' of devotional Hinduism. Elsewhere figures are described which become mythical in their symbolism, such as the 'Earth Woman', whom Chacko invents as a way of explaining the age of the world. More obviously, perhaps, Roy's well-documented environmental concerns (Mukherjee, 2010, p. 102) are signalled 'mythically' in the way she represents the local Meenachal river as a goddess. In the 1969 sections of the novel, the river is untamed, and takes Sophie Mol's life stealthily, almost as a sacrificial gift: 'There was no storm-music … Just a quiet handing over ceremony. A boat spilling its cargo. A river accepting the offering' (p. 293). However, by the 'present-day' sections of the novel, the Meenachal river has been reduced and 'demythologised' by modernity, in the form of a saltwater barrage built further upriver to increase Kerala's agricultural production, which has diminished it to a polluted stream: 'Once it had had the power to evoke fear. To change lives. But now its teeth were drawn, its spirit spent. It was just a slow, sludging green ribbon lawn that ferried fetid garbage to the sea' (p. 124).

The 'mythologising' characterisation of the river in this way is part of Roy's far-reaching critique of the effects of globalisation on Kerala, few of which are positive. In fact, the loss of the Meenachal – as a complex riverine ecosystem understood and respected by both the Ipe children and the fisher people who live on its banks – is one of the contextual tragedies of the novel. Roy suggests that instead of an intimate understanding of nature and a deep localised familiarity with myth as the 'Great Stories', the inhabitants of Ayemenem now have exploitative jobs in the Persian Gulf States and TV satellite dishes purchased with their new 'Gulf Money'. These facilitate the arrival of a new airborne global 'mythology' of the mass media, consisting of 'Blondes, wars, famines, football, sex, music, coups … WWF *Wrestling Mania* [and…] Hulk Hogan' (pp. 27–8) – a new form of entertainment that holds Baby Kochamma and Kochu Maria in a hypnotic thrall. We must not conclude from these details, however, that Roy is uncritical of 'tradition' or wholly nostalgic for some earlier version of rural Kerala. As we have seen, forms of tradition are responsible for the terror at the novel's centre, and it is the alliance of national politics with global capital, and their far-reaching local effects, that Roy condemns.

Reviewing these various instances of the incorporation of fantastical elements into the 'real' world of *The God of Small Things*, it becomes possible to think of their cumulative effects in terms of the slightly vague critical concept of 'tone'. Allied with Roy's incredible power of *noticing*, these techniques change the novel's atmosphere so that it becomes both pin-sharp in its detailing, and yet also hesitates on the edge of a threatening enchantment.

Reading the real as the exotic

Critics have suggested that when books written in English by writers from South Asia, Africa or the Caribbean are marketed globally (to readers in Europe and North America), certain expectations about these fictions come into play. At the time *The God of Small Things* was gaining considerable media attention as a 'miraculous' publishing debut, the critic Timothy Brennan suggested that a certain kind of international fiction that he termed 'literary cosmopolitanism' – defined by an irreverence towards national politics and literatures of national liberation, forms of transculturation and dialogic abundance, and an often magical realist combination of epic scope and personal impressionistic memory (Brennan, 1997, p. 36–44) – was becoming a standard form of what 'enter[ed] metropolitan literature as "third world literature"' (p. 37).

These concerns were also voiced by other commentators, who argued that writing about India was packaged for foreign readers and presented a false image of the subcontinent: a 'slickly exilic version of India' which is 'suffused with nostalgia, interwoven with myth' and 'weighed down with a kind of intellectual simplicity' (Dalrymple, 2005). As a writer who has never moved away from India, and has continued to take a sometimes risky, outspoken part in the political life of the country, Roy has escaped some of the criticisms levelled at other South Asian writers who live abroad but write about India. However, we should still take seriously claims that writing like Roy's – with its verdant, tropical setting, its heightened tone and emotional drama – caters to a certain 'idea' about India prevalent outside the subcontinent. For the critic Graham Huggan, 'the exotic' is a key component of how postcolonial fiction is marketed internationally. Huggan suggests that the exotic is not an inherent quality to be found in people, objects or places; rather it is a 'particular mode of aesthetic perception' which involves both strangeness and similarity (Huggan, 2001, p. 13). When we find something 'exotic', we are actually conferring a value on its strangeness and mysteriousness. Thus, while many readers see the postcolonial novel as having a critical impetus – correcting colonial stereotypes and presenting a truer sense of the material condition of people's lives in places such as south India – we must also consider whether postcolonial fiction sometimes reconfirms stereotypes. Because the postcolonial novel is a commodity – something that needs to be sold – are some of its more formulaic aspects designed to meet the specific tastes and expectations of its readers?

It may be just these expectations that Roy responds to in the Waterstones interview excerpt we looked at earlier, when she denies that her work is magical realism and accuses critics of 'absolving' power through the use of such terms. Also, in *The God of Small Things*, there are clues that Roy is highly aware of the possibility that her writing will be marketed in this way. The 'exotic' advertisement for 'Paradise Pickles & Preserves' on the Ipe's family car – which includes a picture of a Kathakali dancer to provide a 'Regional Flavour', and which Chacko thinks will stand the family in good stead when they enter 'the Overseas Market' (p. 47) – can be read as an extended metaphor for the predicament of the internationally successful postcolonial writer (Tickell, 2003). It is therefore unwise to make any definite judgement about the 'exoticism' of Roy's novel. India's acceleration towards global superpower status in the years since the publication of *The God of Small Things*, and the emergence of a growing readership in India for the English language novel, suggest too that authors like Roy are now involved in a more complicated 'representational' relationship with their Indian subject matter. As you will have realised in working through these module materials, Roy's *The God of Small Things*, however we define its marketability, represents a major formal development in the Indian novel in English.

Conclusion

In your study of Arundhati Roy's *The God of Small Things*, you have explored some significant contexts of the novel and looked at how Roy structures her story and approaches language. You have also thought about *The God of Small Things* in relation to literary realism, and explored the ways in which the novel challenges a critical separation of the real and the fantastic through the incorporation of genres such as the fairy story, the supernatural tale, the fable and religious myth. Additionally, you have reflected on how some aspects of Roy's novel might *seem* magical or extraordinary, simply because of our relative unfamiliarity with them as 'western' readers, and in the final part of the chapter, we returned to this problem and thought about how so-called postcolonial novels such as Roy's are published, promoted and marketed.

References

Set text

Roy, A. (2017) *The god of small things.* London: 4th Estate.

Other references

Bakhtin, M.M. (1981) *The dialogic imagination: four essays.* Edited by Michael Holquist. Translated by C. Emerson and M. Holquist. Austin, Tex.: University of Texas Press. Available online via the OU Library.

Barthes, R. (2009) *Mythologies.* Translated by J. Cape. London: Vintage.

Beaumont, M. (ed.) (2010) *A concise companion to realism.* Chichester: Wiley-Blackwell.

Bowers, M.A. (2004) *Magic(al) realism.* London: Routledge. Available online via the OU Library.

Brennan, T. (1997) *At home in the world: cosmopolitanism now.* Cambridge, Mass.: Harvard University Press.

Dalrymple, W. (2005) 'The lost sub-continent', *The Observer*, 13 August. Available at: https://www.theguardian.com/books/2005/aug/13/fiction.arundhatiroy (Accessed: 13 May 2019).

Huggan, G. (2001) *The postcolonial exotic: marketing the margins.* London: Routledge. Available online via the OU Library.

Mukherjee U.P. (2010) *Postcolonial environments: nature, culture and the contemporary Indian novel in English.* Basingstoke: Palgrave Macmillan. Available online via the OU Library.

Mullan. J. (2006) *How novels work.* Oxford: Oxford University Press. Available online via the OU Library.

Rajan, R.S. (2019) 'The novel of India' in Tickell, A. (ed.) *The Oxford history of the novel in English, volume 10: The Novel in South and South East Asia since 1945.* Oxford: Oxford University Press.

Rao, R. (1993) *Kanthapura.* 2nd edn. New Delhi: Oxford University Press.

Spivak, G.C. (1999) *A critique of postcolonial reason: toward a history of the vanishing present.* Cambridge, Mass.: Harvard University Press.

Tickell, A. (2003) '*The god of small things*: Arundhati Roy's postcolonial cosmopolitanism', *Journal of Commonwealth Literature*, 38(1), pp. 73–89. Available online via the OU Library.

Tickell, A. (2007) *Arundhati Roy's* The god of small things. Abingdon: Routledge.

Waterstones (2017) *Arundhati Roy: The Waterstones interview.* Available at: https://www.youtube.com/watch?v=K0f1MzCajaU&t=1246s (Accessed: 11 April 2019).

Wood, J. (2008) *How fiction works.* London: Jonathan Cape.

Zamora, L.P. and Faris, W.B. (1995) *Magical realism: theory, history, community.* Durham, N.C.: Duke University Press. Available online via the OU Library.

Zipes, J. (1979) *Breaking the magic spell: radical theories of folk and fairy tales.* London: Heinemann.

Žižek, S. (2006) *How to read Lacan.* London: Granta.

Conclusion to Book 1

Jonathan Gibson

The set texts covered in Part One of this module, *Realism*, have ranged far in time and space: from the west of England to the south of India and across a period of more than 150 years. In each, you have encountered vivid depictions of a unique set of characters, events and locations. Each work is, broadly speaking, realist – constructing a fictional world that makes sense as a version of the real world lived in by its author. But as your study of these texts has shown you, realism can take many forms, and the devices used by each author are as varied as the characters, events and locations which form the basis of their narratives. Think again, for example, about the way in which each text opens. In three of them, the reader is addressed by a third-person narrator – though in each case what the narrator is focusing on and the way those things are described is strikingly different. One of these narrators confronts us with the setting of the story, with time, place and weather. Though its sentences are mostly short, the mood is torpid:

> May in Ayemenem is a hot, brooding month. The days are long and humid. The river shrinks and black crows gorge on bright mangoes in still, dustgreen trees. Red bananas ripen. Jackfruits burst.
>
> (Roy, 2017, p. 1)

The details are vivid but they are, we are told, not unique to one particular day in May: this is what May in Ayemenem is always like.

Another of the third-person narrators zooms in on a specific individual. The sentences are much longer, meandering their way through a mildly humorous, rather long-winded description:

> When Farmer Oak smiled, the corners of his mouth spread till they were within an unimportant distance of his ears …
>
> (Hardy, 2002, p. 9)

The other third-person narrator, different again in their strategy, quotes verbatim a snatch of agitated conversation: direct speech accompanied by body language. The reader is whisked swiftly *in medias res* into a room in the Hotel Stentorian:

> 'Undine Spragg—how *can* you?' her mother wailed, raising a prematurely-wrinkled hand ...
>
> (Wharton, 2008, p. 3)

The remaining two texts begin by exposing the reader to the individual consciousness of a key figure in the narrative, though in strikingly different terms:

> I was not anxious to go. An uncertain but unceasing disquiet had been upon me, and when, returning to the officers' mess at Shoreham Camp one Sunday evening, I read the notice that I was under orders for France, I did not hide my feelings.
>
> (Blunden, 2010, p. 3)

> Woooooooo—
>
> (Smith, 2002, p. 3)

As each narrative develops, perspectives shift – the story is framed in relation to one character's point of view or another's, using direct speech, indirect speech or free indirect style, or a mixture. While *Far from the Madding Crowd*, *The Custom of the Country* and *Undertones of War* all tell their stories in a more or less linear way – one event following another in a chronological, though not always straightforward, sequence – *Hotel World* and *The God of Small Things* shift about unpredictably from one time period to another. Each of the five texts includes descriptive passages and dialogue, each in a different style, each picking out different sorts of thing for attention, and each using imagery, narrative voice and register in contrasting ways.

Literary devices do not exist in a vacuum, of course, and you will also have seen in this module book how they are used by the authors of the set texts to address and dramatise complex issues: the political and personal challenges of the caste system in India; the traumas of the First World War; the status of women in early twentieth-century New

York, the relationship between haves and have-nots in late twentieth-century Britain. The chapters in this book have also explored the circumstances in which the set texts were produced and have been read: the pressures of serialisation on Hardy; controversies about autobiographical writing; the difficulty of finding the right words in the wake of political, linguistic and cultural colonisation. As well as the set texts themselves, you have engaged with the voices of critics; and in the later chapters of this module book, you have been introduced to advanced approaches to analysing literature, specifically psychoanalytical criticism and semiotics.

At several points in this module book, you will have noticed chapter authors registering ways in which a set text blurs or expands the boundaries of realism – from Hardy's melodramatic use of coincidence and Wharton's sparky choice of names for her characters, to the relationship of the genre of magical realism to *The God of Small Things*, and the very different use of ghosts in *Hotel World* and *Undertones of War*. Realist fiction has – as the Introduction to Book 1 discussed – sometimes been criticised for taking too simplistic a view of the relationship between text and world, an over confidence about the extent to which a literary text can depict the real world. It has been suggested, for example, that realist novels present 'people as knowable by a number of "outward" signs of "inner" worth … presupposing the possibility of finally discovering the worth or value of a person by reading the external signs' (Bennett and Royle, 2004, p. 62). Having studied a variety of differently realist novels, you are now in good position to assess claims like this, and to consider the extent to which, for example, Hardy and Wharton present Bathsheba and Undine as 'knowable' in this way.

In Part Two of the module, *The Fantastic*, we will move beyond realism altogether, into strange otherworldly narratives. We will also be exploring different ways of telling stories and looking at a wider range of literary genres – in verse and drama as well as in prose. On this journey, you will build on the skills in literary analysis that you have developed in your work on this book, investigating the devices used by authors of 'fantastic' texts to create new worlds.

References

Bennett, A. and Royle, N. (2004) *An introduction to literature, criticism and theory.* Harlow: Pearson. Available online via the OU Library.

Blunden, E. (2010) *Undertones of war.* Edited by Hew Strachan. London: Penguin.

Hardy, T. (2002) *Far from the madding crowd.* Edited by Suzanne B. Falck-Yi, introduction by Linda M. Shires. Oxford: Oxford University Press. Oxford World's Classics.

Roy, A. (2017) *The god of small things.* London: 4th Estate.

Smith, A. (2002) *Hotel world.* London: Penguin Books.

Wharton, E. (2008) *The custom of the country.* Edited by Stephen Orgel. Oxford: Oxford University Press. Oxford World's Classics.

Glossary

adverb

a word, like 'quickly', that can be used to modify a verb (e.g. 'run quickly'). Adverbs can also be used to modify other parts of speech.

agency

the ability of somebody (an 'agent') to act, or do something.

anachrony

anachrony occurs when there is a difference between the order in which events are narrated in a text and the order in which they are imagined to have taken place. The key examples of anachrony are **analepsis** (flashback) and **prolepsis** (flashforward).

analepsis

see **prolepsis**.

authorial narrator

see **narrator**.

Bildungsroman

a type of novel traditional in German literature that focuses on one person's development from childhood to maturity.

binary opposition

a pair of apparently mutually exclusive terms such as on/off, male/female, black/white, etc.

canonical

a literary work is canonical if it belongs to the literary canon, the collection of works traditionally thought to be the best and therefore the most worth studying.

capitalism

an economic system in which the means of producing and distributing goods are privately owned and operated for profit.

characterisation

the techniques a writer uses in creating a character in a **narrative** work.

clause

a part of a sentence usually containing a finite verb. A **main clause** is a clause that can stand alone as a sentence in itself (for example, 'She had put on her best dress'). A subordinate clause is a clause that cannot (for example, 'which I opened, without reading the address').

conventions

agreed ways of doing things in literary **texts** and/or features that appear in many different literary texts. Examples include the convention that novels can be written from the point of view of an **omniscient** third-person **narrator** and the convention that a comedy should end in marriage. Individual works and authors frequently subvert conventions.

dénouement

French for 'unknotting', dénouement is the general term used for the final resolution of a novel, play or other narrative.

dialogic

a term associated with the critic Mikhail M. Bakhtin, who analysed **texts** as made up of the interplay of multiple **voices**.

dialogue

directly quoted speech in a **narrative**.

didactic

didactic literature is literature designed to make a moral point or teach an ethically useful lesson.

discourse

in a narrow sense, 'discourse' can be considered simply as 'language in use'. More broadly it is a term used by critics to refer the socially and politically shaped ways of talking that people 'pick up on' and employ in particular contexts.

disnarration

any parts of a **narrative** that refer to things that have not taken place.

dramatic irony

dramatic **irony** occurs when an audience or reader is in possession of knowledge of which a character is ignorant.

duration

the time in which an event takes place. Often in **narratives** the time spent by the author describing an event is disproportionate to the 'real time' the event would have taken: events happening over a very long time are sometimes narrated very quickly and events taking a very short time are sometimes narrated in great detail over many pages.

exposition

a section of a novel, play or other **narrative** (often the opening section) in which characters are introduced and essential information imparted to the audience.

first-person narrator

see **narrator**.

focalisation

a **narrative** technique whereby, while the third-person **narrator** remains the 'speaker' in a novel or story, a particular character becomes the 'focaliser': the character through whose eyes and perceptions the narrative is mediated.

frame story

a **narrative** device in which one story is enclosed or framed by another. A frame story can also contain multiple embedded narratives: medieval examples include Boccaccio's *Decameron* (1353) and Chaucer's *Canterbury Tales* (*c*.1390)

free indirect style

a type of **focalisation** in a **narrative**, in which a character's speech and/or thoughts are conveyed by the **narrator** but free of any narrator's tags such as 'she thought'. Sometimes called 'free indirect speech' or 'free indirect discourse'.

frequency

the number of times a specific thing happens in a **narrative**. There is often a difference between the number of times something is imagined to have occurred and the number of times it is actually narrated.

Freudian psychoanalysis

a set of theories and therapies developed initially by Sigmund Freud (1856–1939) in the early 1900s and formulated to cure psychological disorders.

genre

French for 'kind' or 'type'. A literary genre is a category or type of literature with its own form and conventions. For example, tragedy is a distinct genre of drama characterised by (among other conventions) an unhappy ending. Comedy, on the other hand, usually has a happy ending. 'Genre' is also sometimes used to refer to non-literary kinds of writing, such as reviews or recipes. Sometimes it is difficult to decide whether something is a genre or **mode**.

genre fiction

popular fiction in an easily identifiable **genre**, such as detective fiction or science fiction.

Golden Age

a time in the past when things were at their best.

Gothic

a **genre** or mode of **narrative** writing characterised by the use of terror and suspense, often accompanied and heightened by elements of the supernatural and by a claustrophobic atmosphere. Writing of this type has appeared in many different periods and places; it was particularly popular from the 1760s to the 1820s.

grand narratives

ambitious historical theories claiming to explain everything.

haiku

a short Japanese poem consisting of three lines of 5, 7 and 5 syllables and often focusing on a specific feeling and **imagery** from the natural world.

historical novel

a novel set in a period earlier than the period in which it was written. Historical novels often include both real-life and fictional characters.

homophone

a word pronounced the same way as another but with a different meaning (for example, 'hole' and 'whole').

idiolect

an individual person's particular speech habits, including the sort of words they use, their use of grammar and their pronunciation.

imagery

a general term for the images that appear in a poem or other literary text. Images are uses of language that evoke strong sense impressions in readers and audiences; often these are visual, creating vivid pictures in the mind. Images can be figurative (e.g. **similes**, **metaphors**) or literal (e.g. sensually vivid descriptions of things in the story).

in medias res

Latin for 'into the middle of things'. A narrative which begins '*in medias res*' starts in the middle of the action, significant events in the story having already occurred.

interior monologue

a form of **narrative** that represents the silent flow of thought as if it were speech. Interior monologue uses **first-person narration**. Interior monologue transmits the thoughts and perceptions of a single character as if directly overheard by the reader. Both interior monologue and **free indirect style** are techniques that can be used to a create **stream-of-consciousness** style.

intertext

a **text** in an intertextual relation with another text. See **intertextuality**.

intertextuality

the interconnecting relationship that a given **text** might have with other texts, in terms of influences or common reference points between texts.

irony

generally speaking, irony involves implying something other than what is explicitly said; it requires readers to read between the lines and, often, to perceive more than a fictional or dramatic character does. See **dramatic irony**, **tragic irony** and **verbal irony**.

liminality

to do with boundaries or thresholds. ('Limen' is Latin for 'threshold'.)

literary allusions

references made by one literary text to an earlier text or author. Often this is done by direct quotation, correct or incorrect. Sometimes the author or text is identified, but often it isn't.

literary theory

the study of general ideas about literature, its nature and its function.

magical realism

a **genre** of prose fiction which mingles realism with fantastic elements.

main clause

see **clause**.

malapropism

humorous misuse of words, named after Mrs Malaprop, a character in Richard Brinsley Sheridan's play *The Rivals* (1775), who habitually used long words incorrectly, muddling up one for another.

meaning potential

the possible meanings of a thing when a viewer or reader tries to make sense of it. Use of the term is a way of recognising that meanings aren't given but are made by readers or viewers on the basis of past knowledge and experience.

melodramatic

this term describes a type of narrative (usually a play) characterised by extravagant emotion and sensational events. Melodrama was a popular dramatic **genre** in the nineteenth century.

memoir

a type of autobiographical writing (writing, that is, in which the author writes about their own life). Memoirs tend to focus on people known and events witnessed by the author.

metaphor

a type of figurative language that establishes an identity between two apparently dissimilar things. When Thomas Hardy describes lightning flashes as 'undulating snakes of green' he is using a metaphor. If he had written 'like undulating snakes of green', he would have been using a **simile**.

mode

a broad kind of literary approach not tied to a particular genre. It is sometimes difficult to decide whether a particular type of literature is a genre or a mode. The word 'mode' is also used to mean more generally 'method' (e.g. 'mode of narration').

modernism/modernist

an umbrella term used to describe late-nineteenth- and early-twentieth-century movements in the arts broadly linked by their interest in experimental form and technique such as **stream of consciousness**.

narrative

a sequence of connected events told by a narrator and arranged in a particular order (or **plot**). Narratives can be in either prose or verse, and can be either fictional or non-fictional.

narrative impact

the effect of particular actions in the **storyworld**.

narrator

the person telling the story in a **narrative**. A **first-person narrator** uses 'I', a **third-person narrator** uses 'he' or 'she'. A first-person narrator is usually also a character in the story. A third-person narrator, on the other hand, usually tells the story from outside/above the characters and events. Third-person narrators often seem to be 'omniscient', or all-knowing, about the story they are telling. They are also often identified with the author (hence the term '**authorial narrator**').

narratology

a branch of literary study that analyses the components and structure of narratives.

naturalism

a nineteenth-century literary movement, initially French, influenced by the scientific theories of Charles Darwin (1809–1882) and depicting fictional characters as subject to external forces such as heredity and environment.

objective

focused on the facts, unaffected by personal bias. Usually contrasted with **subjective**.

omniscient narrator

see **narrator**.

onomatopoeic

Greek for 'name-making'. The use of words to depict a particular sound. Words such as 'moo' or 'whoosh' are onomatopoeic.

pastoral

a literary **genre** or **mode** with a history dating back to ancient Greek and Roman times. Pastoral poems, plays or novels are set in the countryside. The conventional assumption of pastoral is of a rural innocence or purity that provides a moral reference point for the corruption, greed and decadence of cities.

pathetic fallacy

a term invented by the famous nineteenth-century art critic John Ruskin (1819–1900). He used it to attack writing which attributes human feelings to nature. The term is now used without hostile overtones.

persona (pl. personae)

the mask and **voice** adopted explicitly or implicitly by an author, whether in their own person or as some fictive **narrator**, in order to tell a story, provide a description or make an argument. 'Persona' is the Latin word for a theatrical mask.

personification

a type of **metaphorical** writing in which things or ideas are given human form. When Thomas Hardy writes 'Nature, as if offended, lent a hand', he is personifying nature.

plot

the pattern of events in a **narrative**. Usually cause and effect (why things happened) is important in plots, and there can be any number of emphases and distortions: a plot need not arrange events in the order in which they are actually supposed to have happened, for example. A writer normally seeks to structure the plot in such a way as to arouse curiosity (and sometimes **suspense**) in the reader or spectator.

postcolonial

in a hyphenated form, the term post-colonial refers to the historical period after colonialism. However, without the hyphen postcolonial can also refer to a condition of being against, or opposed to, colonialism; or more generally resistant to various forms of political and cultural oppression.

post-modernism

a literary and cultural movement that followed **modernism**, beginning in the period after the Second World War. Whereas modernism involved abandoning traditional art forms in favour of representation of reality as fragmented and discontinuous, post-modernism is more sceptical about the ability of art and literature to depict reality and about **grand narratives**. It foregrounds the **intertextual** elements in art and literature, emphasising the ways in which texts refer to one another rather than to an external reality.

prolepsis

the opposite of **analepsis**. Whereas analepsis is what is popularly called 'flashback', prolepsis can be termed 'flashforward'. Analepsis is a moment when the narrative leaps backwards in time. Prolepsis is a moment when the narrative leaps forward in time, before returning to the original chronological sequence and pacing of events. Both are types of **anachrony**.

pronominal shifters

pronouns (like 'I' or 'me') the meaning of which depends on the context of who is speaking, to whom they are speaking and/or about whom they are speaking.

protagonist

the chief character in a literary work.

realism

the term used to describe literary works characterised by their author's interest in representing human life and experience 'as they really are'.

register

a particular type of language associated with a particular context. Thus, for example, we can talk about formal and informal registers, or registers associated with different professions (legal, medical, academic, and so on). They are often employed by writers in the characterisation of a particular character.

relativism

the idea that such things as morality and truth are not absolute and unchanging but vary according to historical, social and cultural contexts.

Romantic

associated with Romanticism, a movement in the arts and literature which originated in the late eighteenth century and which emphasised inspiration, **subjective** feelings and the primacy of the individual.

satire

a literary work that attacks its subject matter (for example, corrupt politicians) by ridiculing it.

scene

a series of events in a literary work that the reader or spectator experiences complete. In Thomas Hardy's *Far from the Madding Crowd* the chapter in which Bathsheba and Liddy decide to send the valentine (Chapter XIII) is a scene. Most plays consist of a series of 'scenes'. Critics writing on prose fiction sometimes distinguish between scene and **summary**.

semantic

relating to meaning in language.

semiotics

the study of cultural systems as if they are languages.

simile

a comparison of two apparently dissimilar things that uses either 'like' or 'as' to enforce the comparison. Here is an example from Edith Wharton: 'her reflection bloomed out like a flower from the mirror that faced her'.

social realist novel

a realist novel aiming to depict society in a realist way, often with a focus on challenging aspects of everyday life.

sociolect

a form of language (or **register**) characteristic of a particular social class.

storyworld

the world created by and in a particular narrative, whether realist or fantastic.

stream of consciousness

a **modernist** way of depicting the often fragmented flow of inner thought (as opposed to external **plot** events). The chief techniques used are **interior monologue** and **free indirect style** (writers may favour either technique or use both).

style

the key characteristics of a particular writer, **text** or part of text involving things such as choice of words, sentence structure, use of figurative language, rhythms and other devices.

subjective

influenced by a person's invidual feelings, tastes or ideas. Usually contrasted with **objective**.

subordinate clauses

see **clause**.

subplot

a secondary **plot** in a play or narrative that may comment on the main plot in a number of ways.

summary

A narrator's summary of a sequence of events. Sometimes contrasted by critics with **scene**.

surprise

the violation of a reader's or spectator's expectations about what will happen in a narrative.

suspense

uncertainty about the outcome of part of a story. Suspense occurs when a reader or spectator is aware of a number of different possible outcomes and anxious about which one will occur.

text

in one sense, the words of a written work. More generally, novels, plays and poems are often referred to simply as 'texts'.

third-person omniscient narrator

see **narrator**.

tone

the attitude of a speaker or **narrator** towards the topic they are discussing, as shown through their choice of words and other aspects of **style**. Many different types of tone are possible: affectionate, humorous, **satirical**, **ironic**, etc.

tragic irony

a type of **irony** in which the audience is aware of a likely tragic outcome before one or more of the characters involved.

trope

'tropos' is Greek for 'turn'. In English, 'trope' is a general term for any one of a number of literary devices involving some kind of change (or 'turn') in the meaning of words.

uncanny

a feeling of strangeness characteristic of some forms of **narrative**, for example horror stories.

verbal irony

a type of **irony** which occurs when the actual meaning of part of a text is quite different from what its meaning at first seems to be.

verisimilitude

in a fictional **narrative**, the quality of being true to life.

voice

in literary criticism 'voice' can refer simply to a character who speaks in a novel (for example a first-person narrator). (Ali Smith's *Hotel World*, for example, is a **narrative** featuring many 'voices' of this kind.) The word is also used as a short-hand way of referring to the key characteristics of a particular speaker's utterances. Similarly, some critics refer to an author's 'voice' or to the 'narrative voice' characteristic of a particular text.

Acknowledgements

Grateful acknowledgement is made to the following sources:

Chapter 1

Far from the Madding Crowd extracts:

Far from the Madding Crowd by Thomas Hardy. Notes on Text and Explanatory Notes © Suzanne B. Falck-Yi 1993, and Introduction and Bibliography © Linda M. Shires 2002, Oxford World's Classics, Oxford University Press.

Chapter 2

Far from the Madding Crowd extracts:

Far from the Madding Crowd by Thomas Hardy. Notes on Text and Explanatory Notes © Suzanne B. Falck-Yi 1993, and Introduction and Bibliography © Linda M. Shires 2002, Oxford World's Classics, Oxford University Press.

Chapter 3

Far from the Madding Crowd extracts:

Far from the Madding Crowd by Thomas Hardy. Notes on Text and Explanatory Notes © Suzanne B. Falck-Yi 1993, and Introduction and Bibliography © Linda M. Shires 2002, Oxford World's Classics, Oxford University Press.

Chapter 4

The Custom of the Country extracts:

The Custom of the Country by Edith Wharton. Introduction, Note on the Text, Select Bibliography © Stephen Orgel 1995, Oxford World's Classics, Oxford University Press.

Far from the Madding Crowd extracts:

Far from the Madding Crowd by Thomas Hardy. Notes on Text and Explanatory Notes © Suzanne B. Falck-Yi 1993, and Introduction and Bibliography © Linda M. Shires 2002, Oxford World's Classics, Oxford University Press.

Chapter 5

The Custom of the Country extracts:

The Custom of the Country by Edith Wharton. Introduction, Note on the Text, Select Bibliography © Stephen Orgel 1995, Oxford World's Classics, Oxford University Press.

Chapter 6

Hotel World extracts:

Smith, A. (2001) *Hotel World*, Penguin Books. Copyright © Ali Smith, 2001.

Chapter 7

Hotel World extracts:

Smith, A. (2001) *Hotel World*, Penguin Books. Copyright © Ali Smith, 2001.

Ali Smith *Guardian* article extract:

Smith, A. (2013) 'My hero: Lydia Davis by Ali Smith', *The Guardian*, 24th May 2013 [online]. Copyright © 2013 Guardian News & Media Limited.

Chapter 8

Undertones of War extracts:

Blunden, E. (1928) *Undertones of War*, Penguin Books. Copyright © Edmund Blunden, 1928.

Chapter 9

Undertones of War extracts:

Blunden, E. (1928) *Undertones of War*, Penguin Books. Copyright © Edmund Blunden, 1928.

Chapter 10

The God of Small Things extracts:

Roy, A. (1997) *The God of Small Things* 4th Estate. Copyright © Arundhati Roy 1997.

Oxford Dictionary of English definition 'Trauma':

'Trauma', in Stevenson, A. (Ed.) (2015) *Oxford Dictionary of English* (3rd Edition) [online]. Copyright © Oxford University Press.

Chapter 11

The God of Small Things extracts:

Roy, A. (1997) *The God of Small Things*, 4th Estate. Copyright © Arundhati Roy 1997.

Conclusion to Book 1

Far from the Madding Crowd extracts:

Far from the Madding Crowd by Thomas Hardy. Notes on Text and Explanatory Notes © Suzanne B. Falck-Yi 1993, and Introduction and Bibliography © Linda M. Shires 2002, Oxford World's Classics, Oxford University Press.

The Custom of the Country extracts:

The Custom of the Country by Edith Wharton. Introduction, Note on the Text, Select Bibliography © Stephen Orgel 1995, Oxford World's Classics, Oxford University Press.

Hotel World extracts:

Smith, A. (2001) *Hotel World*, Penguin Books. Copyright © Ali Smith, 2001.

Undertones of War extracts:

Blunden, E. (1928) *Undertones of War*, Penguin Books. Copyright © Edmund Blunden, 1928.

The God of Small Things Extracts:

Roy, A. (1997) *The God of Small Things*, 4th Estate. Copyright © Arundhati Roy 1997.

Every effort has been made to contact copyright holders. If any have been inadvertently overlooked the publishers will be pleased to make the necessary arrangements at the first opportunity.

Index

Page numbers in **bold** refer to figures and tables.